"Alister McGrath is one of the most distinguished scholars of the theology of the Reformation in the world academic community, and this splendid volume is a fitting tribute to his achievements. The thoughtful, incisive work in this collection does full justice to the range of McGrath's interests and, collectively, attests to the continued relevance of serious scholarship to the role of Christianity in today's world."

—Andrew Pettegree
University of St. Andrews

"Ngien has assembled a fine collection of well-known theologians and essayists whose contributions reflect the breadth of McGrath's work to Christian theology over many years. This volume is a fitting tribute to McGrath's influential contributions to the study of the Reformation, the spiritual life of Christian faith, the conversation between theology and science, and, of course, to evangelical theology generally. McGrath's many students, readers, and admirers will find much to engage their intellects, encourage their thinking, and enliven their souls here."

—Philip G. Ziegler
University of Aberdeen

"This collection is a fitting tribute to the depth and range of Alister McGrath's life work. Written with verve and clarity, the essays explore some of the most challenging issues confronting Christian thinkers today, offering stimulating and often persuasive solutions. These issues include theodicy: why a good and omnipotent God permits evil to exist, especially natural evil—which is not the consequence of human freedom; the mystery of the holy Trinity, the Atonement, original sin and human freedom, Christology and 'the last things' (eschatology), among others. I have benefited greatly from reading these essays."

—Ian Gentles
Tyndale University College & Seminary, Toronto

"Dennis Ngien has edited a most helpful volume. Leading contributors from a variety of ecclesial homes show us the impact and influence of McGrath's work. Indeed, I am grateful for McGrath's lucid contribution to Christian theology and to Ngien's work in promoting its most salutary dimensions."

—Christopher Holmes
University of Otago, New Zealand

"As one of the doyens of Christian theology in our era, Alister McGrath is a voice of faith and reason. In this compendium, diverse theological themes are addressed by respected scholars who write as if his faithful and influential voice is whispering in their ears. This is a readable, erudite, and highly Trinitarian work that honors the legacy of the Reformation and reveals the importance of the Christian *imaginarium* in our time. In essence this is a work of doxology that places God at the center of all things. A must-read for preachers today."

—ANDREW STIRLING
Senior Minister, Timothy Eaton Memorial Church, Toronto; Fellow of Acadia Divinity College

"Alister McGrath's scholarly output has been both prodigious and diverse. This volume fittingly pays tribute to McGrath's broad scholarly interests through significant articles that represent a wide range of expertise. The contributions bring topics that McGrath has addressed into conversation with contemporary thought in an accessible way that reminds readers of the enduring significance of the questions being examined. This, in turn, appropriately highlights the legacy of McGrath as a scholar who has made a substantial contribution to Christian theological and scientific reflection."

—BRIAN COOPER
Mennonite Brethren Biblical Seminary, Langley

"I love *festschrifts*: the diversity of meaty essays in honor of a distinguished scholarly colleague has always seemed to me an ideal way to share scholarship. This *festschrift* for Alister McGrath is a notable example of this genre: rich theological studies that cover the wide spectrum of Dr. McGrath's own scholarly pursuits and publications. It is indeed a fitting celebration of the literary corpus of a remarkable Evangelical scholar who is equally at home in the twin realms of theology and science."

—MICHAEL A. G. HAYKIN
The Southern Baptist Theological Seminary

"A fitting tribute to the eclectic and penetrating thought of Alister McGrath, this collection of essays engages themes central to the heart and witness of the church. Atonement, Christology, eschatology, mission, reformation, science, theodicy—there is much to ponder here. But what stands out is how human these contributions are. The work of theology is not presented chiefly as a cognitive exercise, but rather as a product of discipleship. Good theology is evident where experience, imagination, and human desire are also caught up in the higher end of loving God and neighbor."

—STEPHEN ANDREWS
Wycliffe College, University of Toronto

"Christianity offers a 'public theology' whereby Christians and non-Christians can enter into a meaningful dialogue. The holder of the Andreas Idreos Professorship in Science and Religion at the University of Oxford, Dr. Alister E. McGrath is the epitome of the interface of science, theology, and religion. Asian Christians and theologians will benefit greatly from Dr. McGrath's works as they embark on such an interdisciplinary approach."

—PETER AU
Canadian Chinese School of Theology

"This fine collection of essays covers the broad array of topics that Alister McGrath has engaged in his prolific career. Often building upon McGrath's own work, this book makes significant contributions to several areas of contemporary and historical theology. Most importantly, the authors undertake their task with the same commitment to rigorous scholarship and faithful churchmanship that McGrath has demonstrated throughout his remarkable career."

—JAMES E. PEDLAR
Tyndale University College & Seminary

"*The Interface of Science, Theology, and Religion* is a *festschrift* in honor of Alister McGrath, scientist, evangelical Anglican, historian of doctrine, systematician, popular apologist, and polymath. The essays mirror his wide range of thought, with a lineup of contributors as illustrious as McGrath himself. 'Missional' is a weary word nowadays, but in a way, via Interface, McGrath's thus engaged with science and its culture, our understanding of nature, the imagination, apologetics, a global Christian awareness, spirituality, and the mysteries of the religions and of evil. Throughout we see how, for McGrath, theology is for 'transformation by the renewing of our minds' (Rom 12:2)."

—GEORGE SUMNER
Wycliffe College, Episcopal Bishop of Dallas

"The *festschrift* reflects everything that we have come to know and appreciate of McGrath: the range of his scholarship, from Reformation studies to the relationship of science and theology, from theodicy to spirituality, etc. In a way, the choice of topics by these renowned contributors makes this collection an appropriate introduction to McGrath's wide-ranging thought."

—SIMON CHAN
Editor of *Asia Journal of Theology*, formerly taught at Trinity Theological College, Singapore

"A superb collection of stellar essays in honor of Alister McGrath, a remarkable scholar whose work has shed light on the Christian story across many disciplines. A worthy tribute to a prolific theologian whose bountiful scholarship continues to bless the church."

—TIMOTHY GEORGE
Beeson Divinity School of Samford University, General Editor of the *Reformation Commentary on Scripture*

# The Interface of Science, Theology, and Religion

# The Interface of Science, Theology, and Religion

Essays in Honor of Alister E. McGrath

*Presented on the Occasion of McGrath's 65th Birthday*

Edited by DENNIS NGIEN
Foreword by GRAHAM TOMLIN

☙PICKWICK *Publications* · Eugene, Oregon

THE INTERFACE OF SCIENCE, THEOLOGY, AND RELIGION
Essays in Honor of Alister E. McGrath

Copyright © 2019 Wipf and Stock Publishers. All rights reserved. Except for brief quotations in critical publications or reviews, no part of this book may be reproduced in any manner without prior written permission from the publisher. Write: Permissions, Wipf and Stock Publishers, 199 W. 8th Ave., Suite 3, Eugene, OR 97401.

Pickwick Publications
An Imprint of Wipf and Stock Publishers
199 W. 8th Ave., Suite 3
Eugene, OR 97401

www.wipfandstock.com

PAPERBACK ISBN: 978-1-5326-4334-7
HARDCOVER ISBN: 978-1-5326-4335-4
EBOOK ISBN: 978-1-5326-4336-1

*Cataloguing-in-Publication data:*

Names: Ngien, Dennis, 1958–, editor. | Tomlin, Graham, foreword.

Title: The interface of science, theology, and religion : essays in honor of Alister E. McGrath / edited by Dennis Ngien ; foreword by Graham Tomlin.

Description: Eugene, OR : Pickwick Publications, 2019 | Includes bibliographical references.

Identifiers: ISBN 978-1-5326-4334-7 (paperback) | ISBN 978-1-5326-4335-4 (hardcover) | ISBN 978-1-5326-4336-1 (ebook)

Subjects: LCSH: McGrath, Alister E., 1953–. | Religion and science.

Classification: BL240.3 .I59 2019 (paperback) | BL240.3 .I59 (ebook)

Manufactured in the U.S.A.    03/04/19

# Contents

*Contributors* | vii
*Foreword by Graham Tomlin* | xi

**Introduction** | 1
—Dennis Ngien

Chapter 1
**Becoming a Christian: Christian Initiation in the New Testament and in British Evangelicalism** | 11
—Anthony N. S. Lane

Chapter 2
**The God Who Sends is the God Who Loves: Missions as Participating in the Ecstatic Love of the Triune God** | 29
—Patrick S. Franklin

Chapter 3
**Luther's Providential God** | 48
—Robert Kolb

Chapter 4
**Did the Death of Christ Appease the Wrath of God?: Luther and Calvin on the Purpose of the Death of Christ** | 66
—Randall C. Zachman

Chapter 5
**Freedom as Salvation: Reformation Insights and Their Significance and Implications for Global Christianity** | 86
—Sung Wook Chung

Chapter 6
**An Edwardsian Quandary Concerning the Atonement** | 100
—Oliver D. Crisp

Chapter 7
**Reality?** | 118
—JONATHAN R. WILSON

Chapter 8
**A Christian Vision of the "End" of Cosmos and Life: Towards a Constructive Eschatology for the Contemporary World** | 137
—VELI-MATTI KÄRKKÄINEN

Chapter 9
**Christology and Creation: Another Kind of Naturalism** | 154
—GRAHAM WARD

Chapter 10
**"Looking for Overland": Fact and Fiction in Children's Literature** | 174
—BENEDICTA WARD

Chapter 11
**Models and Cultures in Science and Theology** | 184
—BETHANY SOLLEREDER

Chapter 12
**Alister McGrath's Theodicy** | 201
—MICHAEL LLOYD

Chapter 13
**Alister McGrath's Exemplary Theology** | 224
—JEFFREY P. GREENMAN

# Contributors

ANTHONY N. S LANE (MA, BD, DD, Oxford) is Professor of Historical Theology at London School of Theology. He has published eight books, including *John Calvin: Student of the Church Fathers* (T. & T. Clark, 1999), *Justification by Faith in Catholic-Protestant Dialogue: An Evangelical Assessment* (Continuum, 2002), and *Bernard of Clairvaux: Theologian of the Cross* (Cistercian, 2013). He has also edited ten books and is the author of almost 100 articles and chapters in books. His main specialism has been John Calvin, and since 1992 he has been a member of the Presidium of the International Congress on Calvin Research.

Bethany Sollereder (PhD, University of Exeter) is a Postdoctoral Fellow in Science and Religion at the University of Oxford. She is the author of *God, Evolution, and Animal Suffering: Theodicy without a Fall* (Routledge, 2018). She has published in both scholarly and popular publications, including *Zygon, Science and Theology, The Expository Times,* and *The Christian Century*. She specializes in theology concerning evolution and the problem of suffering. She is a fellow of the International Society for Science and Religion.

Dennis Ngien (PhD, St. Michael's College in University of Toronto), is a Professor of Systematic Theology, at Tyndale University College & Seminary, and a Research Professor at Wycliffe College at the University of Toronto. He is also the founder of Centre for Mentorship & Theological Reflection, mentoring pastors, professionals, students, scholars, and lay-leaders. He is the author of numerous books, including *Gifted Response: The Triune God as the Causative Agency of Our Responsive Worship* (Paternoster, 2008), *Fruit for the Soul: Luther on the Lament Psalms* (Fortress, 2016), and *Luther's Theology of the Cross: Christ in Luther's Sermons on John* (Cascade, 2018).

The Rt. Revd. Dr. Graham Tomlin (PhD, Exeter University) is the Bishop of Kensington and President of St. Mellitus College in London.

Among past roles he has served as Chaplain of Jesus College Oxford and Vice Principal of Wycliffe Hall, Oxford, where he taught within the Theology Faculty of Oxford University on Historical Theology. He is the author of many books and articles, including *The Power of the Cross: Theology and the Death of Christ in Paul Luther and* Pascal (Paternoster, 1999), *The Provocative Church* (SPCK, 2002), *Looking through the Cross* (the Archbishop of Canterbury's Lent Book – Bloomsbury, 2014), *The Widening Circle—Priesthood as God's Way of Blessing the World* (SPCK, 2017), and most recently, *Bound to be Free: The Paradox of Freedom* (Bloomsbury, 2017) and *Luther's Gospel: Reimagining the World* (Bloomsbury, T. & T. Clark, 2017).

Graham Ward (PhD, Cambridge) is the Regius Professor of Divinity at the University of Oxford and former Head of the School of Arts, Histories, and Cultures at the University of Manchester. Among his books are *Cities of God* (Routledge, 2000), *True Religion* (Blackwell, 2002), *Cultural Transformation and Religious Practice* (Cambridge University Press, 2004), *Christ and Culture* (Blackwell, 2005), *The Politics of Discipleship* (Baker Academic, 2009), and *How the Light Gets In* (Oxford University Press, 2016). He edits three book series: *Christian Theologians in Context* (Oxford University Press), *Illuminations* (Blackwell), and *Studies in Theology and Political Culture* (Continuum). Currently he is completing a four-volume work entitled *Ethical Life* (Oxford University Press).

Jonathan R. Wilson (PhD, Duke University) is the Teaching Fellow of Regent College and Senior Consultant for Theological Integration with Canadian Baptist Ministries. He is the author of eight books, including *Theology as Cultural Critique* (Mercer University Press, 1997), *Living Faithfully in a Fragmented World: From* After Virtue *to a New Monasticism* (Trinity Press International, 1998), *Gospel Virtues: Practicing Faith, Hope, and Love in Uncertain Times* (IVP, 2000), *God So Loved the World: A Christology for Disciples* (Baker Academic, 2001), and *God's Good World: Reclaiming the Doctrine of Creation* (Baker Academic, 2013). He has also edited nine volumes. Four of his books have been translated into Chinese.

Jeffrey P. Greenman (PhD, University of Virginia) serves as the President and Professor of Theology & Ethics at Regent College in Vancouver, British Columbia, Canada. His research and writing has spanned theology, ethics, the history of biblical interpretation, spiritual formation, leadership, world Christianity, and theological education. He is the author or editor of eleven books, including *Understanding Jacques Ellul* (Cascade, 2012) and *The Pedagogy of Praise: How Congregational Worship Shapes Christian Character* (Regent College, 2016).

Michael Lloyd (DPhil, Oxon) is the Principal of Wycliffe Hall, Oxford. His doctoral thesis, *The Cosmic Fall and the Free Will Defence* (Bodleian,

1997), was on the problem of evil, and he has published articles in the area of theodicy and on the theology of G. F. Handel. He is the co-editor of *Finding Ourselves after Darwin: Conversations on the Image of God, Original Sin, and the Problem of Evil* (Baker House, 2018). He is the author of a popular-level systematic theology, entitled *Cafe Theology: Exploring Love, the Universe and Everything* (Alpha International, 2005).

Oliver D. Crisp (PhD, London; DLitt, University of Aberdeen) is a Professor of Systematic Theology in the School of Theology, Fuller Theological Seminary, and a Professorial Fellow of the Institute of Analytic and Exegetical Theology, University of St. Andrews. He is the author of numerous books, including *The Word Enfleshed: Exploring the Person and Work of Christ* (Baker Academic, 2016), *Saving Calvinism: Expanding the Reformed Tradition* (IVP Academic, 2016), and with Kyle Strobel, *Jonathan Edwards: An Introduction to His Thought* (Eerdmans, 2018). He is an editor of the *Journal of Analytic Theology* and co-organizes the annual Los Angeles Theology Conference series with Fred Sanders.

Patrick S. Franklin (PhD, McMaster Divinity College) is an Associate Professor of Theology at Tyndale University College & Seminary in Toronto. He also serves as the Vice President of the Canadian Scientific and Christian Affiliation (CSCA) and as the Book Review Editor for *Perspectives on Science and Christian Faith* (journal of the American Scientific Affiliation and the CSCA). In addition to several journal articles, he is the author of *Being Human, Being Church: The Significance of Theological Anthropology for Ecclesiology* (Paternoster, 2016).

Randall C. Zachman (PhD, University of Chicago) is a Professor of Reformation Studies, Emeritus, at the University of Notre Dame, and is currently the Adjunct Professor of Church History at Lancaster Theological Seminary. He is the author of *The Assurance of Faith: Conscience in the Theology of Martin Luther and John Calvin* (Westminster John Knox, 2005), *John Calvin as Teacher, Pastor, and Theologian: The Shape of His Writings and Thought* (Baker Academic, 2006), *Image and Word in the Theology of John Calvin* (University of Notre Dame, 2009), and *Reconsidering John Calvin* (Cambridge, 2012). He is the North American Co-editor of the *Archive for Reformation History* and is the former President of the Calvin Studies Society and the Sixteenth-Century Society and Conference.

Robert Kolb (PhD, University of Wisconsin), Professor of Systematic Theology, Emeritus, at Concordia Seminary in St. Louis, is co-editor of the new translation of *The Book of Concord* (Fortress, 2000), co-editor of the *Oxford Handbook to Martin Luther's Theology* (OUP, 2014), co-author of *Between Wittenberg and Geneva* (Baker Academic 2017) and *The Genius of Luther's Theology* (Baker Academic, 2008), and author of *Luther's Wittenberg*

*World* (Baker Academic, 2018), *Martin Luther and the Enduring Word of God* (Baker Academic, 2016), *Luther and the Stories of God* (Baker Academic, 2012), *Martin Luther, Confessor of the Faith* (OUP, 2009), and *Bound Choice, Election, and Wittenberg Theological Method* (Eerdmans, 2005).

Sister Benedicta Ward (PhD, Oxon) is Reader Emeritus in the History of Christian Spirituality at the University of Oxford and an Honorary Fellow at Harris Manchester College, Oxford. Sr. Benedicta has written many books, pamphlets, and essays over a long career, including *Miracles and the Medieval Mind* (Scholar, 1982), *Sayings of the Desert Fathers* (Mowbrays, 1981), *Harlots of the Desert* (Cistercian Studies, 1981), *Anselm of Canterbury* (SPCK, 2009), and *The Venerable Bede* (Geoffrey Chapman, 1998). Recently a collection of her essays on spirituality has been published as *Give Love and Receive the Kingdom* (Paraclete, 2018).

Sung Wook Chung (DPhil, Oxon) serves as a Professor of Christian Theology at Denver Seminary in Littleton, Colorado. He has authored *Admiration and Challenge: Karl Barth's Theological Relationship with John Calvin* (Peter Lang, 2002), co-authored *Models of Premillennialism* (Cascade, 2018), and edited *Alister McGrath and Evangelical Theology: A Dynamic Engagement* (Baker Academic, 2003), *Christ the One and Only: A Global Affirmation of the Uniqueness of Jesus Christ* (Baker Academic, 2005), *Karl Barth and Evangelical Theology: Convergences and Divergences* (Baker Academic, 2008), *Jürgen Moltmann and Evangelical Theology: A Critical Engagement* (Pickwick, 2012), and *John Calvin and Evangelical Theology: Legacy and Prospect* (Westminster John Knox, 2009).

Veli-Matti Kärkkäinen (Dr.Theol.Habil., Helsinki) is a Professor of Systematic Theology at Fuller Theological Seminary and Docent of Ecumenics at the University of Helsinki. Among more than twenty-five books written and edited, the most recent ones include the five-volume series entitled *Constructive Christian Theology for the Pluralistic World* (Eerdmans 2013-17): *Christ and Reconciliation* (2013), *Trinity and Revelation* (2014), *Creation and Humanity* (2015), *Spirit and Salvation* (2016), and *Hope and Community* (2017). This project develops a full-scale Christian systematic theology in critical dialogue with the whole of Christian tradition, including the wide contemporary global diversity, natural (and behavioral) sciences, as well as four living faiths (Judaism, Islam, Hinduism, and Buddhism).

# Foreword

GRAHAM TOMLIN

I FIRST MET ALISTER McGrath on the day when he started as a fresh-faced tutor at Wycliffe Hall in the University of Oxford, and I started out as a theological student there in 1983. He went on to teach me Christian doctrine and patristics over the coming years. One-to-one tutorials with Alister were always concise, sharp, and focused. Normally tutorials in Oxford last an hour. With Alister they lasted around forty minutes (you suspected he took the extra twenty minutes to write a few more paragraphs in his latest book), but you often took away more from that shortened time than you did from endless diffuse discussions with other, less focused academics. In my final year I attended his lectures on Luther and the Reformation which made a big impact on me and were instrumental in leading me to do my own doctoral work on Martin Luther and the theology of the cross. I also had the privilege of working alongside Alister as Vice Principal to his Principal at Wycliffe Hall for a number of years.

A glance at the contents page of this volume shows the extraordinary range of academic interests upon which Alister's career has focused. When I first knew him he seemed destined for a career as a specialist Reformation scholar. His book on Luther's theology of the cross (still in print), his subsequent work on the doctrine of justification, and an innovative biography of John Calvin showed an extraordinary grasp of the intricacies of late medieval thought as the background to Reformation theology that would suggest a career just like many sixteenth-century scholars in the years to come. However, that developed into an interest and series of books on the history of Evangelicalism, reflecting on his own journey away from a liberalism that he increasingly felt had "no theological or spiritual core" as he once put it.

Evangelicals always have a tendency to be evangelistic, and so it was not surprising when that developed into a series of books on apologetics.

At this stage, he always kept rather quiet about his scientific background and his previous doctorate in molecular biophysics. I remember a conversation with him when we were both a lot younger, when I asked about his earlier scientific work, wondering how that played into his theological work, and why at that stage he had not written much on science. He replied: "I wanted to wait until I had become a decent theologian before I started to do that." He has made good on his promise. In subsequent years, the project to bring together his scientific work, and particularly his reflections on the philosophy of science, with his theological concerns has yielded a rich array of work to help both the church and the academy to think more clearly and constructively about the complementary nature of these two ventures in human understanding than the work of many of the new atheists had done. He seems to have found exactly the right place now, as Andreas Idreos Professor in Science and Religion in the Faculty of Theology and Religion at the University of Oxford.

Yet Alister was not done yet. This intellectual and spiritual journey and his Belfast upbringing drew him ever closer to another northern Irish Christian thinker, C. S. Lewis. Reading Alister's biography of Lewis can't help make you think of the parallels between them—an Irish background, the setting in Oxford, the journey to Christianity, engaging at both popular and academic levels with sceptics and the robust defense and imaginative presentation of the riches of a classic, orthodox Christian faith.

Alister has always wanted to insist on the experiential core of Christianity. It is not a dry set of ideas, an abstract philosophical system, but an experience of the unexpected presence and mercy of God in Christ. Such an experience gives meaning and purpose to life, stimulates a desire for precise understanding and yet also fires the imagination—an endless fascination that allows and encourages intellectual and spiritual exploration. It also gives a map to the journey of life that can sustain a person over a lifetime and beyond. It is a privilege to be able to count Alister as a friend, someone from whom I have learnt a great deal over the years, from his books and from many laughter-filled conversations, and I am delighted that this book celebrates his sixty-fifth birthday. All his friends, colleagues, and countless others, whose journeys have been helped by his own, will wish him many more.

# Introduction

## Dennis Ngien

Alister E. McGrath currently holds the Andreas Idreos Professorship in Science and Religion in the Faculty of Theology and Religion at the University of Oxford. In celebration of McGrath's sixty-fifth birthday in 2018, this *Festschrift* aims to highlight him as a lauded scholar, who exemplifies an interface of science, theology, and religion. It comprises works by McGrath's theological allies and colleagues. It too presents an opportunity for thinkers from various backgrounds to pay tribute to McGrath, who has risen to a life of significance as a scientist-turned-theologian, professor, author, Christian apologist, and churchman. A word of thanks must be extended to the contributors and endorsers in this volume. I am also indebted to Kate Wong, who helped typeset the manuscript. All their efforts have made my task as the editor a pleasant and rewarding experience.

Theology is not hopelessly irrelevant, as it offers manifold service to the church, and speaks to the world, to culture, and to society in general. First, didactically, theology serves the teaching function of the Christian church. Second, polemically, theology aids in defense of the Christian truth against error within the church or from quasi-Christian movements. Third, apologetically, theology is done in response to the prevailing criticisms of Christianity or in response to questions about ultimate reality allegedly raised by humankind, including science, the new atheism, and religious pluralism. Fourth, spiritually, theology functions as the essential background for the formulation of the principles of piety and application of theological truth to Christian living.[1] Fifth, pastorally, theology—good theology—helps nurture

---

1. Cf. Jordan Aumann, *Spiritual Theology* (Westminster, MD: Sheed & Ward, 1987), 22. Spiritual theology is that branch of theology concerned with the principles and practices of living the Christian life.

souls, especially those of the wounded. McGrath articulates eloquently that the church needs theology precisely for the reasons mentioned above.

Scripture is the norm, but tradition, McGrath writes, "can refer to both the action of passing teachings on to others . . . and to the body of teachings which are passed on in this manner." Tradition is both "a process as well as a body of teaching."[2] The genius of McGrath is his remarkable ability to write in a clear, concise, and lucid manner that draws the readers to participate with the great thinkers of the Christian tradition, past and present. McGrath has not pitted his task as a systematic theologian against the work of the historians, but has sought to build bridges between the two disciplines.[3] Praiseworthy is his emphasis on history, seeing it as essential for understanding the nature of the church and its mission in the world. His reliance of classical Christian orthodoxy on careful historical analysis is evident. All of his scholarship and publications focus on the five categories of historical investigation: tradition, identity, ideas, contexts, and individuals.[4] Individuals and faith communities utilize tradition to inculcate identity, helping those who claim Christian faith to know who they are and where they belong in the church and in the world. As the vehicle for passing on identity and ideas, tradition enables us to inquire what really constitutes a Christian, and what kind of Christianity best defines the nature of the gospel and its implications for the life of the church.

McGrath's colleagues provide glimpses into his vision of how the biblical message has made and continues to make its impact in our world. In the New Testament Christian initiation, becoming a Christian involves repentance and faith. But it also includes baptism and receiving the Holy Spirit. Tony Lane compares that pattern with the evangelistic practice of British Evangelicals in the 1960s, in the current century, and in online materials. He examines books by Billy Graham, John Stott, Michael Green, and David Watson, as well as the much-used booklet *Journey into Life*, all of which were produced in the 1960s. Here the need for repentance and faith is evident, receiving the Spirit is clearer in some accounts than others; baptism is excluded in the process of becoming a Christian. Tony also investigates the

2. *Christianity: An Introduction.* 2nd ed. (Oxford: Blackwell, 2006), 107.

3. See *Christian Theology: An Introduction.* 6th ed. (Oxford: Blackwell, 2017); *The Christian Theology Reader.* 5th ed. (Oxford: Blackwell, 2017). These two books reflect McGrath's attempt to bridge historical and systematic theology; they too have become the seminal texts for an introductory course in systematic theology in several theological schools.

4. See Bill J. Leonard, "Why Study Church History? Listening to Saints and Sinners," in *Theology in the Service of the Church. Essays Presented to Fisher H. Humphreys*, eds. Timothy George and Eric F. Mason (Macon, GA: Mercer University Press, 2008), 62–71.

recent and the frequently used enquirer's courses *Alpha* and *Christianity Explored*, together with two popular booklets. In these materials, the emphasis on the Holy Spirit is more pronounced than their predecessors of the 1960s, but the role of baptism is left unattended. The online resources are less clear on the Holy Spirit and equally ignore baptism. The author offers five possible explanations for this consistent marginalisation of baptism. Finally, he admonishes Evangelicals to apply to their evangelism their declaration about the authority and normative role of Scripture.

Patrick Franklin explores the doctrine of the Trinity and its implications for ecclesial life. More specifically, the participatory approach to missional ecclesiology serves as a corrective to pragmatic, functional tendencies within some of the missional church literature. His fundamental assumption is that the God who sends is identical to the God who loves. This underscores that the mission of God is theologically grounded in God, whose essence is love. The loving Father who initiates his movement toward us through the Son in the Spirit is the same one who draws us into the heavenly sanctuary through the Son in the Spirit. This is borne out in Basil of Caesarea, who stresses the double movement of God in relation to us: the God-humanwardness, in which God first descends to us in the Son and reveals himself by the Holy Spirit as the object of our worship; and the human-Godwardness, in which the Spirit unites us to Christ and draws us to participate in the incarnate Son's communion with the Father (and thus also his ministry and mission). The double movement of the Trinity thus constitutes the condition of the possibility of true worship, faith, and practice.

Dating from the spring of 1979, McGrath was working on Luther at Cambridge University, under the direction of Professor Gordon Rupp.[5] Since then he has become a renowned reformation scholar, resulting in the publication of several major monographs including *Luther's Theology of the Cross*,[6] *A Life of John Calvin: A Study in the Shaping of Western Culture*,[7] *Reformation Thought*,[8] and *The Intellectual Origins of the European Reformation*.[9] Much of what he has written has benefitted the academy and the church; it too has rubbed off on several reformation scholars represented in this volume.

---

5. See McGrath's foreword to my *Luther's Theology of the Cross: Christ in Luther's Sermons on John* (Eugene, OR: Cascade, 2018), ix.

6. Oxford: Blackwell, 1985.

7. Oxford: Blackwell, 1993.

8. Oxford: Blackwell, 1993.

9. Oxford: Blackwell, 2003.

Martin Luther's doctrine of God as Creator, who brings into existence all things *ex nihilo*, without any merits of our own, constitutes the basis of the providential care of the Creator throughout his creation. This doctrine of providence, as Robert Kolb avers, is reflected in Luther's sermons and university lectures. Particularly the psalms and the stories of God's presence and interaction with his people in Genesis and the gospels supplied Luther with the content for an articulation of God's providence. God provides the material blessings sufficient to sustain body and life; his providence also includes the preservation of his human creatures in the face of multiple dangers. God's immanence bestows comfort in illness and persecution while it imparts health and peace at other times. This provision and protection for people occurs through gifts in nature and in the outworking of the callings of daily life to serve the neighbor. Faith perceives and receives God's bountiful blessings; the exercise of that faith encompasses both thanksgivings and petitions.

Both Luther and Calvin, Randall Zachman argues, understand the death of Christ in light of the fortunate or wonderful exchange Christ has made with sinners. Both also claim that God sent Christ to die for us out of sheer free love and mercy, to reconcile the sinful world to God. However, Luther claims that the free love of God frees us from the oppression brought about by our sin, by taking our sin from us and laying it upon Christ, so that Christ might destroy sin, death, and the wrath of God in his death, following Isaiah 53:6. Calvin, on the other hand, interprets Paul's statement that while we were yet enemies Christ died for us (Romans 5:10) to mean that God is as much the enemy of sinners as sinners are the enemies of God. Hence Calvin claims that God sent Christ out of love for sinful humanity in order to appease the wrath of God by his death, so that God could truly love sinners whom God would otherwise be compelled to hate. For Calvin, the death of Christ not only reconciles sinners to God, but it also reconciles God to sinners, by appeasing God's righteous wrath and vengeance against sin, following Isaiah 53:5.

Luther and Calvin, Sung Wook Chung claims, conceive of freedom as the integral aspect of the doctrine of salvation and its implication for public and civil ethics, the former grounds the latter. The reformers rediscovered the authentic and apostolic gospel whose central characteristic was the good news of not only freedom from the negatives — the law, sin, death, hell and the devil but also freedom for the positives — obedience, service and good works. They share the same contents concerning the function of law, which exposes human sinfulness and ultimately leads to Jesus Christ as savior. Through the recovery and restoration of the gospel of freedom, they endeavored to reform the church, and work out the ethical implications for both private and public life. Then the author concludes with applying the Reformation insights to global Christianity in general and Asian Christianity in particular. This shows that the Reformation's theological legacy will be faithfully handed down to next generations, henceforth making a significant contribution to the healthy future of global Christianity.

Oliver Crisp identifies in the New England theologian, Jonathan Edwards, a quandary about the atonement, addressing the question of how Christ in becoming our penal substitute atones for human guilt without compromising his integrity. "Christ does as it were hereby bring their guilt upon himself," Jonathan Edwards wrote, "but not in any blameable sense." Oliver seeks to offer a cogent presentation that addresses this lacuna; and this he does in the spirit of Edwards, as it were, to resolve this puzzle in his atonement theology. He argues that, strictly speaking, Christ does not assume the guilt of fallen humanity. Indeed, he cannot do so because he is not guilty of sin. Nevertheless, Christ can be treated as a representative standing in for fallen human beings. In acting as a representative and a penal substitute he may be said to assume the penal consequences of the sin of fallen human beings. A real union with Christ forms the basis of the legal union with Christ in atonement. This reflects a vicarious act of representation that involves suffering the penal consequences for human sin, though not suffering the punishment for human sin and guilt.

McGrath has written three volumes of *A Scientific Theology*, categorized under three specific titles and topics: nature, reality, and theory.[10] This work explores the issue of theological method rather than specific theological topics. The second volume "Reality" deals with the issue of realism in science and theology. Jonathan Wilson takes McGrath's Reality as a focal point for investigating the question, "What is real?" Jonathan engages Richard Rorty, T. F. Torrance, Roy Bhaskar, and Alister McGrath to argue for a doxological practice rather than an epistemological framing of the question. Jonathan considers it a mistake to frame the work of theology by first giving an account of natural theology and natural sciences because the "object" in question in these three spheres (or practices) is categorically ineffable and incommensurable. The answer to "What is real?" is to be found in the practice of discipleship, which at its core is the disciple community gathered in worship. As such theology is an *a posteriori* discipline, or more accurately, doxological theology offers adequately an account of our being grasped by Reality. The strengths of this doxological practice are briefly suggested, and

---

10. *A Scientific Theology*, 3 vols., *Nature, Reality,* and *Theory* (Grand Rapids: Eerdmans, 2001–03).

this particular practice is set within the gathering of God's people—the community of disciples—and other practices of the community.

Veli-Matti Kärkkäinen argues for a theologically-grounded interdisciplinary account of the wideness of Christian hope. A comprehensive eschatological vision should comprise personal, communal, and cosmic dimensions and engage not only biblical-theological but also scientific—as well as, ideally—religious viewpoints. The author begins to identify the various eschatological constituents and insights in culture, religions, and sciences. Whilst he discerns an eclipse of eschatological hope in modern/contemporary theology, he too delineates some promising new developments on the way to a comprehensive Christian vision. Thereafter the author offers his own vision of a new kind of Christian eschatology in which personal and communal hope, human and cosmic destiny, as well as present and future—orientations are juxtaposed in a dynamic mutual correlation. Because of the oceanic immensity of the end, the eschatologist must accept a certain ambiguity when dealing with events no one has beheld; he too must observe the limit of human language and reason, though not capitulate before the bar of reason. Theological imagination is required to speak of eschatology, in a noetic, metaphorical, and testimonial manner. As McGrath himself states: "From a Christian perspective, the horizons defined by the parameters of our human existence merely limit what we can see; they do not define what there is to be seen."[11]

In his *Re-Imagining Nature*,[12] McGrath proposes that the natural world is to be apprehended through the Christian imagination rather than the rationalistic proofs of the existence of God furnished by the design argument of the 19th century. With McGrath, Graham Ward does not intend to argue for the legitimacy of the necessary association between natural theology and systematic theology. Instead he explores the relationship between Christology and creation, the former is the abiding presupposition of the latter. He develops a theology of "nature" from a distinctly Christological point of view. The content of "nature" flows from and is predicated upon the revelation of God the Creator in Jesus Christ. This essay proceeds through an examination of the *aporias* in both Greek and Latin expressed in and around the Chalcedon formulation of the hypostatic union. It concludes that theology, while prompted always by faith to seek understanding, will never reach a definitive answer to the question of what is "nature" in a doctrine of creation. The task of Christian theology is not to provide answers,

---

11. *A Brief History of Heaven* (Oxford: Blackwell, 2003), 1.
12. Oxford: Blackwell, 2016.

but to question reductive accounts and to evince errors in theo-logic with respect to the operations of God in the redemption of all things created.

Sister Benedicta Ward considers Alister McGrath's work on C. S. Lewis in the ambience of Oxford and the search for truth there in both science and literature, with particular emphasis on children's stories as a guide to ultimate truth. Sister Benedicta extols a positive use of personal imagination in meditation, as seen in history, stretching from Anselm's eleventh century prayers into the modern spiritual, "Were you there when they crucified my Lord?" It is not by "a scientific exploration of the truth of the New Testament but a way of being present within those texts by imaginative participation." While the analysis of facts is essential to the discovery of knowledge, it is often through fiction that true life can be seen. Life consists not so much in the examination of series of molecules for our analysis and use but in a personal pilgrimage from exile towards home, in solitude or in solidarity with others, a journey short or long, sad or glad, known by speaking which is personal and immediate, or by writing which reaches a wider audience and lasts longer. Ultimate truth, Sister Benedicta avers, shines through all attempts to understand both facts and fictions. In this, she praises McGrath for his serious attention to his fellow Oxfordian's novels for children: "Not everything has a name. . . beauty will save the world."

Models help us to better understand complex realities, including the intricate interrelationship of science and theology. Bethany Sollereder takes the idea of two cultures—science and theology — seriously as a means for understanding how practitioners tackle the frustrations of engaging in interdisciplinary work between these two fields. Models of interaction between science and theology tend to concentrate on issues of epistemology, focusing on truth claims and epistemic priority in any given context. The epistemic approach lacks practical advice for how one might go about actually engaging with the other domain of knowledge. Drawing from anthropology and intercultural studies, Bethany claims that cultural models not only furnishes a better description of the complex interrelationship of science and theology, but also that they offer a practical approach to engaging well in scholarship. Intercultural models can provide a practical approach to bridging the two different views of reality provided by science and theology. As an instance, she cites the theodicy of natural disasters represented by theologian David Bentley Hart's *The Doors of the Sea: Where Was God in the Tsunami?* and scientist Robert White's *Who is to Blame? Disasters, Nature and Acts of God.* Spurning isolation in ex-pat communities, challenging the discipline-centric impulse, and progressing towards becoming a 150 percent person are ways to begin to build bridges across these two oft-divided cultures. "To become a 150 percent person is to develop a third culture in oneself: one that is neither wholly the first nor the second. To do so requires the humility to take on an identity that is neither this nor that: to let go of mastery and embrace the uncertainty of the in between." McGrath has demonstrated successfully what it looks like to live as a 150 percent person in science and theology, assuming an identity that is neither wholly the former nor the latter and embracing the two different cultures with enthusiasm and amicability.

Motivated by a pastoral concern for the wounded, McGrath published *Suffering* in 1992.[13] Michael Lloyd provides an appreciation and helpful critique of that book. He approaches the theodical question by erecting a formally inconsistent set of propositions to which atheist philosophers have claimed that theists must be committed: (1) God is omnipotent; (2) God is wholly good; (3) Evil exists; (4a) There are no limits to what an omnipotent thing can do, (4b) Evil in the world is not logically necessary; (5) A good thing always eliminates evil as far as it can. A logically consistent theist must therefore reject one of these propositions. The author describes various approaches to the problem of evil within Christian Theology and categorizes them according to which proposition they reject. It is Michael's persuasion that McGrath rejects proposition 5, and, with Augustine, he presents human freedom as the philosophical legitimacy of why God has not eliminated evil. The Free Will defence, however, fails to account for natural evil. As a remedy, Michael outlines three families of response to natural evil: the Instrumental view, the Inevitable view and the Inimical view. McGrath utilizes both the Instrumental and the Inevitable views. However, these are subject to critique, Michael argues, particularly in light of the way in which Jesus' healing ministry seems to disclose a divine assault upon (and therefore inimical attitude towards) suffering. Finally, McGrath's practical, rather than theoretical, exposition of divine passibility, and why McGrath considers it to be theodically and spiritually helpful, is expounded.

Jeffrey Greenman offers a delightful compendious portrait of McGrath as an evangelical, Anglican, and ecclesial theologian in a consubstantial triad. Greenman proposes a tri-focal vision to penetrate the three interwoven aspects of McGrath's life and work and draw from them the depths and breadth of his contribution to the church, society, and world. He praises McGrath's ability to show how evangelicalism could be enriched by diverse traditions of the forebears without losing its own distinctive identity. Critical yet appreciative is the posture with which McGrath engages with the great tradition of the past. Beyond his evangelical allegiance, McGrath adheres to an Anglican tradition. He reaps from a list of Anglican thinkers, amongst

---

13. London: Hodder & Stoughton, 1992.

whom his favorites are John R. Stott, C. S. Lewis, and James I. Packer, and demonstrates effectively the inner consistency between evangelicalism and Anglicanism, that the former is, historically and theologically, a viable option within Anglicanism, as evident in his reading of the Thirty-Nine Articles, the only document, apart from Scripture, the creeds and the Prayer Book, accepted as authoritative for Anglicans. This too brings to light McGrath as an exemplary ecclesial theologian, fully committed to the centrality and life of the church as basic to his overall evangelical-Anglican vision. As much as he inculcates in God's people the importance of the passionate discipline of the mind, he is critical of pure academic theology that retreats into ivory tower, totally removed from concrete life questions and character formation, and deviations of theology that transcends the core of the historic, credal faith, already confessed by the Christian church. People of all persuasions have sought McGrath "as a clear, consistent and passionate spokesman for a biblically faithful, intellectually grounded, evangelistically attuned, and culturally engaged evangelicalism."

Finally, let me add a personal note. From 1988 to 1993, I was pursuing doctoral study (PhD) at the Toronto School of Theology, University of Toronto. Professor James I. Packer advised me to seek counsel from McGrath, who was at that time the principal of Wycliffe Hall, Oxford University and a widely esteemed theologian. Since 1998, when my Centre for Mentorship & Theological Reflection (Centre) was founded, I have been in frequent correspondence with McGrath. He was honored by the Centre as the Senior Scholar (2009); he too was the plenary speaker for the Reformation 500th anniversary (2017), together with Drs. Victor Shepherd and Dennis Ngien, hosted by the Centre and held at Tyndale University College & Seminary Chapel in Toronto. I often visited with him in Oxford, enjoying consultation with him and informative interactions on various topics ranging from history, theology, philosophy, science, and religion. McGrath has contributed very much to the advancement of my scholarship and spirituality, particularly in Luther's theology.[14]

Gregory Nazianzus' statement befits McGrath's passion as a faithful theologian whose prime interest is the well-being of the people of God: "But the scope of our art is to provide the soul with wings, to rescue it from the world and give it to God."[15] In the spirit of Nazianzus, McGrath bestirs his

14. See McGrath's generous foreword to my *Luther's Theology of the Cross*, ix: "In recent years, Dennis Ngien has established himself as a leading interpreter of Luther, with a most welcome emphasis on the importance of Luther's ideas for the life and witness of the church, as well as for the personal spiritual journeys of individual believers."

15. Gregory of Nazianzus, *Apologeticus de Fuga*, ed., Philip Schaff, *Nicene and Post Nicene Fathers*, Series 2, Volume 7 (Grand Rapids: Eerdmans, 1956), Oration 2.22.

audience through various disciplines to soar on eagle's wings, enabling them to break new ground and reach new height. Recognized as one of the most influential and potent living theologians, his numerous writings have made immense contribution to the on-going task of theology. The depth and breadth of knowledge he possesses, the intellectual rigor and judiciousness with which he writes, the irenic spirit and charity typical of his character—all of this adds to the delight of sitting under his tutelage.

Lord, give us more, like McGrath!

## Chapter 1

# Becoming a Christian
## Christian Initiation in the New Testament and in British Evangelicalism

ANTHONY N. S. LANE

ALISTER MCGRATH IS A theologian of many parts. He has at different times focused on topics as diverse as the doctrine of justification and the relation between theology and science. Among his many publications a number relate to Evangelicalism.[1] It is appropriate, therefore, that a volume dedicated to him should contain a chapter on that topic. Like him, I write as a critical friend, as one who identifies as an Evangelical but is not uncritical of Evangelicalism in all its features. In particular, I want to focus on an aspect of Evangelicalism that is somewhat paradoxical. In any account of Evangelical distinctives, two items are almost certain to appear. A key feature of Evangelicals is their commitment to evangelism, to preaching the gospel, the evangel, the good news. To be an Evangelical is to believe in the need for conversion, whether sudden or otherwise, and the need to be a genuine,

---

1. Richard T. France and Alister E. McGrath, eds., *Evangelical Anglicans: Their Role and Influence in the Church Today* (London: SPCK, 1993), with two chapters by McGrath; Alister E. McGrath, *Evangelicalism and the Future of Christianity* (London: Hodder & Stoughton, 1994); Alister E. McGrath, "Theology and the Futures of Evangelicalism," in *The Futures of Evangelicalism: Issues and Prospects*, eds. Craig Bartholomew, et al. (Leicester: IVP, 2003), 15–39.

living, "born-again" Christian rather than a merely nominal churchgoer. Another key feature concerns the role of Scripture. Evangelicals believe, over against liberals, that the teaching of Scripture is true and normative for the church and that the church should align her teaching with Scripture. Evangelicals also believe, against those from more Catholic sections of the church, that Scripture is not just normative, but is the final norm. That is, while tradition and the teaching of the church are of great value, ultimately they must be tested by the norm of Scripture. In the words of the traditional formula, Scripture is the *norma normans non normata*, the norm or rule that rules but is not itself ruled. It is this that is usually meant by the traditional (though post-Reformation) slogan *sola scriptura*.[2]

My argument in this paper is that most Evangelicals in their practice of evangelism fail to submit their understandings of Christian initiation adequately to the norm of Scripture. Thus, ironically, in one of their most distinctive and central activities they fail to heed one of their most foundational axioms: the normative role of Scripture. What makes this the more embarrassing is that Evangelicals, and often the self-same individuals, are not backward in chiding other traditions for their failure to heed the teaching of Scripture.

I shall begin by outlining the process of Christian initiation as I see it in the New Testament and then compare this with the practice of British Evangelicals in the 1960s, in the current century, and in online resources, before closing with some concluding comments.

## 1. CHRISTIAN INITIATION IN THE NEW TESTAMENT[3]

How does one become a Christian? What must I do to be saved? What needs to happen when someone wishes to respond to the gospel? Or, to use the jargon, what is Christian initiation? Where in the New Testament should we turn for an answer to this? Not to the Gospels as the new covenant had not yet come into effect during the ministry of Jesus. The situation changes with the crucifixion, resurrection, and ascension of Jesus. The response looked for after Pentecost becomes different, though not totally different, from what precedes. There is relevant material in the Epistles, but the clearest answer to our questions is found in the Acts of the Apostles where we see the apostles preaching the gospel to unbelievers. In particular, there are

---

2. Cf. my "Sola scriptura? Making Sense of a Post-Reformation Slogan," in *A Pathway into the Holy Scripture*, eds. Philip E. Satterthwaite and David F. Wright (Grand Rapids: Eerdmans, 1994), 297–327.

3. I am grateful to Conrad Gempf for helpful comments on this section.

fourteen passages where evangelists tell enquirers how to respond or where there is a reasonably full account of the conversion of a person or group.[4] If we look at these passages and ask what was expected to happen, there are four things that are repeatedly mentioned: repentance, faith, baptism, and receiving the Holy Spirit. All four are not mentioned every time, but a clear fourfold pattern emerges.

James Dunn sees three elements only in Christian initiation: repentance, baptism, and the gift of the Spirit. But he then states that repentance and faith are "opposite sides of the same coin."[5] This is confusing and it makes more sense to speak of four elements, as does David Pawson, who links repentance and faith together as our side of initiation, which he calls conversion. He links baptism and receiving the Spirit together as the work of God, under the heading of regeneration.[6]

Faith is mentioned in eleven of the fourteen passages from Acts just mentioned and is found in a variant reading in an twelfth passage (8:37). The only place where faith is missing is in two accounts of Paul's conversion (9:17–18, 22:14–16), though it may safely be assumed that his conversion did involve faith.[7] Baptism is also mentioned ten times, the exceptions including the incomplete address of Acts 3, which was interrupted by the police. The other omissions are 15:7–9, referring to the conversion of Cornelius who *was* in fact baptized according to 10:47–48, the sermon on Mars Hill (17:30–34) and Paul's account of his own teaching in 20:20–21. Receiving the Spirit is mentioned seven out of fourteen times, but should not therefore be seen as an optional extra. The events at Samaria (8:4–17) and Ephesus (19:1–7) show clearly that without the Spirit, initiation was not regarded as complete. The fact that all four things are not mentioned in all fourteen passages reflects the fact that Luke was not a pedant, not that they didn't happen. This can be seen from multiple accounts of the same event (conversions of Paul and Cornelius) where different things are mentioned each time. Also, where the apostles suspected that one of these was missing they took care to remedy the defect (8:15–17, 20–23; 19:1–7).

Tom Wright, in his magisterial biography of Paul, observes that Paul was baptized immediately, "as in some of the other occasions in Acts."[8] This

---

4. Acts 2:37–41, 44; 3:17–20; 4:3–4; 8:12–24, 36–38; 9:17–18; 10:34–35, 43–48; 11:15–18; 15:7–9; 16:14–15, 30–34; 17:30–34; 19:1–7; 20:20–21; 22:10, 14–16.

5. James D. G. Dunn, *Baptism in the Holy Spirit* (London: SCM, 1970), 91.

6. David Pawson, *The Normal Christian Birth* (London: Hodder & Stoughton, 1989), 9–90.

7. In Acts 26:15–18, Paul is instructed at his conversion to preach sanctification by faith.

8. Tom Wright, *Paul: A Biography* (London: SPCK, 2018), 57.

is a remarkably timid statement from one who is well known for his bold claims! The fact is that there is no evidence in Acts that any adult convert was baptized other than immediately. The only convert who was not baptized on the same day as his conversion was the Philippian jailer, and he was baptized the same *night*![9] There is nothing in the rest of the New Testament to suggest that immediate baptism was not the norm.

We see in Acts that baptism is clearly an integral part of Christian initiation, a part of what happens in order for someone to become a Christian. This coheres with the rest of the New Testament, where faith and baptism are like the clichéd two sides of a coin. Baptism is a part of Christian initiation, by which people become Christians, but this is not baptism without faith. Salvation is by faith, but this is not faith without baptism.[10] They thought of faith and baptism as a unity, not just on theoretical grounds but because they came together in actual practice. It was easy, therefore, for them to glide unselfconsciously from talking about the one to talking about the other. A few examples will suffice:

> In Christ Jesus you are all sons of God, through faith. For as many of you as were baptized into Christ have put on Christ. (Gal 3:26–27)

> In him also you were circumcised with a circumcision made without hands, by putting off the body of the flesh, by the circumcision of Christ, having been buried with him in baptism, in which you were also raised with him through faith in the powerful working of God, who raised him from the dead. (Col 2:11–12)

Perhaps the most striking example lies in the very structure of Romans. In chapters 1 to 5, Paul develops his doctrine of justification by faith. In chapter 6, he unselfconsciously turns to a discussion of baptism. Has he completely changed the subject? No. The faith that justifies is the faith that gave birth to baptism at their conversion. The baptism by which they were buried with Christ is the baptism with which they expressed their faith at their conversion. There is a single reality being discussed from two different angles, as is seen from the blending of faith and confession of Christ (in baptism) in 10:9–10.

---

9. Paul's baptism came three days after his blinding experience, but there was no delay once Ananias came to see him (Acts 9:1–19).

10. I am thinking of adults and not wishing to prejudice the issue of infant baptism.

## 2. INITIATION IN THE 1960S

In this section I will review some of the key materials that were used in the sixties, when I was a student. I will look at five works — four evangelistic books and a booklet that were very widely used to lead enquirers into a committed faith.

Billy Graham's *Peace with God* (1954)[11] was a much printed and widely used evangelistic book from the most significant evangelist of the twentieth century. Although its author was not British, he and it exercised a profound influence upon British Evangelicalism and so it is fitting to discuss it here. Like all good sermons, it is in three parts: "The Problem," "The Solution" and "The Results." Most of the teaching about initiation, about embarking on the Christian way, is found in Part Two. An initial analysis of conversion sets out the main elements (95–98). Biblical conversion involves two active steps (repentance and faith) and one passive step (regeneration). It is as you repent and believe, as you open your heart and let Jesus in, that "the Holy Spirit performs the miracle of the new birth" and "Jesus Christ, through the Spirit of God, takes up residence in your heart." There follow chapters on each of these three steps in turn (chs. 9–11). These describe repentance and faith fully, showing how each involves the intellect, the emotions and the will. The new birth is a work of the Spirit and Christ dwells in the regenerate through the Spirit. In Part Two the role of repentance and faith in Christian initiation is paramount and the reception of the Spirit is clear in the account of the new birth. But what of baptism? This is mentioned just once in Part Two, in the chapter on repentance: "The sermon that Peter preached on the Day of Pentecost was, 'Repent, and be baptized every one of you in the name of Jesus Christ for the remission of sins' (Acts 2:38)" (102).[12] But the verse is cited purely as a reference to repentance, with no further mention of baptism.

The place of the church is brought out in Part Three on the results (153) and one of the longest chapters of the book is devoted to it (ch. 15), with one passing mention of baptism: "The church is commanded to 'Go ye into all the world, and preach the gospel,' and to baptize those who believe" (168). The focus is on the church's mission rather than the need for the believing

---

11. Billy Graham, *Peace With God* (Kingswood Tadworth, UK: The World's Work, 1954).

12. To check for references to baptism, in addition to reading the text I made a word search in 2004 on the online version at www.ccel.us/PeaceWithGod.toc.html, which gave the "revised and expanded" 1984 edition. I am assuming that no earlier references to baptism had been expunged in the course of expansion.

reader to be baptized. There is no other mention of baptism in Part Three.[13] Thus readers of *Peace with God* would be aware that they should repent and believe and that they should expect the Holy Spirit to regenerate and indwell them. They would be unlikely, however, to be aware of any need for baptism.

John Stott's *Basic Christianity* (1958)[14] was the leading home-grown contribution to this genre. By 1970 the first edition had sold 300,000 copies and had been translated into over a dozen languages, according to the cover of the second edition. This time there are four parts: "Christ's Person," "Man's Need," "Christ's Work" and "Man's Response." What of Christian initiation? Already at the end of Part Three (Christ's Work) there is the statement that the inner presence of the Holy Spirit is the spiritual birthright and indeed the distinguishing mark of the Christian. All Christians should be filled with the Spirit (100). Part Four (Man's Response) is divided into chapters on "Counting the Cost," "Reaching a Decision" and "Being a Christian." The first of these expounds clearly the need for repentance and discipleship. The next unpacks the step of faith, which goes beyond mental belief to "a decisive act of trust." This is explained at length in terms of Revelation 3:20, the need to open the door of our lives to Christ, with reference to Holman Hunt's famous picture. The prominence of this particular image is in part explained by the fact that the author's own conversion took place in these terms, as he illustrates from his own diary (122, 128–29).[15] Whether or not you are a real and committed Christian depends on the answer to one question: "Which side of the door is Jesus Christ? . . . That is the crucial issue" (129). The chapter concludes with a prayer to be prayed, in three paragraphs: acknowledgement of sins and turning from them in repentance; belief in Christ; opening the door to Christ as Saviour and Lord (129).

Repentance and faith (together with opening the door) are central to "man's response." It has already been stated that Christians receive the Spirit, who indwells them (100) and this is repeated in the final chapter on Being a Christian (134). But what of baptism? This is once portrayed negatively

---

13. In the online version there is a further negative reference to baptism in ch. 19, "Peace at Last": "'Oh,' people say, 'I have joined the church. I have been baptized.' But has Jesus come to live in their hearts?" (p. 216). This is not found in the equivalent chapter of the 1954 edition.

14. John R. W. Stott, *Basic Christianity* (London: Inter-Varsity, 1958). I have used the 2nd edition (1971).

15. For Stott's conversion, cf. Timothy Dudley-Smith, *John Stott: The Making of a Leader* (Leicester: IVP, 1999), 87–96 (94–96 on Revelation 3:20). It was E. J. H. Nash ("Bash") who was instrumental in his conversion, through his preaching and personal counselling. For the prominence of Revelation 3:20 in Bash's evangelism, cf. Dick Knight, "The Speaker," in *"Bash": A Study in Spiritual Power*, ed. John Eddison (Basingstoke, UK: Marshall Morgan & Scott, 1983), 45–53, esp. 51.

in that being baptized and confirmed, even being an ordained minister, is no substitute for opening the door to Christ, without which one is not a real Christian (127). But previously, in the chapter on Counting the Cost, it has been stated that Christians must be ready to confess their faith, beginning with baptism. "Certainly, if not already baptized, the convert must be baptized" (116). Again, in the final chapter on Being a Christian, it is made clear that belonging to a local church is not an optional extra. "Baptism is the way of entry into the visible Christian society.... If you have not been baptized, you should ask your minister to prepare you for baptism" (139). Thus baptism is not ignored, but it occupies a rather minor role as just one of the many implications of being a Christian.

These two works both focus on repentance and faith and both make it clear that the Christian will receive the indwelling Spirit. This is clearly linked to initiation by Graham, who relates it to the new birth, while Stott never mentions it in that precise context. Stott also adds to repentance and faith the imagery of opening the door of our lives to Jesus, the dominant theme of the chapter on "Reaching a Decision." As for baptism, Graham mentions it only in passing and although Stott mentions the need for baptism it is at best marginal to his account of how one becomes a Christian.

To be fair to these two authors we must recognise that they were primarily addressing a nominal Christian audience, the majority of whom had church links at least in their younger years. It is often objected that Revelation 3:20 does not come in an evangelistic context and that it is an abuse to apply it to conversion. There is some truth in this, but it can plausibly be argued that it comes in a context of nominal (or at least lax) Christianity and that it can legitimately be used to summon nominal Christians to commitment.

*Peace with God* and *Basic Christianity* (from the mid to late fifties) are both systematic presentations expounding the Christian message within the context of a clear theological structure. In the sixties society was undergoing profound changes, especially the student society to which British books of this ilk were primarily addressed. Evangelistic books tended to assume less, and especially not to assume that "the Bible says" was sufficient to settle all issues. Michael Green, in particular, wrote a number of racy books seeking to scratch where it itches. Thus *Man Alive* (1967) focused on "the relevance, the challenge, the power of the resurrection to change men's lives and to show the way out from meaninglessness and despair."[16] The problem starts with secularly perceived needs rather than sin and the focus is on the resur-

---

16. Michael Green, *Man Alive* (London: Inter-Varsity, 1967), quoting from the book cover.

rection rather than substitutionary atonement. The narrative is fast moving with frequent reference both to Scripture and to contemporary testimonies. But although the style is very different, there is no shortage of content. Sin and atonement are certainly not ignored. Baptism receives more mention than from Graham or Stott. Of the Corinthians it is said: "Washed in a baptism made effective by Christ's atoning death on the cross, their past was dealt with. And the Spirit of the risen Christ now lived in their bodies, as though they were his temples" (21). Again, the early Christians said that "a man must repent of his sins, believe in the risen Lord, and be baptized in water if he was to be sure of acceptance by God." Baptism is called "the initiation ceremony into world-wide Christendom" (52).

But despite this clear teaching on baptism in the body of the book, it fades from the scene when the reader is invited to respond to the gospel. The book concludes with a four-page section addressed ". . . To The Uncommitted" calling on the reader to respond (92–96). Repentance and a first-hand faith are what is needed. At the very end there is "A Suggested Prayer of Commitment." This focuses on faith, on the cost of becoming a Christian, on our acceptance of Christ's offer and his acceptance of us. Faith is clear and repentance is covered. There is no mention in the prayer (or in this concluding section) of baptism or the Holy Spirit. The better-rounded theology of the body of the book has unfortunately not worked through to the initiatory step of commitment at the end.

Another widely influential book was David Watson's *My God Is Real*.[17] This was first published in 1970, but was based on university mission addresses given during the sixties. The first five chapters examine Christ, sin, hell, the cross and the resurrection. The last three cover the cost, conversion and commitment. The first of these, on the cost, explains with brutal clarity the implications of repentance. The second describes the new birth, with the emphasis on our need to receive it rather than what we should do. The final chapter describes the step of commitment. "Wherever the first disciples went, they preached one message which could be summarised in two words: *repent* and *believe*" (87). Repentance means turning away from sin to a life committed to Christ. Faith involves more than head belief and can be compared to the commitment to one's partner in a marriage service. It is primarily an act of will. There follows a prayer to be used. This contains admission of sin, willingness to turn and follow Christ, thanks for his death on the cross and a decision of will to come to him (90). The new convert is urged to join a Christian fellowship ("you will find it of immense personal

---

17. David C. K. Watson, *My God Is Real* (London: Falcon, 1970). I have used the 2nd edition (1977).

help" (93)) but there is no mention of baptism. The book concludes with the need to be filled with the Holy Spirit, which is the greatest need for the Christian. The convert is urged to pray for this, but the impression given is that this is something for later rather than part of Christian initiation, of becoming a Christian (94–95). Watson effectively reduces initiation to repentance and faith — in keeping with his own summary of the apostolic message. Baptism apparently plays no role at all and receiving the Spirit has moved from being part of initiation to a task for the new convert.

Norman Warren's *Journey Into Life* (1964)[18] is a sixteen-page booklet that has been used in conjunction with countless evangelistic campaigns. Having explained the effects of sin and the death of Christ it explains carefully what is "Your Part" (10–13). You have something to admit: your sin. You should be deeply sorry for it, hate it and be willing to turn from it. You have something to believe: "that Jesus Christ died on the cross bearing all the guilt and penalty of *your* sin." You have something to consider: the cost of discipleship. Finally, you have something to do: "Accept Jesus into your life to be your Lord to control you, your Saviour to cleanse you, your friend to guide and be with you." This is followed by the quotation of Revelation 3:20, with the addition of the comment that there is no handle to the door on the outside. (Holman Hunt is not named, but the source is clear.) After further exhortation, there is a prayer to pray, which expresses sorrow for sin, a turning from it, an acceptance of Christ's death for me and an invitation to him to come into my life.

The ideas of repentance and faith are fairly well expressed, though the latter seems to be excessively focused upon an acceptance of Christ's substitutionary death. The Holy Spirit is mentioned just once in the booklet. "You have said this prayer and meant it," so Christ "now lives in your heart by his Holy Spirit" (14). Baptism is actually mentioned twice, but only negatively. The fact that you are baptized and confirmed proves nothing as "so are thousands who care little about Christ" (3). Those considering whether to open the door of their life to Christ should consider that "you can be baptised, confirmed, go to church, yes, even read the Bible and pray, and still leave Jesus Christ outside the door of your life" (12). Baptism is a snare that can cause nominal Christians not to pray the prayer. There is no hint that it is also expected of Christians and that the previously unbaptized convert should seek it. The convert is told to read the Bible, to pray and to "join a local church at once" (15) — but not told to be baptized. Those following this path of initiation should have a reasonably clear idea of the need to repent

---

18. Norman Warren, *Journey into Life* (Eastbourne, UK: Kingsway [Falcon Booklet], 1964). I have used the revised edition (1980).

and believe. If they pay very careful attention they may be aware that they have the Spirit, though were they to blink at the wrong moment they might like the Ephesian disciples say "we have not even heard that there is a Holy Spirit" (Acts 19:2). They would have no reason for feeling positively inclined towards the idea of baptism.

The picture that emerges from the sixties can be summarised as follows. The need for repentance and faith is clear. This is often expressed through the model of opening the door of one's life to Jesus, based on Revelation 3:20 as interpreted by Holman Hunt. Receiving the Spirit is clearer in some accounts than others. Baptism plays no part in the process of becoming a Christian as set out by these writers, though some of them refer to the need for baptism at other points in their account.[19]

## 3. INITIATION IN THE TWENTY-FIRST CENTURY

The current generation has seen the rise and huge popularity of enquirer's courses. The most famous is Nicky Gumbel's *Alpha Course*. This uses a series of video presentations and there is an accompanying book, *Questions of Life*,[20] which I will cite. The question of how to become a Christian comes near the middle of the course rather than the end and is handled on more than one occasion. The chapter on "Why Did Jesus Die?" ends with a prayer to be prayed "as a way of starting the Christian life" (54–55). This includes sorrow for past sins and prayer for forgiveness, thanksgiving for the gift of forgiveness, the work of Christ and the gift of the Spirit, a commitment to follow and obey and prayer for God to come into my life for ever by his Holy Spirit. Faith is not actually named in the prayer, but the prayer is given for those who are unsure about whether they have ever really believed in Jesus. Repentance, faith and receiving the Spirit are explicit; of baptism there is no mention. The following chapter, on "How Can I Be Sure of My Faith?," contains the almost obligatory use of Revelation 3:20, interpreted again through Holman Hunt's painting (60–61).

---

19. Gordon Kuhrt has pointed out to me that Stott, Green, and Watson all wrote their evangelistic books when they were relatively young and that the first two at least developed their theology over the years. This may have affected their later writings, but it did not affect the revised editions of these books. Also, we see in *Man Alive* the contrast between the developed doctrine of baptism in the body of the book and the failure to mention it in the invitation to respond at the end of the book. Green's later *Baptism: Its Purpose, Practice and Power* (London: Hodder & Stoughton, 1987) develops more fully the positive view of baptism found in the body of *Man Alive*.

20. Nicky Gumbel, *Questions of Life* (Eastbourne, UK: Kingsway, 1993).

What role does baptism play? In the chapter on "Who is the Holy Spirit?" we read that "baptism with water is very important, but it is not enough," because we also need to be baptized in the Spirit (112). Later the account of the Ephesian "disciples" (Acts 19:1–7) is applied to those today who "may have been baptised, confirmed and gone to church from time to time or even regularly" (135).[21] In the chapter entitled "What about the Church?" it is stated that, "Baptism is a visible mark of being a member of the church. It is also a visible sign of what it means to be a Christian. . . . Jesus himself commanded his followers to go and make disciples and to baptise them" (219).

Those following the Alpha Course should have no difficulty in grasping that becoming a Christian requires repentance and faith. Apart from the prayer of commitment, the whole thrust of the course is about the need to believe and convert. That becoming a Christian involves receiving the Spirit is not only stated but also reinforced by the chapters on "Who Is the Holy Spirit?," "What Does the Holy Spirit Do?" and "How Can I Be Filled with the Spirit?" It is made clear that baptism on its own is not enough, though it is also stated that this is a part of what it means to belong to the church.

Nicky Gumbel has also written a twenty-four-page booklet entitled *Why Jesus?*[22] This contains sections on "What's It All About?," "Why Do We Need Him?," "Why Bother With Jesus?," "Why Did He Come?" and "Why Not?," before going on to "What Do We Have To Do?" The answer to this last question is "an act of faith," understood as "putting our trust in a Person" (19). This is summarised by "three very simple words": "Sorry" for sins and turning from them (repentance); "Thank you" to Jesus for dying for your sins and for the offer of forgiveness, freedom and the Spirit; "Please" come and live within by the Spirit. There then follows a prayer which expresses these three things and concludes "Please come into my life by your Holy Spirit to be with me for ever" (19–20). Baptism is not mentioned but the first heading in the concluding section ("What Now?") is "Tell someone." Repentance, faith and receiving the Spirit are clear; baptism is nowhere to be seen.

It is interesting to contrast this with "official policy." Nicky Gumbel's *Telling Others*, in a later edition, has an Appendix entitled "Common Questions," one of which is "What does Alpha teach about the sacraments?" Here

---

21. As was Gumbel's own experience: "I was at times an atheist and at times an agnostic, unsure of what I believed. I had been baptised and confirmed, but it had not meant much to me" (Gumbel, *Questions of Life*, 69).

22. Nicky Gumbel, *Why Jesus?* (Eastbourne, UK: Kingsway, 1991). I have used the 1992 edition.

he states that, "we encourage all new Christians who have not been baptised to be baptised at the end of the course." He also states:

> Teaching on the sacraments is limited, in the sense that we only teach on Alpha what all the major denominations and traditions are agreed about. For example, we teach about the essential meaning and necessity for baptism but we do not go into the divisive issue of infant baptism.... So although the teaching on the sacraments is limited on the course itself, both the teaching and the practice of the sacraments of baptism and Holy Communion form an essential part of the course.[23]

Despite this clear statement, baptism is not mentioned in *Why Jesus?* and plays a very minor role in the Alpha Course.

Another popular model that is often used to explain the gospel to interested folk is found in the *Two Ways to Live* Booklet produced by Philip Jensen in 1989. After a brief account of creation, sin and the work of Christ, there is a description of the two ways to live. The right way is to "submit to Jesus as our ruler" and to "trust in Jesus' death and resurrection."

An increasingly popular alternative to the Alpha Course is *Christianity Explored*, for which I have used both the book and the leader's Study Guide.[24] The latter suggests that participants should be taken through the *Two Ways to Live* booklet and that those wishing to make a commitment to Christ should be taken through four steps (a, b, c, d): accept that they have sinned, believe that Christ died for them, count the cost and "do it" (put their trust in Christ) (35). Both the leader's and the participant's Study Guide end with a suggested prayer of commitment. This contains confession of and sorrow for rebellion and sin, thanks for Jesus' death on the cross so that I can be forgiven, and a prayer for the Holy Spirit to help me to follow Jesus whatever the cost (120). These themes are all prepared for by the material earlier in the course. There is a talk on the Holy Spirit that explains about the Spirit coming to live in Christians (102–103).

---

23. Nicky Gumbel, *Telling Others?* (Eastbourne, UK: Kingsway, 2001 edition), 203–4. I am grateful to James Heard for drawing my attention to this. Also for drawing my attention to an internal HTB document entitled *Questions and Answers*, for the use of staff in responding to queries. This stated, in the context of questions about Alpha and repentance: "We believe the gospel is good news. The overwhelming emphasis of Alpha is on the good news of the gospel. Nevertheless, Christian initiation involves repentance, faith, receiving the Holy Spirit and baptism."

24. Rico Tice and Barry Cooper, *Christianity Explored* (Carlisle, UK: Authentic Lifestyle, 2002); Rico Tice, *Christianity Explored Study Guide: Leader's Edition* (Carlisle, UK: Paternoster Lifestyle, 2001). I have used the 2nd edition (2003).

The book contains a different prayer of commitment (141). This expresses a realization of my sin against God and others, my willingness to turn from self-centeredness to trust in Christ, my thanks for his giving his life for my sin and a request that he become Lord of my life. The reader is then assured that all who respond to Jesus are forgiven, Revelation 3:20 being cited as proof. The book sees initiation in terms of repentance and faith, with the familiar use of Revelation 3:20; the Study Guide is fuller and includes receiving the Holy Spirit. I have yet to find any mention of baptism in either the book or the Study Guide.

## 4. ONLINE RESOURCES[25]

Today there are many online evangelistic resources.[26] The Billy Graham Evangelistic Association has a site called Peace with God,[27] which takes the reader briefly through four steps, followed by a "sinner's prayer" that is explicit about faith and implicit about repentance ("I want to . . . follow Him as Lord, from this day forward"). Those who pray it are offered free resources, including a "church finder," but are not told about baptism or receiving the Spirit. Another key site is Christianity.org.[28] This contains many items aimed at enquirers. A careful search, including reading the pages on "Change and believe" and "Believing and belonging," yielded clear statements about faith and repentance but no mention of baptism.[29] There is a page on "The Spirit of God," which states that the Holy Spirit dwells within Christians, but no mention of receiving the Spirit at conversion. There is a page on "Worship" that refers to "mass, communion, eucharist or a number of other names," as well as "rites of passage such as funerals and weddings," but does not mention baptism.

## 5. COMPARISON

How does one become a Christian? The New Testament answer, we have argued, is by repenting, believing, being baptized and receiving the Spirit. What have we found in our survey of Evangelical patterns of initiation in

---

25. I am very grateful to Rich Powney for guidance in adding this section.

26. For some of these, see https://greatcommission.co.uk/category/act?page=3&topics=369.

27. https://peacewithgod.net.

28. https://christianity.org.uk.

29. Based on my search of the site. If there is in fact a mention in an obscure spot, it is likely to escape the attention of the seeker wishing to know how to become a Christian.

the present and previous generations? Our results can be summarised in a few points:

1. Repentance and faith are clearly taught.

2. These are often summarised in the language of Revelation 3:20, as seen through the portrayal of Holman Hunt. We become Christians by opening the door of our lives to Jesus.

3. Most (but not all) of the materials examined make it clear that the Holy Spirit will indwell the new convert, but most do not portray receiving the Spirit as an aspect of Christian initiation. The danger with this is that it can lead to converts who like the Ephesian disciples "have not even heard that there is a Holy Spirit" (Acts 19:2).

4. Baptism is the missing dimension. While the more theologically grounded Anglicans (Stott, Green, Gumbel) clearly acknowledge its importance, they do not see fit to mention it at the point where they are explaining how to become a Christian. The remainder simply ignore it. It cannot be said that any of the works reviewed *in practice* allow any role for baptism in Christian initiation.

Comparing New Testament initiation (as found in Acts especially) with that found in recent Evangelicalism we have found two weaknesses in the latter. There is a weakness in seeing receiving of the Spirit as part of initiation, a weakness which is liable to create problems at a later stage for these converts. Secondly, there is a complete failure (in practice at least; in theory as well for the majority) to allow any role to baptism in initiation.

Why is baptism thus overlooked or marginalised? A number of reasons spring to mind. *First*, in the sixties the majority of the populace had a Christian background and would have been baptized as babies. This is only a very partial explanation as by no means all enquirers would have been baptized. Graham, as a Baptist, would not have approved of infant baptism as true baptism, but our concern is with its neglect by *British* Evangelicalism. At that stage the main emphasis was on bringing nominal churchgoers or christened non–churchgoers to a living faith. Given that setting it is understandable that reliance upon baptism was often seen as something to be combated.

*Secondly*, in modern times evangelism has often become separated from church life, taking place through para–church organisations such as Christian Unions. One effect of this has been to sideline the church — and even more the sacraments.[30]

---

30. I am grateful to Gordon Margery for making this point.

*Thirdly*, Billy Graham especially was concerned to avoid "divisive" issues in order that his preaching of the gospel would reach as wide an audience as possible. This is probably a contributory motive for his failure to mention baptism — although he could simply have urged his readers to make sure they were baptized according to the way of their particular church. Nicky Gumbel explicitly mentions his concern to avoid controversial teaching on infant baptism.

*Fourthly*, all of the literature reviewed mentions the need to join a church. It could be argued that the authors assume that baptism will be covered at this stage. There may be some truth in this, but the fact remains that these authors do not portray baptism as being part of Christian initiation and their clients would have no reason to suppose that it has anything to do with becoming a Christian.

*Finally*, there was and is a very widespread belittling of the sacraments among British Evangelicals. Two personal anecdotes from the sixties and seventies will illustrate this. On one occasion the issue was raised of students being rebaptized. The wife of an Evangelical Anglican minister protested against this. I was encouraged to think that at least the sacrament was being taken seriously. But no. "It gives far too much significance to an outward sign" was the reason given! The other incident is a comment made in private by a (then) fairly well known Evangelical Anglican rector. "Given all the confusion that they have caused over the ages, wouldn't it be simpler just to scrap the sacraments?" — to which one might respond that Jesus presumably did not think so. Clearly for many "low church" meant (and still means) an extremely low view of baptism. Underlying this is the fear of nominal Christianity, the fear that people will imagine that they are true Christians just because they have been baptized and attend church. This fear can lead to extreme reactions, like those just given. It can also lead to the theologically sophisticated approach of John Stott in one of his last books, *Evangelical Truth*, where the emphasis is that new birth is not identical with baptism and that baptism conveys nothing automatically. Within that negative context Stott does say that "baptism is very important" and that "evangelicals do not (or should not) minimize it."[31] Such a stance was understandable in an age of widespread nominal Christianity, but in the current climate the undoubted Evangelical marginalisation of baptism is perhaps a more pressing issue.

There is little doubt that the basic reason for the silence is that most British Evangelicals simply do not consider baptism an aspect of Christian

---

31. John Stott, *Evangelical Truth: A Personal Plea for Unity* (Leicester: IVP, 1999), 108–10.

initiation, even though the more theologically literate confess the opposite in their theoretical writings. In the New Testament baptism is part of the gospel message. Indeed, in the "Great Commission" of Matthew 28:19–20 baptism is commanded but faith is not even mentioned! For the majority of British (and other) Evangelicals, unlike the New Testament writers, baptism has no place in the gospel message.[32] Much Evangelicalism is fundamentally non-sacramental. To the extent that it is, it departs both from the New Testament and from historic Christianity. Under the latter I include not just the early church fathers but also the Reformers.

My criticism of Evangelical practice is not for the failure to practise baptism at the point of conversion. The pattern of immediate convert's baptism that we see in Acts was soon modified and it is practised today by no major Christian group. How we should react to this and whether and in what way we should seek to move closer to New Testament practice is an interesting and important question, but not the topic of this paper. My criticism of Evangelical practice is for removing baptism from the process of Christian initiation, not for extending the process over a period of time.

At this stage I should pre-empt two objections. Some will oppose the idea of making baptism part of Christian initiation by raising the question of those who through no fault of their own die without baptism. The thief on the cross has a lot to answer for! This objection is basically frivolous. Christian theology, including the most sacramentalist, has always made allowances for such situations. Those who are martyred before their baptism have a baptism of blood and those who intend to be baptized but die first have a baptism of desire. There is all the difference in the world between missing baptism through no fault of one's own and refusing to receive it, between those who *can't* be baptized and those who *won't* be baptized. The fact that some are prevented from receiving baptism is no ground for rejecting the New Testament pattern of initiation. By the same argument one could side-line repentance and faith on the grounds that those dying in infancy are unable to repent and believe. As the lawyers say, hard cases make bad laws.

Secondly, surely it is repentance and faith that are important, not some outward act? It is indeed significant that Mark 16:16 attributes salvation to faith and baptism, but lack of salvation only to unbelief. It is true that ultimately it is the heart that is important rather than outward acts. But to deduce from this that baptism is unimportant and can be neglected when

---

32. This is not true of all. In an email response (11 August 2004) to the first draft of this paper, Michael Green affirmed the role of baptism in initiation and commented: "I have myself baptised people immediately on profession of faith as part of Christian initiation, and done so both in the river, the sea, and by effusion."

it comes to becoming a Christian is to move from a genuine biblical insight to an unbiblical Platonising. Naaman the Syrian had to believe Elisha but it was not until he emerged from the water for the seventh time that his flesh was restored and cleansed (2 Kings 5:14). Is it not somewhat arrogant for Evangelicals to think that they can trim the apostolic pattern of initiation to suit themselves? Surely this is precisely the Liberal path — excising inconvenient aspects of the faith on the grounds that they are not necessary or that other things matter more or that they are uncongenial to people today.

Ironically, while stressing the inadequacy of an outward ritual like baptism to bring salvation, some Evangelicals have replaced it with another outward act, a form of surrogate baptism. Repentance and faith are inward acts that need to be expressed in some way. In New Testament times this way was baptism. The response to the gospel involved an inner belief and an outward confession (in baptism). The practical need for an outward act of commitment and confession has overcome even the traditional evangelical aversion towards externals. The most obvious and direct surrogate baptism was of course the altar call, practised by Billy Graham and adopted by a number of British Evangelicals. Those for whom this was all a little too vulgar often substituted for it the exhortation to go and confess one's faith to a friend.[33]

A more subtle approach is to replace baptism with praying a "sinner's prayer," a prayer of commitment to be prayed by those wishing to become Christians. Many of the works that we have considered conclude with some such form of prayer, but this is a relatively recent phenomenon and it has been argued that it originated in the late nineteenth and early twentieth century.[34] There are earlier examples of prayers for those wishing to turn to Christ. In his *Pilgrim's Progress*, Bunyan represents Faithful as telling Hopeful how to pray, stressing the need to believe in Jesus and rely upon his righteousness.[35] A rather longer prayer is found in Joseph Alleine's *An Alarme to Unconverted Sinners*, first published posthumously in 1672. The sinner is encouraged to pray "in language like this." The prayer that follows places great emphasis on human depravity, on faith and on repentance. There is no mention of baptism (Alleine's target audience, the inhabitants of Taunton, would all have been baptized as infants) or of receiving the Holy Spirit.[36] These prayers anticipate the later neglect of baptism and receiving

33. Warren, *Journey into Life*, 15. Cf. Watson, *My God Is Real*, 92.

34. Paul Harrison Chitwood, "The Sinner's Prayer: An Historical and Theological Analysis," (PhD diss., Southern Baptist Theological Seminary, 2001) 61–63.

35. John Bunyan, *The Pilgrim's Progress* (London: Fount, 1979), 153.

36. Joseph Alleine, *An Alarm to the Unconverted* (Wellington: F. Houlston, 1812), 161–66. This is the title under which it has been most often published.

the Spirit, though (unlike today's "sinner's prayers") they are not intended as quasi-liturgical formulas for regular use.

## 6. CONCLUSION

Our study raises an important point of principle. Evangelicals make a lot of noise about believing in and submitting to the authority of Scripture. They are also very ready to criticise other traditions for failing to do this. Here is a test case. Can Evangelicals at *this* point submit their own traditional practices of initiation to the authority of Scripture? Is the professed allegiance to Scripture just a form of words or does it have a cash value? Is it just a stick to be used to beat others with or is it also a principle to be applied critically to Evangelical traditions and practices?[37]

---

37. I have been asked, by Rich Powney in an email of 25 April 2018, "what it might look like to put this into practice in a local church setting, and what difference that could make." That is a very good question and I hope that others with more experience and expertise in that area will take it up.

Chapter 2

# The God Who Sends Is the God Who Loves
## Mission as Participating in the Ecstatic Love of the Triune God[1]

Patrick S. Franklin

## I. INTRODUCTION

THE GOD WHO SENDS is the God who loves. If we are called to participate in the mission of God then we are called also, and more fundamentally, to participate in the love of God. David Bosch writes, "Mission has its origin in the heart of God. God is a fountain of sending love. This is the deepest source of mission. It is impossible to penetrate deeper still; there is a mission because God loves people."[2] Similarly, Gordon Fee writes, "The *love of*

---

1. This essay was previously published as an article in *Didaskalia* 28 (2017–18) 75–95.

2. David J. Bosch, *Transforming Mission: Paradigm Shifts in Theology of Mission* (Maryknoll, NY: Orbis, 2011), 402. Quoted in Jason S. Sexton, "A Confessing Trinitarian Theology for Today's Mission," in *Advancing Trinitarian Theology: Explorations in Constructive Dogmatics*, eds. Oliver D. Crisp and Fred Sanders (Grand Rapids: Zondervan, 2014), 182.

*God* is the foundation of Paul's view of salvation (Rom 5:1–11; 8:31–39; Eph 1:3–14). The *grace of our Lord Jesus Christ* is what gave concrete expression to that love."[3] And again, in more detail,

> Thus for Paul, human redemption is the combined activity of Father, Son, and Spirit, in that (1) it is predicated on the love of God, whose love sets it in motion; (2) it is effected historically through the death and resurrection of Christ the Son; and (3) it is actualized in the life of believers through the power of the Holy Spirit. This is expressed in any number of ways in Paul, of which Rom 5:5, 8 offers a typical example. The love of God that found expression historically in Christ's dying for us (v. 8) is what the Holy Spirit has poured out in our hearts (v. 5).[4]

Bosch and Fee clearly ground the *missio Dei* (the mission of God) in the *caritas Dei* (the love of God), which in my view is the proper order. This proper ordering, however, has not always been carefully followed in contemporary discussions about the mission of God. In recent years, many have attempted to recover an emphasis on missiology by articulating its significance for theology and ecclesiology. For example, the missional literature describes God as a missional or sending God. Just as the Father sent the Son and the Spirit into the world to accomplish the *missio Dei*, so now God sends the church into the world as "God's instrument for God's mission."[5] While this renewed emphasis on mission is welcome and helpful, it sometimes has the tendency to promote a pragmatic and functional approach to church. The term "missional" has become something of a buzz word in recent years, though its meaning in popular usage is frequently vague and its history not well understood.[6] For example, "missional" is often confused with emerging/emergent church, evangelistic, or seeker-sensitive approaches to church, the church growth movement, a form of consumer ecclesiology, the practice of formulating organizational mission statements, an unbalanced focus on social justice (doing good works in the world is

---

3. Gordon D. Fee, *Pauline Christology: An Exegetical-Theological Study* (Peabody, MA: Hendrickson, 2007), 592; italics his.

4. Fee, *Pauline Christology*, 589.

5. Darrell L. Guder, "Missional Church: From Sending to Being Sent," in Darrell L. Guder, ed., *Missional Church: A Vision for the Sending of the Church in North America* (Grand Rapids: Eerdmans, 1998), 8.

6. See Todd J. Billings, "What Makes a Church Missional? Freedom from Cultural Captivity Does Not Mean Freedom from Tradition," *Christianity Today* 52.3 (March 2008) 56–59; and Alan Hirsch, "Defining Missional: The Word Is Everywhere, but Where Did it Come From and What Does it Really Mean?," *Leadership* 29.4 (Fall 2008) 20–22.

emphasized over gathering to worship), or simply a general, more strenuous emphasis on missions or outreach programs. Ironically, missional ecclesiology arose, in part, as a critique of such church models and trends. However, sometimes its own advocates have contributed to these misunderstandings.

Three brief examples illustrate this tendency. First, Michael Frost argues that *cause creates community*: "We build community incidentally, when our imaginations and energies are captured by a higher, even nobler cause . . . zChristian community results from the greater cause of Christian mission."[7] Frost's intention here is a good one, namely to call the church out of an insular and sentimental Christian subculture mentality. However, his proposal that *cause creates community* potentially reduces the church to a project, a means to a functional end. More seriously it grounds the mission of the church in something other than its intrinsic relational and participatory ontology and *telos*.

Second, Darrell Guder promotes "the preeminence of witness as the fundamental definition of the church," regarding witness as "an all-encompassing definition of Christian existence" and hence subordinating all other functions of the church to witness (including proclamation, community, and service/ministry).[8] Elsewhere, reacting to what he perceives to be Evangelicalism's overemphasis on personal conversation (over-against corporate election for mission), Guder says that "The biblical record places no emphasis on the special significance of conversion stories."[9] In fact, "One

---

7. Michael Frost, *Exiles: Living Missionally in a Post-Christian Culture* (Peabody, MA: Hendrickson, 2006), 108. See also Guder, *Missional Church*, 4–6, 8, 19, 227; and Darrell L. Guder, *Be My Witnesses: The Church's Mission, Message, and Messengers* (Grand Rapids: Eerdmans, 1985), 44.

8. Guder, *Be My Witnesses*, 109, 233, 49.

9. Darrell L. Guder, *The Continuing Conversion of the Church* (Grand Rapids: Eerdmans, 2000), 129. Given the context of Guder's statements, it should be noted that his intention is to overcome a false mission-benefit dichotomy, which he sees in traditional soteriology and ecclesiology. According to Guder, traditional Christian thought (i.e., since Constantine) has focused almost exclusively upon the individual believer's salvation benefits. In contrast to this, Guder wishes to give voice to the missional elements of salvation by defining Christian existence according to the concept of witness. However, rather than transcending the mission-benefit dichotomy, I fear that he succeeds only in shifting the emphasis *from* the benefits of salvation *to* missionary service. Perhaps he actually intensifies the dichotomy by downplaying benefits in favour of mission, as, for example, when he contends that the vocation of Christians to serve includes "their personal blessing, experience, and endowment as something secondary and accessory," which "remains bound to the primary and essential element of their status," i.e., Christ's commission. Similarly, in equating Christian existence with the missional function or task, he gives precedence to doing over being: "Christian existence is 'existence in the execution of this [*missional*] task'" (See Guder, *Continuing Conversion of the Church*, 130).

does not find a concern for 'the establishment of their personal well-being in their relationship with God' in the stories of the call of Abraham, Moses, the prophets, the disciples or Paul. The issue in these encounters is not 'the saving of their souls' or 'their experience of grace and salvation.'"[10]

While Guder's critique of individualistic soteriology has some merit, his correction here is an overcorrection.

Third, several missional writers argue that while traditional theologies of church and mission proceed from Christology to ecclesiology to mission, missional theology must proceed from Christology to missiology to ecclesiology.[11] As Alan Hirsch articulates it, "Christology determines missiology, and missiology determines ecclesiology."[12] Ben Wheatley explains, "Missiology needs to precede ecclesiology because if ecclesiology precedes missiology, mission becomes just a subset of the church."[13] Or, as Graham Cray puts it, "Start with the Church and the mission will probably get lost. Start with mission and it is likely that the Church will be found."[14] Such

---

10. Guder, *Continuing Conversion of the Church*, 129. Guder tends to erect false dichotomies when making his claims. For example: "We must conclude that the *church as an 'institute of salvation'* (Heilsanstalt) has had a greatly **diminished sense of mission** to the world. It has been far more *preoccupied with its inner life*, thereby failing to grasp the essential linkage between its internal life and its **external calling**. Rather than understanding **worship as God's divine preparation for sending**, it has tended to *make worship an end in itself*. Rather than understanding **preaching as the exposition of God's Word to equip the saints for the work of ministry**, for the building up of the body of Christ (Eph. 4:11ff), it has become the *impartation of clerical wisdom to help the saints* prepare for heaven while coping with this 'vale of tears.' In fact, where the *concern for individual salvation* grew and the **focus upon missional calling** decreased in the early medieval church, preaching lost its importance and the *sacraments as holy, reified rites* became central" (Guder, *Continuing Conversion of the Church*, 135; Italics and bold mine to indicate the two sides of the false dichotomy)

11. My own view is that ecclesiology flows from a dialogical and holistic (even systematic) interaction between theological anthropology, soteriology, and missiology, each of which is grounded ultimately in a relational and participatory Trinitarian theological framework. This is the approach that I pursue in my book, *Being Human, Being Church: The Significance of Theological Anthropology for Ecclesiology* (Milton Keynes, UK: Paternoster, 2016).

12. Alan Hirsch, *The Forgotten Ways: Reactivating the Missional Church* (Grand Rapids: Brazos, 2006), 142. See also the discussion of this topic in relation to bounded and centered sets in Michael Frost and Alan Hirsch, *The Shaping of Things to Come: Innovation and Mission for the 21st-Century Church* (Grand Rapids: Baker, 2013), 255; cf. Frost, *Exiles*, 155.

13. Cited by David Fitch (quoting Ben Wheatley), "Missiology Precedes Ecclesiology: The Epistemological Problem," para. 1, *Missio Alliance*, January 8, 2009, http://www.missioalliance.org/missiology-precedes-ecclesiology-the-epistemological-problem/.

14. Graham Cray, ed., *The Mission Shaped Church: Church Planting and Fresh Expressions of Church in a Changing Context* (Brookvale, Australia: Willow, 2005), 116. Quoted in Hirsch, *Forgotten Ways*, 143.

missional thinkers prefer to think about the church as a manifestation or outcome of God's mission. This is a partially helpful move; a good biblical and theological case can be made that missiology is not simply a derivative of ecclesiology or a program of the church but is grounded more deeply in God's own mission to save the world through Israel's Messiah.[15] However, this move does not go far enough to ground the *missio Dei* itself ontologically in the nature of the triune God as ecstatic love. Hence, it potentially falls into reducing the church to a means to a functional end.[16]

To avoid these problems, it is important to envision missional ecclesiology as flowing out of a participatory and relational Trinitarian theology, in which God's redemptive mission is grounded more fundamentally in God's nature as love. God's mission to redeem the world flows from God's prior love for human beings and creation. God's love for human beings and creation is rooted, in turn, in the other-centered, ecstatic, perichoretic love that constitutes God's triune being and reflects the fullness and overflowing quality of the divine life. In what follows, I will outline and commend such a theology. The aim is not to reject or displace missional theology, but to ground it more deeply in a participatory and relational Trinitarian theological framework.

## II. A PARTICIPATORY AND RELATIONAL TRINITARIAN THEOLOGICAL FRAMEWORK

### 1. The Augustinian Mutual Love Tradition

The New Testament declares that God is love (1 John 4:8, 16). In attesting to this, Augustine believes that Scripture speaks of love not merely as an aspect of God's character or a description of how God normally acts (though both of these statements are true); more fundamentally, love defines God's *essential* nature. Now if love is God's essential nature then it must be true that love has always characterized God, even before the creation of human

---

15. See Christopher J. H. Wright, *The Mission of God: Unlocking the Bible's Grand Narrative* (Downers Grove, IL: IVP Academic, 2006).

16. To be fair, in talking about "ecclesiology," Hirsch seems to mean not the ontology of the church but its functional expression and structures: "By my reading of the Scriptures, ecclesiology is the most fluid of the doctrines. The church is a dynamic cultural expression of the people of God in any given place. Worship style, social dynamics, liturgical expressions must result from the process of contextualizing the gospel in any given culture. *Church must follow mission*" (Hirsch, *The Forgotten Ways*, 143; italics his). Similarly, Frost writes, "Too many churches begin by trying to artificially develop an ecclesiology, determining first where to meet, what songs to sing, what to preach, how to have small groups and leadership structures" (Frost, *Exiles*, 155).

beings or other creatures (on earth or in the heavenlies). If love is essential to God's nature, then love is constitutive of the divine life itself and God is eternally a loving Being. As an essentially loving Being, God exists not as an isolated individual deity but in the eternal communion of Father, Son, and Holy Spirit. Thus, the One God exists as three subsisting persons; and, as three divine persons-in-relation, the Father, Son, and Holy Spirit subsist eternally as the One God.

The insight that God is love led Augustine to formulate his mutual love model of the Trinity. According to Augustine's mutual love model, the Father eternally generates the Son (without beginning or end) and the Holy Spirit proceeds from the Father and the Son and subsists as their mutual love.[17] Augustine begins his discussion with a reflection on the nature of love as depicted in 1 John 4:16: "God is love, and those who abide in love abide in God, and God abides in them." He discovers that love implies a Trinity of relationships and can serve as something of an analogy for the Triune God: "There you are with three, the lover, what is being loved, and love. And what is love but a kind of life coupling or trying to couple together two things, namely lover and what is being loved?"[18] This analogy does not

---

17. Identifying the Spirit as the bond of love shared between the Father and the Son is not unique to Augustine or even to the Western tradition. For example, we find this connection in Athenagoras of Athens, Athanasius (who says that the Spirit constitutes the union between Father and Son), Basil (the Spirit is the communion of the Father and Son, the bond of their union), Gregory of Nazianzus (the Spirit is the intermediate between Father and Son), and Epiphanius (the Spirit is in the midst of the Father and Son as the Bond of the Trinity). See Thomas F. Torrance, *The Christian Doctrine of God: One Being Three Persons* (New York: T. & T. Clark, 2001), 167. Augustine himself presents this teaching as having been passed down to him from his theological predecessors. On this point, see Lewis Ayres, *Augustine and the Trinity* (Cambridge: Cambridge University Press, 2010), 88.

18. Augustine, *The Trinity* VIII/5.14 (255). We must be somewhat careful with the word "analogy," especially if we are tempted to think that Augustine is trying to *explain* the mystery of the triune life. His "analogy" does not simply proceed from something created to something divine, but employs a theological pattern (discerned from Scripture) already and necessarily operating in the created order itself (perhaps we might say that Augustine employs analogy in a kind of sacramental way, rather than merely an illustrative/symbolic, deductive, or inductive way). As Lewis Ayres writes, "Moving from the created analogue towards the Trinity is done well, then, when it is recognized as, and performed as, a move towards that which defeats the exercised mind. The advance towards understanding is one that is only appropriately founded in humility before the divine mystery." And, "The description of a triad in the act of love . . . is based on the assumption that love is necessarily triune *because* love is God. The description is part analogy, part invitation to use the language of faith to explore that which one *thinks* one understands." Thus, "Augustine's account is not an analogy between a structure of loving in the created order and the loving that constitutes the Trinitarian life, but a description of the manner in which we love in and because of the Spirit's presence. It

espouse tritheism, as if there are three gods loving each other, but rather illustrates that God is love and as such exists in complexity and differentiation. In contrast, human beings image God in this manner only in a partial sense, for, as Augustine says, "it is not the case that anyone who loves himself is love except when *love* loves itself."[19] For the human individual, love is not its own (hypostasizing) subject, but only gains transcendence in the encounter with another human person. However, Augustine implies that there is a kind of inter-subjectivity within God, because in God (and in God alone) "love loves itself."[20] Love takes on such an all-encompassing reality as to be a transcendent Subject.[21] For Augustine and the Augustinian mutual love tradition, the Holy Spirit is love personified.[22] For Christians, love in

---

is a description of a structure of loving in the created order, founded in the divine love that will also illustrate the nature of the Trinitarian love *per se*." See Ayres, *Augustine and the Trinity*, 141, 283, 284.

19. Augustine, *Trinity* IV/1.2 (272). Emphasis added.

20. Augustine, *Trinity* IV/1.2 (272).

21. Not to be confused with what we find in the creaturely realm, i.e., the human person as an autonomous individual. Rather, the Spirit's "subjectivity" has to do with agency, as the Spirit works inseparably together with Father and Son. Lewis Ayres is helpful here: "The Spirit is the communion of Father and Son which . . . is a mutual act of adherence and love; the Spirit is the love and fount of love between Father and Son who eternally gives himself; the Spirit, as also 'God from God,' shares in the simple mode of divine existence in which he is what he might be thought to possess. Thus, . . . Augustine presents the Spirit as the agent identical to the act of communion between Father and Son" (Ayres, *Augustine and the Trinity*, 258).

22. Augustine's process of thinking this through is complex, involving several important mutually dependent affirmations, and thus difficult to capture in a brief summary. First, given the classical tradition's emphasis on divine simplicity, implying that God IS as God acts, for God *to be* is the same as *to be wise, to be loving, to be just*, and so forth (whereas for creatures being is not necessarily identical with the predicates attached to it). As Ayres explains it, "Lacking any accidents [in the Aristotelian sense], God must be any qualities we predicate of God" (Ayres, *Augustine and the Trinity*, 216). Second, as a consequence, God's act of love must be identical with God's being love. Thus, the triune God—Father, Son, and Holy Spirit—IS love (since, for God to be is to be loving, to be love). Third, the love that comes to us from God is God's very self, God from God, love from love, and thus one of the divine persons, either the Son or the Spirit (because both are sent, while the Father is not sent). Fourth, Augustine identifies this divine person as being the Spirit, because the Spirit is the one that God sends to indwell us as gift (John 15:26; Rom 8:9) and as God's own love (e.g., Rom 5:5, "God's love has been poured into our hearts through the Holy Spirit that has been given to us"). Fifth, to say that the Spirit is love is not to imply that the Spirit is impersonal or passive; rather, the Spirit is the active presence and activity of God, who actively loves and draws us to participate in that love and drawing us into active communion with God and others (e.g., Gal 4:6: "God has sent the Spirit of his Son into our hearts, crying, 'Abba! Father!'"). Finally, it is helpful to note that this movement of God's love follows from the doctrines of the unity of inseparable divine operations and the pattern of

its deepest sense is not simply an emotion or a sentiment; rather, love is the divine Spirit who indwells us, awakens love within us, and draws us into loving communion with God and others.

To depict simultaneously the essential unity of God and the interrelatedness of Father, Son, and Spirit, the Greek fathers of the early church employed the concept of *perichoresis*. This term was first used by Gregory of Naziansus to express the way in which the divine and human natures in the one person of Christ co-inhered without the integrity of either being diminished. In subsequent Trinitarian theology, *perichoresis* came to depict the mutual indwelling, co-inhering, or inter-penetrating of Father, Son, and Holy Spirit.[23] As Catherine Mowry LaCugna explains it, *perichoresis* illustrates that the three persons "mutually inhere in one another, draw life from one another, 'are' what they are by relation to one another."[24] According to T. F. Torrance, this move had deep and far reaching implications not only for the Christian understanding of God but also for the Christian understanding of the human person, with ripple effects influencing the development of conceptions of personhood. This new understanding of personhood distinguished Christian thinking from classical Greek ontology in which being (*ousia*) had been conceived as something static and unchanging, as for example in Aristotle's distinction between substances and accidents and his restriction of relation to the latter category. Conversely, by admitting the category of relation into the concept of being the Cappadocians reconceived being itself (*ousia*) in dynamic and relational terms. In the new Christian understanding, "With God, Being and Communion are one and the same" and being could now be conceived as being-in-relation.[25]

The New Testament speaks of Christians experiencing the *koinōnia* of the Holy Spirit, a word which is often translated "fellowship" but also includes the idea of partnership or participation.[26] To experience the fellow-

---

divine appropriation in Scripture, such that the manifestation of God's being and acting as love in the created order follows the eternal, internal processions within God: thus, God's love comes to us *from* the Father *through* the Son and *in* the Spirit. For a detailed and nuanced discussion of Augustine's theological exposition of the Spirit as love, see Ayres, *Augustine and the Trinity*, chapter 10.

23. On the historical development of *perichoresis*, see James. D. Gifford, Jr., *Perichoretic Salvation: The Believer's Union with Christ as a Third Type of Perichoresis* (Eugene, OR: Wipf and Stock, 2015; Kindle edition), chapter 3.

24. Catherine Mowry LaCugna, *God for Us: The Trinity and Christian Life* (San Francisco: Harper, 1991), 270–71.

25. Torrance, *Christian Doctrine of God*, 104.

26. I. Howard Marshall, *New Testament Theology: Many Witnesses, One Gospel* (Downers Grove, IL: InterVarsity, 2004), 290. For this theme in Paul, see Michael J. Gorman, *Becoming the Gospel: Paul, Participation, and Mission* (Grand Rapids: Eerdmans, 2015), 30–31.

ship of the Holy Spirit is not just to commune with the Spirit; it is actually to participate in the Spirit and thereby to experience communion with God and each other. The same Spirit who proceeds as the mutual love between the Father and the Son, thus completing or perfecting the ecstatic and perichoretic relational unity of the Trinity, also unites Christian brothers and sisters together by drawing them to share in the divine love, and thereby to participate in God's own Trinitarian life. In the economy of salvation the Spirit's mission corresponds with his manner of procession (as love and gift) in the immanent Godhead;[27] So, the Spirit as the bond of love, brings believers into union with Christ (and thus the Father) and with one another.[28]

By participating in the Spirit, Christians share together in the Trinitarian love of the Father, Son, and Holy Spirit. As Stan Grenz puts it, "Through the Spirit, we participate in the love that lies at the heart of the triune God himself."[29] Or as James Torrance exclaims, "By sharing in Jesus' life of communion with the Father in the Spirit, we are given to participate in the Son's eternal communion with the Father and hence in the Trinitarian life of God."[30] Through their sharing and participating together in the love of the Trinity, Christian brothers and sisters have unity in the Spirit and the church community begins to reflect the communion of the triune God.[31]

---

27. As John Webster states, it is important to remember that, "as with all God's external works, the economic mission of the Spirit refers back to the Spirit's antecedent deity and personhood, in which the mission has its ground. Missions follow processions; the character of the work is determined by the nature of the one who works" (John Webster, "Illumination," *Journal of Reformed Theology* 5 [2011] 329). For Augustine's affirmation of and dependence on this notion, see Ayres, *Augustine and the Trinity*, 181, 183.

28. This insight is crucial for grasping the relational ontology of the church, which grounds and makes possible both its internal communal life and its external mission in the world. See Patrick S. Franklin, *Being Human, Being Church* (Milton Keynes, UK: Paternoster, 2016), chapters 3 and 6.

29. Stanley J. Grenz, *Theology for the Community of God* (Grand Rapids: Eerdmans, 1994), 484.

30. James B. Torrance, "The Doctrine of the Trinity in Our Contemporary Situation," in *The Forgotten Trinity*, ed. Alasdair I. C. Heron (London: BCC/CCBI Inter-Church House, 1989), 7. Quoted in Stanley J. Grenz, *The Social God and the Relational Self: A Trinitarian Theology of the Imago Dei* (Louisville: Westminster John Knox, 2001), 325.

31. Reflecting on Acts 4:32 ("They had one soul and one heart toward the Lord"), Augustine writes: "[if] many souls through love are one soul, and many hearts are one heart, what does the very fountain of love do in the Father and the Son? . . . If, therefore, 'the love of God [which] has been poured forth in our hearts by the Holy Spirit who has been given to us' [Rom 5:5] makes many souls one soul and many hearts one heart, how much more does [the Spirit] make the Father and the Son and the Holy Spirit one God, one light, one *principium*" (Tractate 39.5; quoted in Ayres, *Augustine and the Trinity*, 257)?

This is why the church cannot simply be a means to an end, simply an instrument deployed functionally to achieve God's mission. With Bonhoeffer (and against some missional writers), we must affirm that the church is both means and end; it exists simultaneously for the sake of its own community and for the sake of the world.[32] It exists for its own sake (as an end) because God's missional intention is to establish a new creation, a community of love and new life, in which people live in restored communion with God and one another.[33] Yet, the church also exists for the world instrumentally (as a means), as the "church for others" because its Lord Jesus Christ, the "man for others," is conforming it to his image, which includes being-free-for-others and for the world.[34] The church exists to experience and share the reconciliation and intimate communion that the gospel makes possible; everything it is and does bears witness to this.

In a sense, the church community images the Trinity and God's own Trinitarian life becomes a model for human relationships in the church. Being bound together in the Spirit, we have become united in a way that is analogous (not identical) to the unity of Father and Son. As Jesus prayed to the Father, "My prayer for all of them is that they will be one, just as you and I are one, Father—that just as you are *in* me and I am *in* you, so they will be *in* us, and the world will believe you sent me" (John 17:21; emphasis added).[35] It is important for us to notice the "in" references in John as pointing to the mutual indwelling of the Trinitarian persons. The Holy Spirit, who will be "in" Jesus' disciples, will place them "in Christ," who is "in" the Father.[36] Reflecting on this passage, Andreas Köstenberger and Scott Swain write,

> The model for this unity is found in the Father and the Son, specifically, their mutual indwelling or perichoresis (17:21, 23, 26). Just as the unity of the Father and the Son is manifest in their mutual indwelling (14:10–11), so Jesus asks that the unity

---

32. See my discussion of this in my article "Bonhoeffer's Missional Ecclesiology," *McMaster Journal of Theology and Ministry* 9 (2007–2008), 118–25.

33. Köstenberger and Swain write, "Communion in the Son's eternal life of love, glory and giving with the Father in the Spirit constitutes the ultimate blessing of the gospel" (Andreas J. Köstenberger and Scott R. Swain, *Father, Son and Spirit: The Trinity and John's Gospel* [Downers Grove, IL: InterVarsity, 2008], 178).

34. Dietrich Bonhoeffer, *Letters and Papers from Prison*, vol. 8, *Dietrich Bonhoeffer Works*, trans. Isabel Best, et al., ed. John W. de Gruchy (Minneapolis: Fortress, 2010), 501, 503.

35. For a detailed exposition of the theme of participation in Paul, see Gorman, *Becoming the Gospel*, 21–49.

36. On the "in" language in Paul, see Gorman, *Becoming the Gospel*, 29.

of the apostolic community will be manifest as they come to experience the mutual indwelling of the Father and the Son (cf. 14:17, 23). The effect of this new perichoretic communion will be that the world will 'know that you sent me and have loved them even as you have loved me' (17:23).[37]

The church does not reflect the image of the Trinity simply because it is a community that tries to imitate the triune relationships.[38] It reflects the image of the Trinity because it is comprised of individual human beings (exocentric persons-in-relation) whom the Spirit of God indwells and thereby frees to love and serve God and others genuinely.[39] Just as God created individual human beings in the divine image to be other-centered and to find their fulfilment in relationship with God and other human beings, so now God redeems and transforms human beings to cultivate relational fulfilment with God and others in the church community (though complete fulfilment awaits eschatological consummation).

One implication of the foregoing discussion of Christian life as participating together in the life of the Trinity is that Christian soteriology must be conceived relationally rather than merely individualistically.[40] Being in the church is thus intrinsically related to the believer's salvation; it is not just a secondary application—not because the church is an institutional dispenser

---

37. Köstenberger and Swain, *Father, Son and Spirit*, 176. Ladd writes, "The idiom of abiding is usually called mysticism, but it is difficult to define. There is a mutual abiding of the believer in Christ (16:56; 14:20, 21; 15:5; 17:21) and Christ in the believer (6:56; 14:20, 23; 15:5; 17:23, 26). This is analogous to the Son abiding in the Father (10:38; 14:10, 11, 20, 21; 17:21) and the Father abiding in the Son (10:38; 14:10, 11, 21; 17:21, 23). Once it is said that believers are in both the Father and the Son (17:21); and once it is said that both Father and Son will come to make their abode in believers (14:23)" (George E. Ladd, *A Theology of the New Testament*, ed. Donald A. Hagner [Grand Rapids: Eerdmans, 1993], 313–14. Quoted in Gifford, *Perichoretic Salvation*, Kindle loc. 1342).

38. What I am proposing is not "social Trinitarianism" *per se* (at least as usually understood), but a relational ontology of personhood informed by Trinitarian theology, which proceeds not simply from Trinity to human community, but from Trinity through theological anthropology and soteriology to ecclesial community.

39. I am drawing here on Wolfhart Pannenberg's notion of exocentricity discussed in his *Anthropology in Theological Perspective*, trans. Matthew J. O'Connell (Edinburgh: T. & T. Clark, 1999).

40. Robert Sherman writes, "The Triune God does not save by plucking individuals up to heaven or by us establishing a particular social agenda or political regime following Jesus's example. Rather, salvation is the fruit of God's embedding persons in a community called and sanctified (which is to say, set apart) by the Holy Spirit to be a witness to God's own fulfillment of creation's ultimate goal in the work of Jesus Christ" (Robert Sherman, *Covenant, Community, and the Spirit: A Trinitarian Theology of Church* (Grand Rapids: Baker Academic, 2015), 41).

of salvation but because it is the community in which reconciliation is embodied and transformation takes place. It is the social context in which redeemed human persons practice and live out concretely their restored relationships with God and others. The church is the phenomenological manifestation of what God has achieved ontologically. As Bonhoeffer argues, Christian communion is not a human ideal that we strive to achieve; it is a divine reality established by Christ in which we participate by the Spirit.[41]

## 2. Basil and Other Patristic Writers on Participation

In a recent book on ecclesiology, Robert Sherman writes, "It is the Holy Spirit who acts as the effective agent of the Father in communicating Christ's benefits to us, *and* it is the Holy Spirit who acts as the effective agent in us to enable and strengthen our grateful human response."[42] Similarly, Lesslie Newbigin once wrote, "The Spirit is the Spirit of the Father and of the Son. His work is to enable us to participate in Christ's Sonship, to be one with him in his obedience to the Father. And only he can enable us to participate in, and thereby be the occasions of, his witness."[43] New Testament scholar Gordon Fee explains,

> The *participation in the Holy Spirit* continually actualizes that love and grace in the life of the believer and the believing community. The koinwnía *(fellowship/participation in) of the Holy Spirit* is how the living God not only brings people into an intimate and abiding relationship with himself, as the God of all grace, but also causes them to participate in all the benefits of that grace and salvation—that is, by indwelling them in the present with his own presence and guaranteeing their final eschatological glory.[44]

These statements represent well the patristic doctrine of participation.[45] In this final section, I will draw on patristic sources, especially Basil's

---

41. Dietrich Bonhoeffer, *Life Together*, vol. 5, *Dietrich Bonhoeffer Works*, trans. Daniel W. Bloesch and James H. Burness, ed. Geffrey B. Kelly (Minneapolis: Fortress, 1996), 35–38.

42. Sherman, *Covenant, Community, and the Spirit*, 57.

43. Leslie Newbigin, *Trinitarian Doctrine for Today's Mission* (Eugene, OR: Wipf & Stock, 2006), 50. Quoted in Sexton, "A Confessing Trinitarian Theology," 183.

44. Fee, *Pauline Christology*, 592.

45. E.g., "[T]he Son himself partakes of no one and that which is partaken from the Father is the Son. We partaking of the Son himself are said to partake of God.

*De Spiritu Sancto*, to elucidate what it means to participate in the missional activity of the triune God.[46]

In his work *De Spiritu Sancto* Basil reflects theologically on two doxological statements that were being used in the church: (1) the doxology *to* God the Father *with* the Son *together with* the Holy Spirit; and (2) the doxology *to* God the Father *through* the Son *in* the Holy Spirit. Basil seeks to defend the first statement against his interlocutors, who took issue with the term "with" but not with terms "through" and "in" used in the second statement.[47] Basil finds problematic both their rejection of the first statement and their reasons for affirming the second. They reject the first statement due to their tritheistic and subordinationist leanings (since "with" implies unity and equality of the Spirit with the Father and Son, which they rejected) and therefore they affirm the second statement but in a way that rejects the orthodox position. As Basil explains,

> By the term '*of* whom' they wish to designate the Creator; by the term '*through* whom,' the subordinate agent or instrument; by the term '*in* whom,' or '*in* which,' they mean to shew [sic] the time of place. The object of all this is that the Creator of the universe [the Son] may be regarded as of no higher dignity than an instrument, and that the Holy Spirit may appear to be adding to existing things nothing more than the contribution derived from place or time.[48]

Basil sets out to defend the legitimacy of both statements and to clarify their true meaning in light of Scripture and the orthodox tradition. Against his opponents' interpretation of the second statement, Basil shows that the prepositions 'of,' 'through,' and 'in' are each applied to all three persons of the Trinity in the Bible: 'through' and 'in' are applied to the Father, 'of' and 'in' are applied to the Son, and 'of' and 'through' are applied to the Spirit.[49] While the meanings associated with these prepositions in the second statement are in one important sense distinct, they emphatically do not refer to ontological separation of or subordination within the Trinity. This

---

This is what Peter said: 'That you might become partners of a divine nature' [2 Pet. 1:4]" (Athanasius, *Orations against the Arians*, Book 1.16. Quoted from *The Trinitarian Controversy*, trans., ed. William G. Rusch (Philadelphia: Fortress, 1980), 79).

46. As a guide to my reading of the primary text from Basil (*De Spiritu Sancto*; NPNF2-08: *Basil: Letters and Selected Works*), I have learned much from Dennis Ngien, *Gifted Response: The Triune God as the Causative Agent of Our Responsive Worship* (Milton Keynes, UK: Paternoster, 2008), 1–34.

47. Basil, *De Spiritu Sancto* II.4 (NPNF2-08, 4).

48. Basil, *De Spiritu Sancto* I.3 (NPNF2-08, 3).

49. Basil, *De Spiritu Sancto* III.5; I.IV.6; I.V.7–12 (NPNF2-08, 4–8).

is because the statement refers not to the immanent divine essence but to the economic activity of God *ad extra* in drawing that which is not God to participate in God's creative, redemptive, and perfecting activity.[50] Basil explains,

> I say that the Church recognizes both uses, and deprecates neither as subversive of the other. For whenever we are contemplating the majesty of the nature of the Only Begotten, and the excellence of His dignity, we bear witness that the glory is *with* the Father; while on the other hand, whenever we bethink us of His bestowal on us of good gifts, and of our access to, and admission into, the household of God, we confess that this grace is effected for us through Him and by Him.[51]

For Basil, both statements are valid; indeed, both are necessary to safeguard the unity of the economic trinity and the differentiation of the divine persons. As Dennis Ngien explains, the second statement (which includes 'through' and 'in') "admits of the way the Triune God deals with us in the economy of salvation," while the first statement ('with') "admits of the immanent unity and close communion of the members of the Trinity."[52] The second statement makes possible theological expressions of appropriation (e.g., the three articles of the Creed following Father, Son, and Spirit) while the first statement reminds us both of the oneness and equality of the Godhead and of the unity of the divine operations or activity *ad extra* (i.e., each of God's acts is one act with a threefold pattern, where external missions follow internal processions). Thus, when used doxologically, Basil argues that "the one phrase 'with whom' is the proper one to be used in the ascription of glory, while the other, 'through whom,' is specially [sic] appropriate in giving thanks."[53] Basil's analysis of the economic significance of the prepositions 'of,' 'through,' and 'in' fits the pattern we find in New Testament texts such as Titus 3:54b-6, "He [God] saved us *through* the washing of rebirth and renewal *by* the Holy Spirit, whom he poured out on us generously *through* Jesus Christ our Savior," and Ephesians 2:18, "*Through* [Christ], we both alike have access *to* the Father *in* the one Spirit" (emphasis added; notice that both of these statements concern God's economic activity *ad extra*, either toward us or in drawing us to participate in the double movement

---

50. The theological formula *opera ad extra trinitatis indivisa sunt* ("the external works of the Trinity are undivided") expresses a theme that is common to the patristic writers and has its roots in the writings of Athanasius (Sherman, *Covenant, Community, and the Spirit*, 41n4).

51. Basil, *De Spiritu Sancto* VII.16 (NPNF2-08, 10).

52. Ngien, *Gifted Response*, 2.

53. Basil, *De Spiritu Sancto* VII.16 (NPNF2-08, 10).

of divine grace). Basil's analysis is also consistent with common patristic formulations.[54] Consider the following:

> Irenaeus: One God, the Father, who is over all and through all and in us all. For over all is the Father; and through all is the Son, for by means of Him all things were made by the Father; and in us all is the Spirit, who cries Abba Father, and fashions man into the likeness of God.[55]

> Irenaeus: And for this reason the baptism of our regeneration proceeds through these three points: God the Father bestowing on us regeneration through His Son by the Holy Spirit."[56]

> Gregory of Nyssa: But in the case of the Divine nature we do not similarly learn that the Father does anything by Himself in which the Son does not work conjointly, or again that the Son has any special operation apart from the Holy Spirit; but every operation which extends from God to the Creation, and is named according to our variable conceptions of it, has its origin from the Father, and proceeds through the Son, and is perfected in the Holy Spirit.[57]

> Ambrose: And of the Father, too, you may rightly say "of Him," for of Him was the operative Wisdom [the Son], Which of His own and the Father's will gave being to all things which were not. "Through Him [the Son]," because all things were made through His Wisdom. "In Him [the Spirit]," because He is the Fount of substantial Life, in Whom we live and move and have our being.[58]

> Augustine: Not that the Father should be understood to have made one part of the whole creation and the Son another and the Holy Spirit yet another, but that each and every nature has been made simultaneously by the Father through the Son, in the Gift of the Holy Spirit.[59]

---

54. As Lewis Ayres reports, "pro-Nicene accounts of inseparable operation frequently move beyond asserting merely that each of the divine three is involved in every act, by emphasizing the Father works through the Son and in the Spirit. Such assertions both emphasize the fact of Trinitarian order, and they begin to specify how we may conceive of the three as being unified" (Ayres, *Augustine and the Trinity*, 70).

55. Irenaeus, *The Demonstration of the Apostolic Preaching* 5, trans., ed. Armitage Robinson (New York: MacMillan: 1920), 74.

56. Irenaeus, *Demonstration of the Apostolic Preaching*, 75.

57. Gregory of Nyssa, *Letter to Ablabius: On Not Three Gods* (NPNF2-05, 334).

58. Ambrose, *On the Holy Spirit* II.IX.92 (NPNF2-10, 126).

59. Augustine, *De Vera Religione* 7.13 (Corpus Christianorum, Series Latina 32.196; quoted in Ayres, *Augustine and the Trinity*, 62).

Having clarified the meaning of the second statement, including its proper relation to the first statement, we can now explore its implications for a theology of participation. For example, reflecting on the significance of Basil's thought for Christian worship, Dennis Ngien writes, "The saving import of the Spirit's deity lies in this: the Spirit places us in Christ so that our worship, as a participation in the Son's communion with the Father, is found pleasing. The believer, 'the place of the Spirit,' is enabled to offer doxology to God." In light of this, "The Church's worship is truly ours insofar as it participates in the Spirit's unitive movement through the only begotten to the Father."[60] As Basil asserts, "it is impossible to worship the Son, save by the Holy Ghost; impossible to call upon the Father, save by the Spirit of adoption."[61] Similarly, Nazianzus says, "[I]t is the Spirit in whom we worship and through whom we pray . . . Worshipping, then, and praying in the Spirit seem to me to be simply the Spirit presenting prayer and worship to himself."[62]

Thus, as James Torrance argues, a thoroughly Trinitarian theology of worship recognizes a "double movement of grace": first, "a God-humanward movement, from (*ek*) the Father, through (*dia*) the Son, in (*en*) the Spirit," and second, "a human Godward movement to the Father, through the Son in the Spirit."[63] It is important to note that both of these movements occur within God; in the second movement we are not entirely passive but neither are we entirely active and we certainly do not initiate the human-Godward movement. Rather, by the Spirit we are placed "in" the Son so that we can participate in *his* efficacious offering. As Ngien points out, all of this depends upon God's triune soteriological activity achieved in time in the economy of salvation: "The divine descent presupposes the sending of the Son; the human ascent presupposes the homecoming of the Son to glory, but with our humanity eternally attached. The Spirit is the power of efficacy of both movements in us."[64] Thus, worship is the gift of participating by the Spirit in the incarnate Son's communion with the Father.[65] In fact, all of Christian being and doing must be understood theologically as participat-

60. Ngien, *Gifted Response*, 2.

61. Basil, *De Spiritu Sancto* XI.27 (NPNF2-08, 18).

62. Gregory of Nazianzus, *On God and Christ: The Five Theological Orations* 5.31.12, trans. Frederick Williams and Lionel Wickham (Crestwood, NY: St. Vladimir's Seminary Press, 2002), 125–26

63. James B. Torrance, *Worship, Community & the Triune God of Grace* (Downers Grove, IL: InterVarsity, 1996), 32.

64. Ngien, *Gifted Response*, 31.

65. This is a slightly modified version of James Torrance's definition of worship (Torrance, *Worship, Community*, 30).

ing in the triune God. For example, patristic writers speak in participatory terms about human knowledge of God, holiness, and spirituality. Consider the following representative quotations:

> Basil: Thus the way of the knowledge of God lies from One Spirit through the One Son to the One Father, and conversely the natural Goodness and the inherent Holiness and the royal Dignity extend from the Father through the Only-begotten to the Spirit.[66]

> Origen: As now by participation in the Son of God one is adopted as a son, and by participating in that wisdom which is in God is rendered wise, so also by participation in the Holy Spirit is a man rendered holy and spiritual. For it is one and the same thing to have a share in the Holy Spirit, which is (the Spirit) of the Father and the Son, since the nature of the Trinity is one and incorporeal.[67]

> Basil: Shining upon those that are cleansed from every spot, [the Spirit] makes them spiritual by fellowship with Himself. Just as when a sunbeam falls on bright and transparent bodies, they themselves become brilliant too, and shed forth a fresh brightness from themselves, so souls wherein the Spirit dwells, illuminated by the Spirit, themselves become spiritual, and send forth their grace to others.[68]

With respect to participating in God's mission, I suggest that mission is the gift of participating by the Spirit in the Son's missionary activity of establishing the Kingdom of God the Father. Our mission is, first and foremost, God's mission; it is the *missio Dei*. Our mission is a participation in God's mission, made possible through our union with Christ in the Spirit. We minister and do mission in Christ by the Spirit; Christ is the true Minister and Missionary. All that we proclaim to the world and demonstrate with our lives as a living hermeneutic of the gospel comes *from* God the Father *through* the priestly and salvific mediation of Christ the Son *in* and *by* the new-creation power, illuminating guidance, and personal, fruit-bestowing presence of the Holy Spirit. Correspondingly, all that we offer and accomplish as we participate in God's mission (that is, all that *genuinely* participates in God's missional activity) we do *in* and *by* the Spirit through the sole priesthood of Christ (in which we participate as his kingdom of priests, purchased by his blood; Rev. 5:9–10) to the glory and honor of the

---

66. Basil, *On the Holy Spirit* XVIII.47 (NPNF2-08, 29).
67. Origen, *On First Principles* IV.32 (ANF04, 379).
68. Basil, *De Spiritu Sancto* IX.23 (NPNF2-08, 15).

Father, in obedience to "the mystery of his will according to his good pleasure, which he purposed in Christ" (Eph. 1:9).

## III. SUMMARY CONCLUSION

In this essay I have argued that the mission of God is properly grounded in the ecstatic, loving being and act of the Trinity. The argument can be summarized in four steps. First, God's mission to the world is rooted in God's love for the world. This idea is supported in Scripture and in tradition, though it is not always explicit in the contemporary missional literature. Second, God's love for the world is itself rooted in God's own essential nature as love. Third, through God's mission, we are lovingly drawn into union with Christ and one another by the Spirit, who is the very love and gift of God. Finally, by virtue of our union with Christ, we participate in God's mission. This involves a threefold economic pattern of human participation in divine activity, a double movement of grace that takes place in Christ by the Spirit. The God-humanward movement proceeds from the Father through the Son in/by the Spirit, while the human-Godward movement takes place in/by the Spirit through the Son to the Father.

While I do not have the space to develop the many practical implications this theological framework has for the church, some of these include: (a) the importance of spiritual discernment (and spiritual direction) for pastoral ministry, church leadership, and missional engagement; (b) the importance of the church's immersion in the biblical narrative, indwelling the text so as to embody its patterns and see the world through it (as Gorman suggests, the church must 'become' the gospel); (c) due attention to discipleship and being/becoming and doing (thus a grace-based, holistic character ethics), since true missional witness calls the church to be and become by participating in the Spirit that which it proclaims and does "in Christ" (e.g., Matt. 5:13-16); (d) a renewal of worship and liturgy shaped by the Trinitarian *patterns* outlined in this essay (not just dropping the world 'Trinity' here and there, or simply referring to Father, Son, and Spirit; thus the *structure* of our songs, prayers, and sermons must be Trinitarian, not just the verbal content), informed by the whole of Scripture, and articulated contextually and missionally; (e) a renewed theology of vocation, conceived missionally within a participatory Trinitarian framework, so that the *whole people* of God can bear witness of the *whole gospel* to the *whole world*; and (f) a deeper understanding and outworking of a sacramental approach to theology, ecclesiology, and mission, within which the church I seen to be the sacramental presence of God in the world (this, in turn, has implications for how we understand and practice preaching, worship, the sacraments, Christian ministry and service within the church, solidarity with the suffering and marginalized, social action and community engagement, and so forth; in short, we are participating concretely in something God is mysteriously and graciously initiating, sustaining, and completing; e.g., Phil. 1:6; 2:12–13; 3:12; 4:8–9).

## Chapter 3

# Luther's Providential God

Robert Kolb

Many have seen Martin Luther as a Christomonic theologian—if not Christomanic.[1] It is indeed true that Luther believed that no one has seen God, but the Only-Begotten of the Father has made him known. He would have agreed with the words of a German preacher two generations ago who said, "We Christians do not believe in a 'higher power.' We Christians believe in God close by and the God who made himself so small that he found his way through the doors of this world, under the yoke that pressed down upon his neck and bowed him down under the burden of our guilt and death, heavy as a mountain."[2] For Luther, God's revelation of himself as he assumed humanity as Jesus of Nazareth formed the focus and heart of the reformer's orientation to life.

Luther had come to know God's merciful heart and his all-embracing concern and care for his human creatures though the incarnation of the second person of the Holy Trinity. But Luther was a Trinitarian theologian, with a strong doctrine of the Holy Spirit as the *Spiritus Creator* of the new life in Christ, and his recognition of God as Creator undergirded his entire

---

1. This essay was originally delivered as a lecture at Greenville Presbyterian Theological Seminary, Greenville, South Carolina, USA, on March 14, 2017.

2 Karl Hartenstein, "Predigt zum 4. Advent über Philipper 4,4–7," in *Vom Wachen und Beten. Ein Jahrgang Predigten*, 2nd ed. (Stuttgart: Evangelischer Missionsverlag, 1956), 26.

proclamation of the work of Jesus Christ as true God and true human being and his proclamation of activities of the Holy Spirit. Luther believed that God is indeed present, and not only in the unique manner of his presence in the Lord's Supper. He is present in the pages of Holy Scripture, from which he addresses readers and hearers with the power of his gospel. He is present and experienced in the world of everyday existence, as he provides the gifts that flow naturally from his essence as a loving, and thus giving, God. That presence exhibits itself as he directs the course of natural events and presides over human history.

## 1. GOD PROVIDES

In teaching the children of the German-speaking lands the fundamentals of the faith in his *Small Catechism*, he confessed God as a Creator whose initial creation formed the basis of a never-ceasing, ongoing relationship with his creatures. In the Wittenberg reformer's explanation of the first article of the Apostles' Creed, the children were taught to trust that "God has created me together with all that exists." The Creator's relationship with each child who could view himself or herself, therefore, as the product of God's own creative word, did not end, however, with an initial creation. Luther continued, "God has given me and still preserves my body and soul: eyes, ears and all limbs and senses; reason and all mental faculties." And it was not just a matter of installing the hardware, the hardwiring: Luther reminded the children of God's regular and reliable interaction with their daily needs: "In addition, God daily and abundantly provides shoes and clothing, food and drink, house and farm, spouse and children, fields, livestock and all property—along with all the necessities and nourishment for this body and life." God not only provides things: "God protects me against all danger and shields and preserves me in the face of all evil." Finally, there is an explanation, of sorts, as to why God does this. "And all this is done out of pure, fatherly and divine goodness and mercy, without any merit or worthiness of mine at all!" Oswald Bayer suggests that this is an echo of the Ockhamist insistence on the complete dependence of creatures upon their Creator.[3] God's creative act and his continuing provision for all of life had its implications for the response of the human creatures whom he had made his children. Luther concluded, "For all of this I owe it to God to thank and praise, serve and obey him."[4]

3. Oswald Bayer, *Martin Luther's Theology: A Contemporary Interpretation*, trans. Thomas H. Trapp (Grand Rapids: Eerdmans, 2008), 171–73.

4. *Die Bekenntnisschrfiten der Evangelische-Lutherischen Kirche*, ed. Irene Dingel

Luther reinforced this view of God's continuous providing presence in the children's lives when he explained the fourth petition of the Lord's Prayer. Earlier he had followed the medieval line of interpretation that viewed this petition as a prayer for the daily bread of God's word. Luther had abandoned this interpretation by 1529 when he composed his catechism.[5] Luther defined "daily bread" there as "everything included in the necessities and nourishment for our bodies, such as food, drink, clothing, shoes, house, farm, fields, livestock, money, property, an upright spouse, upright children, upright members of the household, upright and faithful rulers, good government, good weather, peace, health, decency, honor, good friends, faithful neighbors, and the like."[6]

Luther's rather optimistic perception that God indeed provides all that we need for this body and life reflects in part his own situation. His paternal grandparents had been relatively prosperous peasants, and his maternal grandparents merchants in a small town—not to be counted among the rich, but certainly comfortable in terms of earthly blessings. His own situation placed him in danger of losing his life after his papal excommunication and imperial banning as an outlaw, both capital judgments, but his own rulers offered him protection—and a good salary. As a resident of Wittenberg, he shared with his fellow citizens times of food shortages and the flooding of the Elbe, but in general life had been good for him. His Ockhamist background led him to think of God as almighty and also reliable, for the Creator's promises in his various covenants, including that of Noah that future flood waters would do limited damage, prepared Luther to accept a certain stability in the world taken care of by a reliable God.

Thus, for Luther, God's omnipresence and omnipotence were not abstractions, but experiences, encountered in the course of daily life, in God's word, and to be sure, above all, in the presence of Christ as he came in the proclamation of forgiveness, life, and salvation, but also in the blessings of the created order.

Luther confessed God's intimate involvement in the regular working of the world. Jesus demonstrated with the feeding of the four thousand in Mark 8:1–9 that God "is a rich and powerful lord and provider; indeed, he is a rich miller and baker, better than any other upon the earth that has learned his trade perfectly . . . He plows, harvests, threshes, grinds, and bakes in a

---

(Göttingen: Vandenhoeck & Ruprecht, 2014 [henceforth BSELK]), 870/871,9–18; *The Book of Concord*, ed. Robert Kolb and Timothy J. Wengert (Minneapolis: Fortress, 2000 [henceforth BC]), 354–55.

5. Paul Robinson, "Luther's Explanation of Daily Bread in Light of Medieval Preaching," *Lutheran Quarterly* 13 (1999) 435–47.

6. BSELK, 878/879,8–12; BC 357.

twinkling of the eye."[7] Jesus supplying the tax payment to Peter in Matthew 17:27 further illustrates how God continues to create and give in the midst of daily life, for he brings bread and water out of rocks:

> We are to be sure familiar with the fact that grain grows yearly out of the earth, and through this familiarity we are so blinded that we do not esteem such work. For what we see daily and hear, that we do not regard as miraculous. But indeed it is just as great. To speak correctly, it is a greater miracle that God should give us grain out of the sand and the stone than that he here feeds the masses with seven loaves.[8]

## 2. WHAT GOD PROVIDES

According to Luther, God provides both material blessings and the protection that preserves the order and stability necessary to enjoy those blessings. An excellent overview and summary of Luther's understanding of God's providential care occurs in his comments on Psalm 147:12–20. While suffering one of his periodic bouts of "the buzzing and weariness of my head" in late 1531, the professor received an invitation from a friend at Elector John's court at the other end of Wittenberg's main street. Hans Löser, an important advisor of the elector, invited him to indulge in some physical exercise and accompany him on the hunt. Never much one for hunting, Luther confessed, "I did some spiritual hunting on my own as I sat in the carriage. I bagged Psalm 147, *Lauda Jerusalem*, together with its exposition, and this was my happiest hunt and grandest game." He added that having brought the psalm home and butchered it, he was sharing it in print with Löser, as friends do with a bountiful prize from the hunt.[9]

One presupposition for Luther's entire understanding of God's providence lay in his conviction that God acts through his word, as he did from the beginning in Genesis 1. Verse 15 of Psalm 147 announces that God "sends forth his command to the earth; his Word runs swiftly." Luther observed that God can get along without "forge, hammer, anvil, or tongs, . . . brick or mortar . . ." He could easily dispense with "women [as childbearers], merchants, or manufacturers of coinage" to bestow wealth and

---

7. *D. Martin Luthers Werke* (Weimar: Böhlau, 1883-1993 [henceforth WA]), 22:120,18–28; *Luther's Works* (St. Louis/Philadelphia: Concordia/Fortress, 1958–1986 [henceforth LW]), 78:257; *The Complete Sermons of Martin Luther*, ed. John Nicholas Lenker (1905–1909; Grand Rapids: Baker, 2000 [henceforth CP], 4:218; 78:257).

8. WA 22:120,35–121,22; CP 4:219; LW 78:257–58.

9. WA 31,1:430,4–431,20; LW 14:110.

happiness upon his children. His word could simply command wheat stalks to bear fruit without any plows. "It only takes one little word from him, and that word is *fiat* ["let it happen"]." "Unless God creates with his Word, all our work and effort is in vain." Nonetheless, God works through his gifts—seed and plow and plowman—to feed us. Everything that he has created serves as means of his providence. In this manner his word that brings blessings creates trust that withstands the gates of hell (Matt 16:18) and banishes fear. But too often, Luther reminded readers, "we do not believe that God is for us. We are unbelieving, ungrateful, shameful, wicked children!"[10]

Verse 13, "he strengthens the bars of your gates," reminded Luther that "God guards and keeps the gates of the city so that people can dwell there in safety and quiet." The Creator's protection of humankind by keeping order among his creatures is a great gift, beyond "human intelligence or power," but one which most take for granted, causing God to remind them of this "noble gift" by sending "war, thieves, robbers, revolution, fire, flood, pestilence, and other such catastrophes."[11] Connected with this blessing of public stability was the gift of a city full of people, "well populated and well built." Human might does not make that possible. A city that is at peace but is constructed poorly and lacking many people will not experience the gifts that human society requires: manpower, livestock, skills. Luther expressed his gratitude to God for Wittenberg's water supply and for the fact that its "children [were] fat as snails" even though their parents earned little.[12]

Related to this protection is the gift of peace (verse 14). This peace is characterized by the ability to raise crops and livestock in a secure environment, which includes reliable neighbors and properly-behaving nobles and peasants. Here Luther broke into a paean of "God-fearing, faithful neighbors," with quotations from Terence, Aristotle, and Cato. Patience and good-will are required for this peace to take place in town or village. In addition, a government must lead its people in preparing good roads and fortifying the towns. But peace also includes physical health in a world filled with the plague, floods (which Wittenberg often experienced, lying on the Elbe river as it does), fires, poison, and other misfortunes.[13]

Along with peace, Psalm 147:14 speaks of "filling you with the finest wheat." Daily bread also is taken for granted, Luther noted, in a call for repentant and grateful reactions to God's rich temporal blessings. In one of his typical monologues the professor addresses the grain: "O splendid grain!

10. WA 31,1:445,1–447,2; LW 14:123–25.
11. WA 31,1:434,15–435,23; LW 14:112–14.
12. WA 31,1:437,20–439,13; LW 14:116–17.
13. WA 31,1: 439,15–443,11; LW 14:117–21.

God gives you to us in abundance out of his great goodness. And withwhat great power he protects you! What dangers you have overcome from the moment you were sown until you are placed on our table. What mighty power that God has displayed in snatching you from the devil's fingers and hands, which grabbed you to spoil you so that we would starve." Without God's protection Satan would deprive human beings of their daily physical sustenance, Luther was certain.[14]

Finally, Psalm 147:16–18 provided the occasion for thankfulness for good weather. Luther was apparently no friend of winter, when the land is barren and bleak. "If the devil regulated the frost, winter would last forever and everything would turn to ice in a day." But, Luther concluded, one and the same God stands by his people in summer and winter even though his expression in winter "appears as death, anger, and all evil," whereas summer has the appearance of "life, grace and all good things." Only God could make provision for human survival in winter, without warmth, when even the grain cannot grow. Believers should cling in trust to the God who annually delivers them from both winter and flooding, he claimed. For he provides the delights of summer so that they may recognize how good he is and give him thanks since, according to verse 18, "he sends forth his Word and melts [the snow and ice]" and sends the winds that bring the thaw. Luther turned this in an allegorical direction, for the wind that is the Holy Spirit uses the winter-like law to convert his enemies and bring them into the summer of the gospel.[15] Luther concluded his comments on Psalm 147 with thanksgiving based on the final two verses for the blessing of God's word with its power to save that remains and upholds believers when temporal blessings are gone, even when death removes us from their realm.[16]

This theme continued throughout Luther's life. In 1542, lecturing on Genesis 27:39–49, he informed his students of the earthly blessings which the patriarchs had enjoyed, including those which Isaac bestowed on Jacob (Gen 27:39–40), observing that God gives "sumptuously and luxuriously."[17] As a result Jacob offers an example of the kind of life Luther expected would come in reaction to God's giving: Jacob was content to serve the Lord in the lowliest of earthly tasks, herding his sheep, tending to the needs of his family. The professor held him up as a model his students and their future hearers to follow.[18] His contentment grew from his confidence in God's love

14. WA 31,1:443,12–444,37; LW 14:121–23.
15. WA 31,1:447,3–452,21; LW 14:125–31.
16. WA 31,1:452,22 –456,21; LW 14:131–35.
17. WA 43:523,16–524,31; LW 5:138–40.
18. WA 43:617,36–619,4; LW 5:274–76; cf. WA 43:642,33–39; LW 5:310–11.

and his commitment to the welfare of his people; such contentment marks the life of the faithful.

In preaching on the disciples' great catch of fishes, Luther described the connection between God's provision of temporal blessings and faith. Trust in Christ produces gratitude and contentment as well as joy in believers: "all who believe will have enough for their temporal needs, but those who do not believe can never get enough and have no rest in scheming how to secure riches, by which they fall into all kinds of vice."[19] "Peter might well have thought since he had fished so long and caught nothing, 'now God will let the stomach languish.' But he does not despair. He continues to work and stands and hopes that God would give it to him although he might delay.... even if God should delay a little and let you toil in your sweat, so that you imagine that your labor is now lost, you must be wise and learned to know your God and to trust in him."[20]

God's temporal blessings were to shape the way those who heard Luther's preaching led their lives each day, also in the way in which they thought about and reacted to the injustices and evils which they encountered. Resisting temptation and evil is aided by the fact that "we have received such an ample supply of good from God, both eternal and temporal, that we can easily help the neighbor."[21] Discontent with what God has provided stifles and smothers the practice of love and care for others "with the result that a person does good for no one but scratches together everything only onto his own pile."[22] But "if one believes, God gives him so much that he is able to help all people, outwardly with his property and gifts, from within by going further, teaching others and making them inwardly rich also, for such a person cannot keep silent but must declare to others what he experienced."[23]

The Creator serves not only as provider but also as protector amidst all kinds of perils and threats. Luther treasured the presence of God in his life that had defended him against foes of all kinds. Scripture offered many examples of God's entering the battle against such foes. In the case of Jacob as he returned home and had to confront Esau (Gen. 32), the brother whom he had cheated out of his inheritance, Luther claimed that the outcome of their meeting demonstrates that God indeed delivers to his people more good than evil despite their experience of evils that plague them. Believers must concede that Jacob's experience with evil suggests that "a very small

---

19. WA 10,3:228,13–21; CP 4:133; LW 78:205.
20. WA 10,3:231,16–26; CP 4:136; LW 78:210.
21. WA 45:699,37–700,9; LW 24:261.
22. WA 10,3:229,14–18; CP 4:134.
23. WA 10,3:234,3–9; CP 4:139.

part of life is subjected to the devil's power."[24] In every case, God is in charge. The impious may ignore their Creator and his commands, but he directs and controls them along with the pious in what they do.[25]

Yet Luther did not turn a blind eye to the poor, the orphans, and the widows, who suffer violence and injustice. They were to find comfort in knowing that their Creator is the "father of such orphans and the avenger of such widows, that he is not far away but close by, and does not need to be sought in Jerusalem or Rome."[26]

Luther's assertions about God's presence and provision in the midst of all kinds of threats was in part autobiographical. God's promise to "return justice to the righteous" and to stand up for his people against evildoers (Ps 94:15–17) led Luther to recall the particularly dangerous days after his excommunication and banning as an outlaw by Emperor Charles V. With those factors in mind, he told Queen Mary of Hungary in 1526, "If it had depended on my own resources and those of others, it would have been over for me." Feeling deserted, and with his heart beating fast, Luther had experienced that God had given him patience and informed him beyond his own ability to reason, that "he would bring down his enemies."[27]

A decade later the reformer sketched a short commentary on Psalm 23 at the evening gathering around his table. The claim of the psalmist in verse 1 that God's people will not be wanting provides readers and hearers of the psalm "a confidence, comfort, and sense of security that the word 'father' and others provide when attributed to God." For "a sheep must live completely on the basis of its shepherd's aid, protection, and care." Dangers and death threaten the impotent little beast, which loses its way and cannot find food if it is separated from the shepherd. It must take refuge in the shepherd's ability to find good pasture and ward off threats. Like sheep, "we poor, weak, miserable people cannot feed ourselves spiritually and find our way on the right path or with our own might protect ourselves against every evil and find aid and comfort for ourselves when under attack and in affliction."[28]

Some fifteen years earlier Luther had composed a postil sermon for the festival of Saint Stephen, on Matthew 23:37, which uses the metaphor of the text, the hen giving her chicks shelter from threats out of the sky, to sketch a picture of God's providential protection. Fred Meuser has suggested

24. WA 44:67,9–10; LW 6:90.
25. WA 44:68,1–27; LW 6:92.
26. WA 8:8,3–19; LW 13:6.
27. WA 19;591,34–592,6; LW 14:253.
28. WA 51:271,19–274,8; LW 12:152–55.

that Luther may have been meditating on the text while gazing at the birds who had free rein in the courtyard of the Wartburg Castle, where he was in protective custody, safe, he hoped, from imperial troops and other foes searching for an excommunicated imperial outlaw.[29] The cast of the drama included the mother-hen in the role of Christ, the chicks play his faithful people, and the hawks are cast as the devils and evil spirits which intend to swoop down and carry off the hapless believers as their prey. The chicks are somewhat witless, but they do know that they have to depend completely on the mother-hen, that is, Christ's righteousness, as their shelter and shield. They creep, snuggle, and crouch in Christ's sheltering love and place their confidence in him. The mother-hen not only finds them food and attempts to cajole them into eating; she exemplifies the concern that sounds from Christ's voice, for like her, he stretches out his wings of merit over these chicks, warms them with the warmth of his body, which represents the Holy Spirit, and shields them with his body from the attack of the devil, the hawks. Luther embellished Jesus' metaphor by adding wild boars to the tale. Both hawks and hogs intend to chase the chicks, rip them open, and munch them down, but their plans come to naught. God protects and provides.[30]

The world may pursue its own will in defiance of God, Luther announced to the hearers in Wittenberg in 1537, but God is in charge of human history and protects his people against the worst in the attacks of those whom Satan makes his tools. With memories from twelve years earlier of the murder and theft wrought by rebellious peasants Luther said:

> Daily, too frequently, we see and experience that the common rabble among burghers, peasants, and noblemen submit reluctantly and unwillingly and would much rather shake off the yoke of obedience and restraint. Therefore, there must be another power that upholds kings and lords in their rule and suppresses the mob with its malice and disobedience. Otherwise everything would go to wrack and ruin. That is what happens when God becomes angry, when the measure of iniquity of tyrants and of the populace is filled to overflowing, when they ungratefully persecute God's Word and the Christians, destroy them, and silence their prayers. Then it is time to put an end to it. Then God closes his eyes and lets matters take their course. Then prince, mayor, mob, and all tumble in a heap like an old house that collapses. Then it is clear how well the world can

---

29. Fred Meuser, *Luther as Preacher* (Minneapolis: Augsburg, 1983), 62.

30. WA 10,1,1:280,5–282,3; LW 52:96–97; this passage is taken from Robert Kolb, *Luther and the Stories of God, Biblical Narratives as a Foundation for Christian Living* (Grand Rapids: Baker, 2012), 179.

govern when left to itself . . . the world goes its way in abysmal ignorance, for it is blind and possessed by the devil.[31]

Shortly before this sermon, Luther had had as his text John 14:11. Christ's claim that he and he Father are one led the preacher to remind the Wittenberg congregation of all that God does to help and save his people, as he daily reveals by preserving all his creatures, bestowing so many blessings on the whole world, and bountifully pouring out his good gifts, except when of necessity and for the sake of the godly he must punish and restrain the wicked. But his manner of governing shows that even physically his people always experience more of his grace and blessing than of his wrath and punishment. Luther ventured that for every hundred thousand healthy people there is only a single ailing, blind, deaf, paralytic, or leprous person, a bit of homiletic exaggeration indeed. He reasoned that even if one member of the body has a defect, the entire person, still endowed with body and soul, reveals nothing but God's goodness.[32]

## 3. HOW GOD PROVIDES

As Luther affirmed in his comments on Psalm 147, he believed that God has the whole world and all that is within it in his hands. He does not only work through the agency of natural forces, behind which always stands his word; he works through his people, and their prayers help direct his providential hand. Two examples of Luther's combination of prayer to God and both admonition and consolation for the ill reveal how Luther himself used these tools for mediating God's care for his people. Consultations with Saxon officials in Weimar on the bigamy of Landgrave Philip of Hesse in 1540 had exhausted Luther's colleague Philip Melanchthon and brought him near death. Elector Johann Friedrich summoned Luther to Weimar for discussions of other pressing concerns, but Luther also went to the sickbed of his friend, who had lost consciousness. Martin Brecht sketches Luther's response to Melanchthon's condition: "He turned at first to the window and stormed God in a manner that was unusual and outrageous, even for him."[33] He berated God for imposing this suffering on him and, in Luther's words, "I rubbed God's ears with all the promises that he would hear prayer, which I could recall from Holy Scripture, telling him that he had to listen to me if I

---

31. WA 45:534,24–535,2; LW 24:81.

32. WA 45:527,27–37; LW 24:73.

33. Martin Brecht, *Martin Luther. Dritter Band. Die Erhaltung der Kirche,* 1532–1546 (Stuttgart: Calwer, 1987), 209–10.

were to trust his promise any other time." He took Melanchthon's hand and told him, "you will not die." Deathly sick though Melanchthon was, Luther commanded his colleague not to give an inch to the spirit of depression, or else he would be a murderer himself. As Melanchthon became conscious, he had no appetite. Luther ordered him to eat, or "I will excommunicate you." Luther wrote to his wife Katherine that Philip had really been dead and like Lazarus had risen from the death, for God had heard his prayer.[34]

Four years later their mutual friend Georg Spalatin, pastor in Altenburg, Luther's companion and counselor in the earliest days of the reform movement when Spalatin had served Elector Frederick the Wise as an advisor, was suffering from "a spirit of sadness," melancholy or depression. Luther received word that this friend was also on the edge of death. "God does not want the sinner to die but to live and turn to him," he wrote his friend, whose conscience was being plagued by guilt over his approval of the marriage of a fellow pastor with the step-mother of his dead wife. Luther had the pastoral wisdom to take Spalatin's feelings of sin and guilt as seriously as Spalatin himself did. He assured Spalatin of forgiveness for his bad judgment, arguing that if he viewed himself as a real sinner, he should believe that Christ is a real savior. Spalatin was drenched in comfort and consolation, not only from Luther but also from their mutual friends Nikolaus von Amsdorf and Melanchthon, who sent assurance that also Elector Johann Friedrich was graciously disposed toward the Altenburg pastor. In fact, Spalatin did not fully recover and lived only five more months after this bout with depression.[35] God hears the pleas of his people, and their prayers are part of his plan for providing for his church and world, Luther was convinced.

God also is at work through human beings as his agents in making the world work according to his plan, to supply the good for his people but also to bring judgment upon them in a call for repentance, as the professor remarked commenting on Isaiah 10:15 in 1527. Rulers are no more than "God's scepter," in God's hand. Isaiah ridiculed the king of Assyria "who to himself seems made of iron . . . because he is not even made of wood, and his effort is futile. He is indeed both God's saw and God's ax so long as God employs him as his instrument to discipline a disobedient people." Otherwise, the king is no more than stubble ready for the fire. "He can do

---

34. Brecht, 3:210, cf. Luther's report to his wife, WA Briefe 9:168, 172, 22–24, WA 50:215.

35. WA Briefe 10:638–640.Number. 4021, cf. Stephen Pietsch, *Of Good Comfort. Martin Luther's Letters to the Depressed and Their Significance for Pastoral Care Today* (Adelaide: ATF, 2016), and Ute Mennicke-Haustein, *Luthers Trostbriefe* (Gütersloh: Gütersloher Verlagshaus, 1989).

neither good nor evil apart from the Lord's drawing him or cutting and striking with him."[36]

Nonetheless, God also provides blessings and preserves the existence of his world through human beings within his structures of the walks of life into which he has cast human life. In these situations all human beings exercise the responsibilities to which their Creator has assigned them. Luther adapted the medieval social theory that viewed this configuration of life together into three "situations" or "walks of life"—often translated "estates"—in which God gives every individual responsibilities—often translated "offices"—in which people hold certain positions or roles and are assigned specific functions. The walk of life designated to teach [*Lehrstand*] was the church [*ecclesia*]; it taught the truth to the society; priests, monks, and nuns comprised this walk of life, which was also labeled an "order." The walk of life designated to preserving public order and protecting the populace [*Wehrstand*] consisted of those to whom the public life of the "*polis*," society, was entrusted, especially those of public governance [*politia*]; this "situation in life" kept order, administered justice, and provided defense against external enemies. The rest of the population made up the walk of life that supplied nourishment or sustenance for physical existence [*Nährstand*], or household [*oeconomia*]; the bulk of the population lived in families that rendered services and made products available for the entire society. Each individual was placed in one of these situations to exercise their offices or responsibilities for the benefit of the whole society.[37]

Luther altered the concept of "office" or "responsibility" in at least two ways. He regarded all people as having responsibilities in all three walks of life, not just one. Furthermore, he asserted that Christians realize that they are given these responsibilities through a "call"—a "*vocatio*" from God, who places them in the "order"—"*ordo*"—of each walk of life. He thus appropriated two terms which had been reserved for priests, monks, and nuns in medieval thinking, and he applied them to all.[38] Luther expressed his thanks for these situations and responsibilities in his exposition of Psalm 111, composed in autumn 1530. "These divine walks of life and orders have been established by God in the world to insure a stable, orderly, peaceful life and the practice of justice." Luther equated this with natural law.

---

36. WA 31,2:78,16–27; LW 16:110.

37. Gustaf Wingren, *Luther on Vocation*, trans. Carl C. Rasmussen (Philadelphia: Muhlenberg, 1957), 1–77.

38. Timothy J. Wengert, "Per mutuum colloquium et consolationem fratrum," Monastische Züge in Luthers ökumenischer Theologie, in *Luther und das monastische Erbe*, eds. Christoph Bultmann et al. (Tübingen: Mohr/Siebeck, 2007), 243–68.

Life in society is dependent on God's institution and preservation since discontent lurks in every heart. Such discontent needs the disciplines of God's structures for life and their own enforcement mechanisms. Servants covet the position of master, peasants that of the prince, and children want to exercise the roles of their parents. Without God keeping order through his structures, the human condition would be worse than that of animals in the wild.[39] God has established human communities and there he "each day creates, maintains, and makes things grow so that his people can remain at home and beget children and educate them," Luther mused as he began comments on Psalm 82:1. It provided assurance that God is present among his people, that he "accepts them as the product of his hand, his creation, and he takes care of them, protecting and upholding them . . . For who could possess or keep a cow or a coin if God did not give it and lend his help and protection?"[40]

In these callings or vocations Christians realize that God has made his human creatures agents of his providence, "masks" behind which he is present to provide, protect, and preserve his creatures. "God could easily give you grain and fruit without your plowing and planting." He does not run his world in this manner, however. "You are to plow and plant and then ask his blessing and pray, 'Now let God assume responsibility. Give us grain and fruit, dear Lord. Our plowing and planting will not accomplish this. It is your gift." He continued, noting that God could place children in this world without using human beings as parents. He chose instead to "join man and woman so that it appears to be the work of man and woman, and yet he does it under the cover of such masks."[41] So Luther concludes in a criticism of "lazy bums": "Work, and let him give the fruits. Govern, and let him provide blessing. Fight, and let him take the victory. Preach, and let him win hearts. Take a husband or wife, and let him produce the children. Eat and drink, and let him nourish and strengthen you . . . He is to work through us, and he alone is to have the glory from it," citing 1 Corinthians 3:7 as proof.[42]

Luther had made precisely this point in comments on Psalm 37 in the booklet prepared for Queen Mary of Hungary at the death of her husband, King Louis II, in battle against the Turkish invaders in 1526. On verse 5, "commit your way to the Lord; trust in him, and he will act," Luther added, "this does not mean that you should be lazy. . . . Committing our way to God does not mean that we do nothing. It means that . . . we remain on task, . . .

---

39. WA 31,1:408,35–409,30; LW 13:368–69.
40. WA 31,1:194,13–27; LW 13:47.
41. WA 31,1:435,36–436,6; LW 14:114.
42. WA 31,1:437,3–19; LW 14:115.

entrusting our whole cause to God, who will make it come out right on both sides."[43] God acts, but human beings must also act.

The report on the great catch of fish illustrated this simultaneous action of God and human creature in a different way. The disciples' toil and trouble did not accomplish anything in the night, when the fish are easiest to catch, but in broad daylight Christ was able to give them so many fish that their nets broke. Luther addressed the phenomenon that there seems to be no correlation between human effort and human gain; he ignored the seeming injustice and saw it as an example of Psalm 127:2, "so he gives it to his beloved in sleep," which he paraphrased "it is in vain that you fret and plague yourself with cares and labor, day and night, in order to provide what is needed in the home. Much may be needed there; but it does not depend on your hands and work at all. Nothing will come of your effort unless God himself is the housefather and makes it possible for you to say, 'God bestows his gifts overnight.' Grain and all food from the earth, indeed, all that a person has or may acquire must be given him by God." All that human creatures have is a gift from the Creator. This protects believers from covetousness and from anxious cares for the body and the present life.[44]

Luther also used the opportunity of the story of the great catch of fish for a deconstruction of the monastic piety and reverence for the clerical estate that still had a firm hold on the imagination of the people in the early 1520s. They glorified escape from work, but God had assured Adam that he would earn his bread in the sweat of his face (Gen. 3:19). No roasted dove will fly into the mouths of those who do not work. And even when want and deprivation descend, hope for God's provision should be steadfast in hope despite delays in God's provision. Believers take refuge in the wisdom that counts on God.[45]

Following his Ockhamist instructors, Luther held that God is almighty, and thus he is truly responsible for all that takes place in his universe. But Luther also had learned from those instructors that human beings must exercise their responsibilities as well. He did not attempt to solve the mystery of the humanity that is totally dependent on God and yet so created in his image with mind, will, and emotions, that God can hold them responsible for their actions and attitudes. In the human creature's exercise of these responsibilities, God is at work, providing for others.

---

43. WA 19:555,29–556,3; LW 14:212–13.
44. WA 22:76,20–36; CP4:144–45; LW 78:206.
45. WA 22:75,35–76,8; CP4:135–36; LW 78:210.

## 4. WHEN GOD SEEMS ABSENT

Luther was soberly realistic about the fact that God often seems absent, not providing but either angrily refusing to help believers or just ignoring their plights. Luther had more than one approach to such dilemmas. One presented such predicaments as tools through which God builds faith and patience by delaying the delivery of his aid. This Luther concluded in a sermon on Luke 5:1–11, the catch of fish, from 1534. In it he reiterated and expanded on the thoughts of his 1522 sermon on the same text. Believers learn to pray in such times, but God gives his gifts all the more abundantly in such situations.[46] Trust in God for salvation lays the basis for trusting his providential intent for his people, for, as Jesus had said in Matthew 6:33, his people are to seek his rule and righteousness first, and temporal blessings will be piled on top. God's supplies his blessings for the needs of daily life, providing help and comfort along with the stuff of daily life. He provides protection and deliverance as well. When we are in great need, and all our efforts are in vain, it is precisely in such need and weakness that "he gives and helps in richer measure than could be accomplished by all human power, skill, and assistance."[47] The feeding of the four thousand in Mark 8:1–9 gave Luther the opportunity to reiterate that those who trust God "entrust the stomach to God for his care and believe that he will not allow us to come to distress because of the lack of temporal things." The four thousand clung to God alone and confessed that he "will indeed feed us. . . . they commended themselves to him and freely laid all that they needed upon him."[48]

Luther knew that it is not always the believer's experience that God truly provides. His theology of the cross answered in part the theodical questions raised by the impoverishment and hunger of his people. God and Satan, the Lord's truth and the devil's deception, are locked in a continuing eschatological conflict because God has chosen to fend off the Evil One's assault on his lordship and his creation with what seems to the world and human reason to be the weakness and foolishness of the cross and of the message of its salvation, which is God's wisdom and power (1 Cor. 1–2). That God's strength is made perfect in his people's weakness (2 Cor. 12:9) explains those times of want and need as no more than the devil's hatred for the believer's faith.[49] Luther was using this part of his hermeneutical frame-

---

46. WA 22:84,3–27; CP 4:154–55; LW 78:213.
47. WA 22:75,35–76,8; CP 4:143–44; LW 78:205.
48. WA 12:636,23–637,4; CP 4:207.
49. Vitor Westhelle, "Luther's *theologia crucis*," in *The Oxford Handbook of Martin Luther's Theology*, eds. Robert Kolb et al. (Oxford: Oxford University Press, 2014), 156–67; Gerhard O. Forde, *On Being a Theologian of the Cross: Reflections on Luther's Heidelberg Disputation, 1518* (Grand Rapids: Eerdmans, 1997).

work in the early 1520s. In preaching on Luke 16:19–31, the rich man and Lazarus, he reminded hearers that Satan rules "in the world, and he is the enemy of Christ and of his church, and since they themselves do not seek the things of this world, they must suffer that to be taken out of their mouths and be robbed of that which belongs to them." But Christ, who has secured eternal life through the forgiveness of sins for his elect, will be present with them precisely in the midst of Satanic attack.[50]

Luther suggested that Christ says to his people, "It does not sound appealing to say that all the world should be directed to discard all its wisdom, for example, to surrender its own ideas about the Godhead or about the way he created heaven and earth, governs the world, and performs other works."[51] But, indeed, that is simply the way it is. Thus, to preserve its own systems and principles the world often has to persecute believers. "Let the angry princes or the ranting and raving bishops persecute the gospel. Let the learned people abandon it! It is necessary for the gospel to be despised outwardly by the world, to be trodden underfoot and persecuted, . . . There is, after all, another power which preserves this teaching."[52] Luther believed that God used such evils to the benefit of his people. "If all the devils, the world, our neighbors, and our own people are hostile to us, revile and slander us, hurt and torment us, we should regard this as no different from applying a shovelful of manure to the vine to fertilize it well, cutting away the useless wild branches, or removing a little of the excessive and hampering foliage."[53]

In both bad times and good the person of the providing God—that same person who rescues and restores sinners in the incarnation of the second person of the Trinity and the death and resurrection of the Word made flesh—was present with is people. He provides, protects, and preserves. Therefore, they had every reason to enjoy the peace of Christ and the contentment that trust in God's providence creates. Contentment expresses itself in thanks. It demonstrates not an attitude of passive resignation but a joyful acknowledgement that God has the whole world in his hands. Luther closely connected trust in Christ for eternal life with trusting him for temporal blessings. In his sermon preached in 1522 on the disciples' great catch of fish (Luke 5:1–11) he associated unbelief with a lack of contentment regarding the things of this earth, which, he noted, ignored Paul's admonition in 1 Timothy 6:6–10 and Jesus' in Matthew 6:25–26.[54] Those who strive for

50. WA 10,3:181,26–184,24; CP 4:20–22; LW 78:57–58.
51. WA 33:185,6–25; LW 23:120.
52. WA 33:248,12–21; LW 23:158.
53. WA 45:641,7–11; LW 24:198.
54. WA 10,3:228,6–229,12; CP 4:133–34.

more and more possessions fall into the temptations and traps of the devil, the curse of unbelief. Here again, Luther was interweaving the seemingly contradictory poles of hope and trust in God's giving nature with his commands to work within the callings he bestows within human society. "If you wish to lead a truly Christian life, let your God see to it how the fish come into your net, and go and take up some calling in life so that you may work."[55]

This text also served as the basis for an attack on greed and the worries that lack of trust in God produce. Christ (Matt 13:22) and Paul (1 Tim 6:9–10) condemn such worries in the face of God's goodness and gifts, Luther reminded hearers and readers. In contrast to trust, which "fills the heart with such goodness, peace and joy that it may be called the root of all good things, unbelief with all its cares and covetousness shall have this as its reward, that it is not bettered thereby but inevitably falls into all sorts of traps through many harmful lusts and desires." Those who, like David (Psalm 37:25), think that they have never gone to bed hungry even though they are living in the midst of affliction and poverty, are upheld by their trust in God. This trust preserves them from wounding themselves among the thorns, which the cares for temporal things are. Instead, believers sit in the pleasure garden of roses. Without such faith people practice "robbery, they skin others for every cent they are worth, they impose levies and practice usury, etc. to such an extent that God and conscience are set aside for the sake of a miserable penny." The result is that they benefit no one in their callings but only spread "harm, misfortune, and misery."[56] Luther spared no one from his critique of greed, neither clergy nor ruling officials. He sharply condemned the exploitation of "destitute pastors, with their children, widows and orphans" by such rulers, who also "flay and tax their poor subjects to such an extent that they themselves fall into worries and difficulties, which must bring poverty and ruin upon themselves, their land, and their people." Or they bring ruin upon themselves in some other way.[57] Without the trust in God that breeds contentment, life invites misery upon itself.

This goal of contentment in everyday life stood at the foundation of Luther's interpretation of Ecclesiastes. He began his comments on the book in its 1532 publication by telling students that "Solomon wants to put us at peace and give us a quiet mind in the affairs of daily life and its activities so that we live in contentment in the present without worry and fussing about the future and are, in Paul's words, free from care and apprehension (Phil.

---

55. WA 10,3:230,11–15; CP 4:135–36.
56. WA 22:78,23–32; CP 4:145–47; LW 78:206–7.
57. WA 22:78,16–79,31; CP 4:147–49; LW 78:207–9.

4:6). It is useless to burden oneself with apprehension about the future." Luther used 1 Timothy 4:4–5 to remind readers of the goodness of all of God's creation, and he called it wicked and foolish to fulminate against God's good created gifts, including "glory, power, social position, wealth, gold, fame, beauty, or women," for that rejects what God created and gives. They are to be reasons for thanking God and instruments to enjoy his gift of life. It is the "depraved affection and desire" of the discontented that is sinful because it clings to these things for the security that God alone can give.[58]

Therefore, Solomon condemns the efforts that possess people to make their acquisition of temporal blessings the most important thing in their lives. That breeds discontent and dismissal of God's gifts as unimportant. Ecclesiastes was written to cultivate thanksgiving so that "we may use the things we have and God's creations that are generously given to us and bestowed upon us by God's blessing," following his admonition "to eat and drink and enjoy life with the wife of our youth." For if a person compares the blessings in his possession with the evils that have not befallen him, he will perceive what a treasure-chest of blessings he has.[59] Believers are blessed with the gift of contentment for what they have, and they are able to use them "with thanksgiving and joy."[60]

Thanksgiving and joy flow from the trust that knows God through his revelation in Christ's death and resurrection. That trust opens human eyes to see God's presence in their life and to experience his goodness, Luther frequently reminded his hearers and readers, as the completion of the comfort and peace Christ came to give. The Wittenberg reformer found the heart of the biblical message for sinners in the liberating and recreating work of Christ, who died to bring sinful identities to an end and rose to restore righteousness to his chosen people (Rom 4:25, Rom 6:3–4). But Luther's faith embraced the Creator, who provided for daily life by his own design throughout human history, from creation on. His preaching focused on this God, who provides, protects, and preserves as a means of bringing assurance, contentment, and trust in him to the everyday existence and experience of the believer.

---

58. WA 20:9,3–11,31; LW 15:7–8.
59. WA 20:13,18–34; LW 15:10–11.
60. WA 20:100,37–101,2; LW 15:86.

## Chapter 4

# Did the Death of Christ Appease the Wrath of God?

## Luther and Calvin on the Purpose of the Death of Christ

Randall C. Zachman

Both Luther and Calvin understand the death of Christ in light of the fortunate or wonderful exchange Christ has made with sinners. According to Luther, "By this fortunate exchange with us He took upon Himself our sinful person and granted us His innocent and victorious Person."[1] Calvin describes Christ in a similar way: "This is the wonderful exchange which, out of his measureless benevolence, he has made with us, . . . that, taking the weight of our iniquity upon himself (which oppressed us), he has clothed us with his righteousness."[2] This similarity is not at all surprising, given

---

1. Martin Luther, *Lectures on Galatians 1535*, edited by Jaroslav Pelikan and Walter Hansen (St. Louis: Concordia, 1963), 284; henceforth Galatians 1535, LW 26:284.

2. Inst. IV.xvii.2, *Calvin: Institutes of the Christian Religion*, edited by John T. McNeill and translated by Ford Lewis Battles (Philadelphia: Westminster, 1960), Volume 2, 1362; henceforth LCC 2:1362.

the influence that Luther's treatise on Christian freedom had on Calvin's conversion to the evangelical movement. For in *The Freedom of a Christian* Luther describes the death of Christ in light of the metaphor of the "royal marriage" that he received from Johann von Staupitz.[3] "By the wedding ring of faith he shares in the sins, death, and pains of hell which are the bride's. As a matter of fact, he makes them his own and as if he had sinned; he suffered, died, and descended into hell that he might overcome them all."[4] Calvin echoes this picture of Christ's death in one of his first writings as an evangelical teacher. "For, he was sold, to buy us back; captive, to deliver us; condemned, to absolve us; he was made a curse for our blessing, sin offering for our righteousness."[5]

However, for all of their similarities, there are significant differences in the ways Luther and Calvin understand the meaning and purpose of the death of Christ, especially regarding the relation of the love of God to the wrath of God in that death. Both of them claim that God sent Christ to die for us out of sheer free love and mercy, to reconcile the sinful world to God. According to Luther, "God appears as nothing but the merciful One who did not spare His own Son but gave Him up for us all (Rom 8:32)."[6] Similarly, according to Calvin, "God, therefore, *confirms*, i.e., declares His love toward us to be certain and true, because He did not spare Christ His Son for the sake of the ungodly."[7] However, Luther claims that the free love of God frees us from the oppression brought about by our sin, by taking our sin from us and laying it upon Christ, so that Christ might destroy sin, death, and the wrath of God in his death. "But the true theology teaches that there is no more sin in the world, because Christ, on whom, according to Is. 53:6, the Father has laid the sins of the world, has conquered, destroyed, and killed it in His own body."[8] Calvin, on the other hand, interprets Paul's statement that while we were yet enemies Christ died for us (Rom 5:10) to mean that God is as much the enemy of sinners as sinners are the enemies of God. Hence Calvin claims that God sent Christ out of love for sinful humanity in order to appease the wrath of God by his death, so that God

---

3. Heiko Oberman, *Forerunners of the Reformation* (Philadelphia: Fortress, 1981), 186–91.

4. *The Freedom of a Christian*, LW 31:352.

5. Preface to Olivetan's New Testament, *Calvin: Commentaries*, translated by Joseph Haroutunian (Philadelphia: Westminster, 1958), 69.

6. *Galatians 1535*, LW 26:42.

7. Commentary on Romans 5:8, *Calvin's New Testament Commentaries*, edited by David W. Torrance and Thomas F. Torrance (Grand Rapids: Eerdmans, 1959–72), Volume 8, 109; henceforth *CNTC* 8:109.

8. *Galatians 1535*, LW 26:286.

could truly love sinners whom God would otherwise be compelled to hate. "God, to whom we were hateful because of sin, was appeased by the death of his Son to become favorable towards us."[9] For Calvin, the death of Christ not only reconciles sinners to God, but it also reconciles God to sinners, by appeasing God's righteous wrath and vengeance against sin.

We can see this difference between Luther and Calvin in the verses from Isaiah 53 that they favor in their interpretation of the meaning of Christ's death. Luther favors the statement in Isaiah 53:6, that the Lord has laid on his servant the iniquities of us all; whereas Calvin prefers the statement in Isaiah 53:5, that God's chastisement of the servant is our peace, for by his stripes we are healed. These different perspectives inform the way they interpret John the Baptist's message that Jesus is the Lamb of God who takes away the sins of the world (John 1:29). Luther interprets this message in light of Isaiah 53:6, and so he claims, "In other respects He was a man like all other human beings, but God made Him a Lamb which should bear the sins of all the world."[10] Calvin, on the other hand, interprets John's preaching in light of Isaiah 53:5, meaning that God's chastisement of Christ in his sacrificial death appeases the wrath of God. "Christ certainly bestows other blessings upon us, but the chief one, on which all the others depend, is that by appeasing the wrath of God He brings it to pass that we are reckoned righteous and pure."[11]

In what follows, we will trace Luther and Calvin's understanding of the relation of the love of God to the wrath of God in their portrayals of the purpose and meaning of the death of Christ. We shall attend in particular to the way Luther inseparably links the love of Christ for sinners with the love of the Father for sinners, thereby raising the question of the source of the wrath of God for him. Luther's attempt to divorce the wrath of God from the love of God the Father will lead him to hypostasize and personify the Law of God, making it the agent of the suffering and death of Christ in much the same way as earlier theologians like Augustine and Irenaeus made the devil the agent of Christ's suffering and death. "For the Law exercised its full function over Christ; it frightened Him so horribly that He experienced greater anguish than any other man has ever experienced."[12] Calvin, on the other hand, clearly associates wrath with God the Father, so that Christ really suffers under the wrath of his Father, but this leads to the apparently contradictory claim that the Father sent Christ out of love for sinners so

---

9. Inst. II.xvii.3, LCC 1:531.
10. *Sermons on the Gospel of John*, LW 22:162.
11. *Commentary on John 1:29*, CNTC 4:32.
12. *Galatians 1535*, LW 26:372.

that Christ could appease the wrath of God against sinners. "For, in some ineffable way, God loved us and yet was angry toward us at the same time, until he became reconciled to us in Christ."[13]

## 1. "THE LORD HAS LAID ON HIM THE INIQUITY OF US ALL" (IS. 53:6): MARTIN LUTHER ON THE PURPOSE OF THE DEATH OF CHRIST

As we have already noted, Luther roots the purpose of the death of Christ in the free, gratuitous, and utterly unmerited love of God for sinful humanity. "God, the heavenly Father, had compassion on us and in His mercy and pity gave us His Son. Add to this the fact that we did not deserve it but that it was done, not in view of any piety or merit in us but out of sheer grace."[14] Indeed, Luther makes it clear that sinners deserved the opposite of love, which makes the mercy and love of God in Christ all the more astonishing, for Christ is "graciously bestowed upon us unworthy men out of God's sheer mercy, although we have rather deserved wrath and condemnation, and hell also."[15] Luther is at pains to show the depth of God's love by insisting that by giving God's Son for sinners, God has given us nothing less than Godself. "But no, He gives us Himself. He gives us His Son, who is very God."[16] He is also at pains to show that this love is truly shown to those who know in their consciences that they have deserved the opposite of love. "I have often experienced, and still do every day, how difficult it is to believe, especially amid struggles of conscience, that Christ was given, not for the holy, righteous, and deserving, or for those who were his friends, but for the godless, sinful, and undeserving, for those who were his enemies, who deserved the wrath of God and eternal death."[17]

The love of God in Christ is made known especially in the way it freely bears burdens not its own, and freely gives blessings to those who do not deserve them. Luther clearly situates his understanding of the meaning of the sending of Christ to die for us in the context of the revelation of sin, death, and the wrath of God by the Law of God. Once the Law reveals sin, the conscience finds itself profoundly oppressed by the burden of sin, and the consequences of sin in death and wrath. Luther does not want to identify the God of Jesus Christ with our oppressive captivity under the Law, but

13. Inst. II.xvii.2, LCC 1:530.
14. *Sermons on John*, LW 22:373.
15. *Sermon on Two kinds of Righteousness*, LW 31:298.
16. *Sermons on John*, LW 22:374.
17. *Galatians 1535*, LW 26:36.

rather treats this oppression as being brought about by a hostile power, in much the same way that Pharaoh oppressed the Israelites. God's love leads God to free us from the oppressive burden of sin, death, and wrath in much the same way that love led God to free the Israelites from oppression in Egypt. God does this by sending his own Son, who is truly God of God and light of light, to become a sinless human who can thereby bear the burden of our sin, and by bearing it, bear it away. "God wishes to say this to us: 'I see how the sin oppresses you. You would have to collapse under its heavy burden. But I shall relieve and rid you of the load—when the Law convicts you of, and condemns you for, your sin—and from sheer mercy I shall place the weight of your sin on this Lamb, who will bear them.'"[18] Luther thereby distinguishes the love of God that removes sin from the Law of God that reveals sin, thereby distinguishing the Law from God. "It is extremely important that we know where our sins have been disposed of. The Law deposits them on our conscience and shoves them into our bosom. But God takes them from us and places them on the shoulders of the Lamb."[19] As we noted earlier, Luther interprets the description of Jesus as the Lamb of God who takes away the sin of the world by means of Isaiah 53:6, which speaks of the Lord laying the iniquity of us all upon him. "Is. 53:6 speaks the same way about Christ. It says: 'God has laid on Him the iniquity of us all.' These words must not be diluted but must be left in their precise and serious sense. For God is not joking in the words of the prophet. He is speaking seriously and out of great love, namely, that this Lamb of God, Christ, should bear the iniquity of us all."[20]

Christ freely obeys the will of the Father by taking our sin on himself. "Christ did not take our sins by His own will but by the will of the Father who had mercy on us."[21] However, Christ obeys the will of the Father to be the one who bears the iniquity of us all, because he acts out of the same love for sinners that motivates his Father. "For He does in fact bear all our evils, because God the Father, as Isaiah says (53:6), 'has laid the iniquity of us all on *Him*.' And He willingly took them upon Himself. For He was not guilty, but He did this in order to do the Father's will, by which we would be sanctified eternally." This willingness of Christ to act as our slave bearing our sin reveals the true depth of the love of God, which surpasses all understanding, according to Luther, for "the human heart is too limited to comprehend,

---

18. *Sermons on John*, LW 22:166.
19. *Sermons on John*, LW 22:169.
20. *Galatians 1535*, LW 26:278–79.
21. *Lectures on Isaiah*, LW 17:226.

much less to describe, the great depths and burning passion of divine love toward us."[22]

Once Christ freely obeys God and willingly takes our sin upon himself, the full power of sin, death, and the curse of God attack him and seek to put him to death, supported by the power of the Law to condemn sinners. "Now the Law comes and says, 'I find Him a sinner, who takes on Himself the sins of all men. I do not see any other sins than those in Him. Therefore let Him die on the cross!' And so it attacks and kills Him."[23] In this way, Luther avoids saying that God the Father willed the death of Christ, as it is the Law that put him to death, once he took upon himself the sins that the Father laid on him. However, Luther also ascribes the death of Christ to the monstrous and destructive power of sin, death, and the curse and wrath of God, resulting in what he calls the "wondrous duel." Christ bears our sin in his body, and the power of sin puts his body to death. The same thing happens with the power of death—it also puts his body to death. Finally, the curse of God slays him, for he willingly placed himself among those placed under the wrath of God revealed in the Law. "For unless He had taken upon Himself my sins, your sins, and the sins of the entire world, the Law would have had no right over Him, since it condemns only sinners and only holds them under a curse."[24] However, Christ is also the eternal Son, who is divine by nature; and so he combats the destructive power of sin with the greater power of his righteousness, and puts sin to death in his death. "In this duel, therefore, it is necessary for sin to be conquered and killed, and for righteousness to prevail and live. Thus in Christ all sin is conquered, killed, and buried; and righteousness remains the victor and the ruler eternally."[25] In the same way, the divine life of Christ combats the power of death, and puts death to death, and emerges alive from the tomb. Finally, Christ combats the curse and wrath of God by means of the divine mercy and blessing that is his own. The curse fails to damn the blessing, but is rather conquered by it, for the blessing is divine.

The death of Christ therefore does not appease the wrath of God, as we will see in Calvin, but rather defeats and conquers the wrath of God as though the wrath of God were an enemy of God, in the same way that his death conquers sin and death. "If you look at this Person, therefore, you see sin, death, the wrath of God, hell, the devil, and all evils conquered and

---

22. *Galatians 1535*, LW 26:292.
23. *Galatians 1535*, LW 26:280.
24. *Galatians 1535*, LW 26:284.
25. *Galatians 1535*, LW 26:281.

put to death."[26] Christ's victory over sin, death, and the curse and wrath of God shows that he must be divine by nature, for only a divine power could defeat and annihilate the destructive powers of sin, death, wrath, and hell, and replace them with righteousness, life, blessing, and heaven. Moreover, the annihilation of sin, death, and wrath seems to be what Luther means by the satisfaction or payment made by Christ. Once the Law attacks and kills Christ, Luther says, "By this deed the whole world is purged and expiated from all sins, and thus it is set free from death and from every evil."[27] Moreover, it is the Law, and not God the Father, that terrifies Christ in Gethsemane, and causes him to cry out that God had forsaken him. And once again, Christ does not appease God's wrath by suffering such anguish, but rather combats the destructive power of the Law when it puts him to death, and then conquers the Law by putting it to death. "By performing and bearing the Law He conquered it in Himself."[28] Thus the free love of God, and the gracious love of Christ, free us from sin, death, wrath, and the Law by abolishing all of these oppressive and destructive forces in the death of Christ. "Therefore it is Christ's true and proper function to struggle with the Law, sin, and death of the entire world, and to struggle in such a way that he undergoes them, but, by undergoing them, conquers them and abolishes them in Himself, thus liberating us from the Law and from every evil."[29]

The love of the Father removes from us the sin that oppresses us and places it on his incarnate Son, and the love of the Son leads him to obey the will of God in bearing our sin away unto death and annihilation. "Therefore Christ was not only crucified and died, but by divine love sin was laid upon Him. When sin was laid upon Him, the Law came and said, 'Let every sinner die!'"[30] Since both the Father and Christ lovingly will the removal of sin from sinners, Luther insists that it is impossible to distinguish between the love of Christ for sinners, and the love of his Father for sinners. "Christ wants to prevent us from thinking of Him as separate from the Father. Therefore He again directs our mind from Himself to the Father and says that the Father's love for us is just as strong and profound as His own, which is reflected in His sacrificial death."[31] The danger according to Luther is that we would think that although Christ loves us, the Father might be wrathful to us. This is why it is crucial that we see that it is the will of God to place

26. *Galatians 1535*, LW 26:282.
27. *Galatians 1535*, LW 26:280.
28. *Galatians 1535*, LW 26:373.
29. *Galatians 1535*, LW 26:373.
30. *Galatians 1535*, LW 26:279.
31. *Sermons on John*, LW 22:355.

our sin not on us, but on his Son Jesus Christ. "Now I can confidently say: If God loved me so that He gave His only Son for my salvation, why should I fear His anger?"[32]

The problem is that the sense of God's wrath is an essential aspect of the human experience, especially in light of the apparent signs of God's wrath in sickness, war, famine, and sudden death. "The consciousness that God is angry and that He is an irate Judge of sin is innate in the human heart. His wrath is evident in the world; we see Him punishing one here, another there."[33] This is why it is essential to see the love of the Father in the love of the Son for sinners, and to see the Father as the one who takes sin from us and places it on his only Son to free us from its oppressive and destructive power. Luther therefore hears Christ saying, "The Father and I condemn no one. God is not angry; for I am the pledge and the certain Token, yes, the Gift and the Present to show you that God is not angry with us."[34] According to Luther, the devil will try to take advantage of our anxiety that the Father is in fact wrathful, over against the mercy and love of Christ, and so he exhorts us to pay no attention to such talk of God's wrath. "He will torture you with thoughts of predestination, and the wrath and the judgment of God. Then you must say: 'I don't want to hear or know anything else about God than that He loves me. I don't want to know anything about a wrathful God, about His judgment and anger, about hell, about death, and about damnation. But if I do see God's wrath, I know that this drives me to the Son, where I find refuge; and if I come to the Son, I also have a merciful Father.'"[35] This is why Luther will never say that God the Father is angry with or hates sinners, as that would divorce the love of God from the love of Christ, and would lead us to conclude that God does hate us when we see evidence of God's wrath. "I ought to feel nothing in my heart except the sense of the mercy of God, and when our heart is filled with that awareness and feeling of mercy, it is enough for it to fight against sin, hell, the wrath of God, the warnings of the Flood, Satan, and the power of sin."[36]

Luther succeeds in eliminating the question of the wrath of God in relation to Jesus Christ by abstracting the Law from God the Father, thereby seeing God only in light of the love of the Son, and not also in light of God's wrath against sin. But this raises the question of who exactly sends the Law, and reveals God's wrath and curse against sin? Calvin attempts to solve this

32. *Sermons on John*, LW 22:366.
33. *Sermons on John*, LW 22:375.
34. *Sermons on John*, LW 22:375.
35. *Sermons on John*, LW 22:368.
36. *Lectures on Titus*, LW 29:81.

problem by identifying God's wrath against sin with God the Father, and he reads Romans 5:10 as describing the situation this identification creates, wherein sinners are enemies of God, and God is the enemy of sinners. If this is the case, then not only do sinners need to be reconciled to God, but God also needs to be reconciled to sinners, and this takes place by the death of Christ, which appeases the wrath of God. But how can the death of Christ be the cause of God's love for sinners, when Calvin also agrees with Luther that the death of Christ is the effect of God's free and gracious love? Moreover, one can only speak of God the Father's wrath against sinners if one abstracts God the Father from his Son Jesus Christ, and views the will of the Father independently of the Son. Luther will not do this, because it could lead us to conclude that God is wrathful and does not love us the way Christ does. But Calvin cannot follow Luther here, for he insists that God is wrathful and hates sinners, until the wrath of God is appeased by the death of Christ. Thus Calvin will consistently run into the same apparent contradiction that he will try to resolve in different ways. How can the death of Christ simultaneously be the effect and the cause of God's love for sinners? And how can God simultaneously love and hate sinners?

## 2. "THE CHASTISEMENT OF OUR PEACE WAS UPON HIM; AND WITH HIS STRIPES WE ARE HEALED" (IS. 53:5): JOHN CALVIN ON THE PURPOSE OF THE DEATH OF CHRIST

John Calvin agrees with Martin Luther that the ultimate cause of our reconciliation with God by the death of Christ is the free and unmerited love of God. "God, therefore, *confirms*, i.e., declares His love toward us to be most certain and true, because He did not spare Christ His Son for the sake of the ungodly. Herein is His love manifested, that without being influenced by any love of ours, He first loved us of His own good pleasure, as John tells us (John 3:16)."[37] Calvin insists that "there is no calm haven where our minds can rest until we come to God's free love," which reveals God's love for those who are perishing in sin "because the heavenly Father does not wish the human race that He loves to perish."[38] The only cause of this love is found in the eternal goodness of God, and not in human beings, for Paul tells us "that this love was founded on 'the good pleasure of his will' (Eph.1:5),"

---

37. *Commentary on Romans 5:8*, CNTC 8:109.
38. *Commentary on John 3:16*, CNTC 4:73.

and not on anything in us which would be deserving of this love.[39] Indeed, God loved us in Christ both before we were even born, as well as in the depravity of our nature after we were born.[40] "Christ is such a shining and remarkable proof of the divine love toward us that, whenever we look to Him, He clearly confirms to us the doctrine that God is love."[41] The love of God that leads Christ to die for sinners therefore expresses the nature of the goodness, mercy, and love of God, for God "will never find in us anything worthy of His love, but He loves us because He is kind and merciful."[42] Like Luther, Calvin will stress the fact that the love shown in Christ is the same love that God the Father has for us. "And it is proper to both; for, on the one hand, the Father by His eternal purpose decreed this atonement and in it gave this proof of His love for us that He spared not His only-begotten Son but delivered Him up for us all. And Christ, on the other hand, offered Himself as a sacrifice to reconcile us to God."[43]

The love of God for sinners seeks to remove the obstacles to God's love, especially human sin, so that sinful humans might be reconciled to God: "that nothing might stand in the way of his love toward us, God appointed Christ as a means of reconciling us to himself."[44] Thus God resolves out of free love to remove our unrighteousness, which creates a conflict with God's righteousness. "Therefore, to take away all cause for enmity and to reconcile us utterly to himself, he wipes out all evil in us by the expiation set forth in the death of Christ; that we, who were previously unclean and impure, may show ourselves righteous and holy in his sight."[45] According to this understanding of God's love, God is not led to love us by the death of Christ, but rather God loves us, and so freely removes from us all that is within us that leads God to hate us. "It is a wonderful goodness of God and incomprehensible to the human mind, that He was benevolent towards men whom He could not but hate and removed the cause of the hatred that there might be no obstruction to His love."[46]

However, we can already see in Calvin's understanding of the love of God the dynamic that leads God to love those whom God also hates, leading God to remove the cause of God's hatred in sinners, so that God and sinners

---

39. *Commentary on John 3:16*, CNTC 4:73.
40. *Commentary on 1 John 4:10*, CNTC 5:291.
41. *Commentary on 1 John 4:9*, CNTC 4:290.
42. *Commentary on Titus 3:4*, CNTC 10:381.
43. *Commentary on Galatians 1:4*, CNTC 11:11.
44. Inst. II.xvii.2, LCC 1:530.
45. Inst. II.xvi.3, LCC 1:506.
46. *Commentary on John 17:23*, CNTC 5:149–50.

can be fully reconciled. In a paradoxical way, God seeks in mercy to set forth the means of placating the wrath of God in the death of Christ. When Paul speaks of God setting forth Christ as a propitiation, Calvin claims that "Paul is referring to the mercy of God in having appointed Christ as our Mediator to reconcile the Father to us by the sacrifice of His death."[47] Calvin interprets this act of propitiation by means of Isaiah 53:5, which he takes to mean that Christ appeases the wrath of God the Father by suffering the chastisement and punishment that is due to us. "This could be accomplished only by His suffering in our place the punishment that we were unable to endure. 'The chastisement of our peace,' says Isaiah, 'was upon Him' (Is. 53:5)." However, the suffering of Christ can only appease God's wrath because of God's love and mercy, "because expiation depends on the eternal goodwill of God, who chose this way of reconciliation."[48] God can only truly love sinners once the punishment suffered by Christ appeases God's wrath, but this punishment only appeases God's wrath because God willed it to do so in God's mercy. "Apart from God's good pleasure Christ could not merit anything; but did so because he had been appointed to appease God's wrath with his sacrifice, and to blot out our transgressions with his obedience."[49] This then sets forth the central paradox that Calvin will seek to resolve, which is created by his interpretation of Romans 5:10. The sending of the Son to die for sinners is the unsurpassable revelation of the free love of God for sinners (Rom 5:8), but God can only truly love sinners once God's anger against sinners has been appeased by the death of Christ.[50] "But since it is also needful for us to know that Christ came forth to us from the fountain of God's free mercy, Scripture explicitly teaches both; the Father's wrath has been placated by the Son's sacrifice and thus the Son was offered for the expiation of men's sins, because God has had mercy on them and has made this sacrifice the pledge of His receiving them into His favor."[51]

There are times when Calvin seeks to find the ground for God's love in human beings, over against his other insight that the love of God is grounded in the nature of God, and not in something loveable in us. "But because the Lord wills not to lose what is his in us, out of his own kindness he still finds something to love. However much we may be sinners by our own fault, we nevertheless remain his creatures. However much we have brought death upon ourselves, yet he has created us unto life. Thus he is

---

47. *Commentary on Romans 3:25, CNTC* 8:75.
48. *Commentary on Romans 4:25, CNTC* 8:102.
49. Inst. II.xvii.1, LCC 1:529.
50. Inst. II.xvi.2, LCC 1:504.
51. *Commentary on 2 Corinthians 5:19, CNTC* 10:78–79.

moved by pure and freely given love of us to receive us into grace."[52] Calvin is conflicted about this claim, however, for even as he says that God "does not recognize as his handiwork men defiled and corrupted by sin"[53] he also claims that "God does not hate in us His own workmanship, that is, the fact that He has created us as living beings, but He hates our uncleanness, which has extinguished the light of his image."[54]

The other way in which Calvin seeks to explain the way that God both loves and hates sinners is by appealing to the hidden love of God's eternal election, for God both loves us (John 3:16) and hates us (Romans 5:10) until God is reconciled to us in the death of Christ.[55] "My answer to this is that because God hates sin, we are also hated by Him in so far as we are sinners. But in so far as He receives us into the body of Christ by His secret counsel, He ceases to hate us. Our return to grace, however, is unknown to us, until we attain it by faith. With regard to ourselves, therefore, we are always enemies, until the death of Christ is interposed to propitiate God."[56] The free and gracious love that leads God to send Christ is not revealed in Christ, but is rather a "secret love" that is unknown to sinners, who rather experience the reality of God's wrath and hatred. "For since He necessarily hates sin, how shall we be convinced that He loves us until those sins for which He is justly angry with us have been expiated? Thus before we can have any feeling of His fatherly kindness, the blood of Christ must intercede to reconcile God to us."[57] Calvin is convinced that God's free love for us that leads God to send Christ to die for us cannot itself break the impasse created by God's hatred of sin. "God interposed His Son to reconcile Himself to us (*ad se nobis reconciliandum*) because He loved us. For we were yet enemies to God, continually provoking His wrath."[58] God can only truly love the sinners God would otherwise also hate when Christ actually dies to appease God's wrath and win God's favor for sinners. "See how we are both enemies and friends until atonement has been made for our sins and we are restored to favor with God!"[59]

Calvin accentuates the ability of the death of Christ to appease God's wrath by describing it as the reality which was set forth in the types of Israel's

---

52. Inst. II.xvi.3, LCC 1:506.
53. Inst. II.vi.1, LCC 1:341.
54. *Commentary on Romans 3:25*, CNTC 8:76.
55. Inst. II.xvi.4, LCC 1:506.
56. *Commentary on Romans 5:10*, CNTC 8:110.
57. *Commentary on John 3:16*, CNTC 4:74.
58. *Commentary on 1 John 4:10*, CNTC 5:292.
59. *Commentary on John 17:23*, CNTC 5:150.

sacrifices of expiation. "It was not in vain that God of old willed, through expiations and sacrifices, to attest that he was Father, and to set apart for himself a chosen people. Hence, he was then surely known in the same image in which he with full splendor now appears to us."[60] Israel was taught that they could only appease God's wrath by offering to God a sacrifice of expiation that would atone for their sin. "By this symbol God wanted to show that he who procures grace for us must be furnished with a sacrifice. For when God is offended, the price of satisfaction is required to pacify Him."[61] Calvin will therefore use Israel's sacrifices of expiation as the way of demonstrating how and why the death of Christ appeases the Father's hatred of sinners. "He offered as a sacrifice the flesh he received from us, that he might wipe out our guilt by his act of expiation and appease the Father's righteous wrath."[62] The sacrificial death of Christ is therefore the way God breaks the impasse between God's love and hatred of sinners. "We have been reconciled to God by the death of Christ, Paul holds, because He was an expiatory sacrifice by which the world was reconciled to God."[63] This is why Christ must be without sin, for only such a pure victim is capable of appeasing God.[64] The sacrifice must also include the shedding of blood, for without blood it is not possible to appease the wrath of the Father. "The one way of pacifying is by the atonement of blood, and hence no pardon of sin can be hoped for unless we bring blood."[65] Thus the "principle point on which, he knew, our whole salvation turns" is the sacrifice Christ offers in his death, as only in this way can God love the sinners whom God otherwise also hates. "But God's righteous curse bars our access to him, and God in his capacity as judge is angry toward us. Hence, an expiation must intervene in order that Christ as priest may obtain God's favor for us and appease his wrath. Thus Christ to perform this office had to come forward with a sacrifice."[66]

As we have seen, Calvin interprets the meaning of the death of Christ in terms of his understanding of Isaiah 53:5, which he takes to mean that God is placated by the punishment that Christ suffers at the hands of God. "Christ was the price of 'our chastisement,' that is, of the chastisement which was due to us. Thus the wrath of God, which had been justly kindled against us, was appeased; and through the Mediator we have obtained 'peace,' by

60. Inst. II.ix.1, LCC 1:423.
61. *Commentary on 1 John 2:1*, CNTC 5:243.
62. Inst. II.xii.3, LCC 1:466-67.
63. *Commentary on Romans 5:10*, CNTC 8:110.
64. *Commentary on Hebrews 9:14*, CNTC 12:121.
65. *Commentary on Hebrews 9:22*.
66. Inst. II.xv.6, LCC 1:501.

which we are reconciled. We draw from this a universal doctrine, namely, that we are reconciled to God by free grace, because Christ has paid the price of our 'peace.'"[67] Whereas Luther sees Christ as the one on whom God has laid the sins of the world, Calvin sees Christ as the one who is severely punished by God for our guilt, thereby appeasing the very wrath that afflicts him so terribly. Over against those like Osiander who claim that God would have become human even without sin, Calvin insists that the sole reason the Son became human was to appease the wrath of God by taking on himself the chastisement of our peace. "In short, the only reason given in Scripture that the Son of God willed to take on our flesh, and accepted this commandment from the Father, is that he would be a sacrifice to appease the Father on our behalf."[68] Thus when 1 Peter speaks of Christ bearing our sins, Calvin takes this to mean that he took on our punishment, and he cites the way Isaiah says that Christ was smitten, wounded, afflicted and broken for our sake, so that the chastisement of our peace was laid upon him. "Peter's intention has been to set forth the same truth by the words of this verse, namely that we are reconciled to God on this condition, that Christ made Himself the surety and the guilty one for us before His judgment-seat in order to suffer the punishment due to us."[69]

Thus, whereas Luther thinks that Christ's experience of the abandonment by God was due to the Law exceeding its just bounds, Calvin insists that Christ experienced the full wrath and vengeance of God against the guilt of our sin, for only in this way could God's wrath be appeased. "If Christ had died only a bodily death, it would have been ineffectual. No—it was expedient at the same time for him to undergo the severity of God's vengeance, to appease his wrath and to satisfy his just judgment."[70] Thus when Christ cries out on the cross that God has forsaken him, Calvin interprets this cry by means of Isaiah 53:5, and sees it as the chastisement that appeases God's wrath. "This is what we are saying: he bore the weight of divine severity, since he was 'stricken and afflicted' [cf. Is. 53:5] by God's hand, and experienced all the signs of a wrathful and avenging God."[71] However, the Son must also be the beloved of God, for otherwise his death would not appease God's wrath. Therefore, just as human sinners are both loved and hated by God, so also, to free sinners from the impasse of God's love

---

67. John Calvin, *Commentary on Isaiah 53:5*, henceforth *CTS* (Edinburgh: Calvin Translation Society, 1844-56), 16:116.

68. Inst. II.xii.4, LCC 1:468.

69. *Commentary on 1 Peter 2:24*, CNTC 12:278.

70. Inst. II.xvi.10, LCC 1:515.

71. Inst. II.xvi.11, LCC 1:517.

and hatred, Christ himself must not only experience God's vengeance, but must also be loved by God.[72] "He could not be outside God's grace, yet He endured His wrath. For how could He reconcile Him to us if He regarded His Father as an enemy and was hated by Him? Therefore the will of the Father always reposed in Him. Again, how could he have freed us from the wrath of God if He had not transferred it from us to Himself? Therefore He was smitten for our sins and knew God as an angry judge."[73]

Calvin insists that the punishment Christ experienced under the curse and wrath of God is sufficient to make full satisfaction for our sin and guilt, by paying to God's justice what we owed but could never pay ourselves. "Accordingly, our Lord came forth as true man and took the person and the name of Adam in order to take Adam's place in obeying the Father, to present our flesh as the price of satisfaction to God's righteous judgment, and, in the same flesh, to pay the penalty that we deserved."[74] Calvin makes it clear that this satisfaction and payment is directly related to the death of Christ under the curse of God. "The Father destroyed the force of sin when the curse of sin was transferred to Christ's flesh. Here, then, is the meaning of this saying: Christ was offered to the Father in death as an expiatory sacrifice that when he discharged all satisfaction through his sacrifice, we might cease to be afraid of God's wrath."[75] The appeasement of God's wrath is therefore the primary meaning of Christ's death for Calvin. "This is our acquittal: the guilt that held us liable for punishment has been transferred to the head of the Son of God [Isa. 53:12]. We must, above all, remember this substitution, lest we tremble and remain anxious throughout life—as if God's righteous vengeance, which the Son of God has taken upon himself, still hung over us."[76]

This issue is so important to Calvin that he added an entire section to the 1559 edition of the *Institutes* which attempts to demonstrate that, by the mercy of God, the death of Christ truly satisfies God's righteous judgment and pays the penalty we owed, so that God's wrath might be appeased by his death, and God's love and mercy might be won for us. "Isaiah's testimony is also clear: 'The chastisement of our peace was laid upon Christ, and with his stripes healing has come to us' [Isa. 53:5 p.]. For unless Christ had made satisfaction for our sins, it would not have been said that he appeased God

---

72. Inst. II.xvi.11, LCC 1:517.
73. *Commentary on Galatians* 3:13, CNTC 11:55.
74. Inst. II.xii.3, LCC 1:466.
75. Inst. II.xvi.6, LCC 1:510.
76. Inst. II.xvi.5, LCC 1:509–10.

by taking upon himself the penalty to which we were subject."[77] The willingness of Christ to take on himself the punishment we deserved truly merits the grace and favor of God for us, by paying to God what we owed. "I take it to be a commonplace that if Christ made satisfaction for our sins, if he paid the penalty owed by us, if he appeased God by his obedience—in short, if as a righteous man he suffered for unrighteous men—then he acquired salvation for us by his righteousness, which is tantamount to deserving it."[78] By paying to God what we owed but could never pay, Christ makes it possible for God to love those sinners whom God would otherwise justly hate, which Calvin takes to be the meaning of Paul in Romans 5:10. "The meaning therefore is: God, to whom we were hateful because of sin, was appeased by the death of his Son to become favorable toward us."[79]

By reading Romans 5:10 the way he does—that God was the enemy of sinners until God was reconciled to them by the death of Christ—Calvin creates a contradiction not found in Luther, which he tries in various ways to resolve. For Calvin knows, as we have seen, that the death of Christ is the greatest pledge and proof of the love of God for sinners, especially in light of the claim of John 3:16, but also in light of Romans 5:8. How can the death of Christ be the cause of God's love, by appeasing the wrath of God against sinners, if the death of Christ is the effect of God's love, and is in fact the greatest demonstration of that love? We have seen above that Calvin attempts to resolve this contradiction by means of the hidden love of God in eternal election, and the revealed love of God in Christ, but this still creates a contradiction, because what is revealed in Christ is the appeasement of God's wrath, making it possible for God to love those whom God would otherwise necessarily hate. Another way Calvin tries to reconcile this contradiction is by seeing the statements of Scripture regarding the meaning of the cross from two different perspectives. How can Scripture say that God is our enemy until God is reconciled to us by the death of Christ (Romans 5:10), when Scripture also says that God so loved the world that he gave his only Son (John 3:16)? "These two statements seem to contradict each other, but it is easy to reconcile them, for in the second we are viewing the thing from God's side, and in the first from our own. For God, as far as He Himself is concerned, loved us from before the foundation of the world and redeemed us solely because He loved us, but we, when we look at ourselves, see nothing but sin which provokes God's wrath, and we cannot grasp God's

---

77. Inst. II.xvii.4, LCC 1:532.
78. Inst. II.xvii.3, LCC 1:530–31.
79. Inst. II.xvii.3, LCC 1:531.

love without a Mediator. Thus, as far as we are concerned, Christ's grace is the beginning of God's love."[80]

But this still raises the question: does God truly hate sinners until God is appeased by Christ? If so, then how can God be said to love sinners before the creation of the world? And if God really does love sinners before Christ dies, then why does God punish Christ so severely to reconcile himself to sinners (Is. 53:5)? Calvin keeps trying to say that the solution to this dilemma is to be found in the perspective Scripture is representing, the divine or the human, but even as he advances this position, he keeps hitting upon the objective reality of God's hatred of sinners apart from Christ. "I reply that when Christ is said to have reconciled the Father to us, it is to be referred to our feeling; for as we are conscious of sin, we can only conceive of God as angry and hostile until Christ absolves us from guilt. For whenever sin appears, God wants His wrath and the judgment of eternal death to be felt."[81] If God wants sinners to be aware of God's hatred of them, then it seems that God really does hate sinners until God is appeased and reconciled by Christ's death, "for sin, which reigns in us, renders us hateful to God and Him in turn to us."[82] Calvin acknowledges as much even when he thinks he has reconciled this contradiction by means of the divine and human perspectives. "We now see that the variety of expressions occurring in Scripture and corresponding to the different aspects, is most appropriate and useful for faith. God interposed His Son to reconcile Himself to us ... because He loved us. For we were yet enemies to God, continually provoking His wrath. . . . Therefore, as to the feeling of our faith, God began to love us in Christ."[83] It does not seem that the two perspectives resolve the contradiction after all, for according to Calvin we really were enemies of God continually provoking God's wrath before Christ appeased God's wrath by taking God's vengeance upon himself. And Christ certainly experienced in his soul the full force of God's vengeance against sin, for it led him to cry out in anguish that God had forsaken him. "This is what we are saying: he bore the weight of divine severity, since he was 'stricken and afflicted' [cf. Isa. 53:5] by God's hand, and experienced all the signs of a wrathful and avenging God."[84]

Another way Calvin tries to resolve the contradiction his interpretation of Romans 5:10 creates for him is to see it in light of two different ways

---

80. *Commentary on 2 Corinthians 13:14*, CNTC 10:177.
81. *Commentary on 1 John 4:10*, CNTC 5:291.
82. *Commentary on 1 Peter 1:21*, CNTC 12:250.
83. *Commentary on 1 John 4:10*, CNTC 5:292.
84. Inst. II.xvi.11, LCC 1:517.

human beings can view God. According to Calvin, we can either view God apart from Christ, or we can view God in Christ. If we view God apart from Christ, we cannot help but be aware that God hates us because of our sin. The statements of Scripture about God being reconciled to us by the death of Christ have to do with our knowledge of God apart from Christ. "My answer is that we were loved from before the foundation of the world, but not apart from Christ. But I do agree that the love of God was first in time and in order also as regards God; but, as regards us, His love has its foundation in the sacrifice of Christ. *For when we think of God apart from a mediator, we can only conceive of him as being angry with us, but when a mediator is interposed between us*, we know that He is pacified towards us."[85] Calvin uses these two different ways of viewing God—apart from Christ and in Christ—throughout his theology, beginning with his distinction between the knowledge of God the Creator and the knowledge of God the Redeemer. "In this ruin of mankind no one now experiences God either as Father or as Author of salvation, or as favorable in any way, until Christ the Mediator comes forward to reconcile him to us."[86] He makes the same point in his transition to the knowledge of God the Redeemer in Book II: "Therefore, since we have fallen from life into death, the whole knowledge of God the Creator that we have discussed would be useless unless faith also followed, setting forth for us God our Father in Christ."[87] All of this indicates that Christ really does change the relationship God has with us, from hating us as sinners apart from Christ, to loving us after being appeased by the death of Christ, even though God also sent Christ to die for sinners because God loved us before the foundation of the world. "But since it is also needful for us to know that Christ came forth to us from the fountain of God's free mercy, Scripture explicitly teaches both; the Father's wrath has been placated by the Son's sacrifice and thus the Son was offered for the expiation of men's sins, because God has had mercy on them and has made this sacrifice the pledge of His receiving them into His favor. To sum up: wherever there is sin there is also God's wrath for God is not propitious towards us until He has blotted out our sins by not imputing them."[88]

Calvin's most well-known attempt to solve this contradiction comes in three paragraphs he added to the final edition of the *Institutes*, to address a question addressed to him by Socinus. "But, before we go further, we must see in passing how fitting it was that God, who anticipates us by his

---

85. *Commentary on 2 Corinthians* 5:19, CNTC 10:78; my emphasis.
86. Inst. I.ii.1, LCC 1:40.
87. Inst. II.vi.1, LCC 1:341.
88. *Commentary on 2 Corinthians* 5:19, CNTC 10:78–79.

mercy, should have been our enemy until he was reconciled to us through Christ."[89] Calvin's response is to say that the statements in Scripture about Christ appeasing God's wrath by his suffering the punishment we deserved are rhetorical statements accommodated to our capacity, so that we might understand how miserable our condition would be without Christ. According to this rather astonishing explanation, when Scripture tells us that when we were lost sinners under wrath "Christ interceded as [our] advocate, took upon himself and suffered the punishment that, from God's righteous judgment, threatened all sinners," and that Christ as intercessor "has appeased God's wrath," this is simply a rhetorical strategy employed by God to make us "even more moved" by our redemption in Christ given the greatness of our calamity.[90] Even this interpretation depends on two views of God, one outside of Christ, and one in light of Christ: "we are taught by Scripture to perceive that apart from Christ, God is, so to speak, hostile to us, and his hand is armed for our destruction; to embrace his benevolence and fatherly love in Christ alone."[91]

However, Calvin knows that his understanding of the death of Christ is severely undermined if the claim that God is reconciled to us in Christ is only an accommodated statement that is deeply modified by a "so to speak" qualification. Hence he immediately says, "Although this statement is tempered to our feeble comprehension, it is not said falsely. For God, who is the highest righteousness, cannot love the unrighteousness that he sees in us all. All of us, therefore, have in ourselves something deserving of God's hatred."[92] Thus, even though God "is moved by pure and freely given love to receive us into his grace," the righteousness of God makes it necessary for God to hate the sinners God also freely loves, until God sets forth the death of Christ as the expiation of our sins. "But until Christ succors us by his death, the unrighteousness that deserves God's indignation remains in us, and is accursed and condemned before him. Hence, we can be fully joined with God only when Christ joins us with him."[93] He concludes this discussion with a long quotation from Augustine, which maintains that God "loved us even when he hated us."[94]

Thus, in spite of all of Calvin's different attempts to reconcile the contradiction he creates between John 3:16 and his reading of Romans 5:10, he

---

89. Inst. II.xvi.2, LCC 1:504.
90. Inst. II.xvi.2, LCC 1:505.
91. Inst. II.xvi.2, LCC 1:505.
92. Inst. II.xvi.3, LCC 1:505.
93. Inst. II.xvi.3, LCC 1:506.
94. Inst. II.xvi.4, LCC 1:507.

ends up consistently maintaining that God hates sinners even as God loves sinners, either because they are God's creatures or because they are elected in Christ from before creation. Hence, according to Calvin, God can only fully embrace sinners with God's love once Christ appeases the wrath of God by his death. "For, in some ineffable way, God loved us and yet was angry toward us at the same time, until he became reconciled to us in Christ."[95]

---

95. Inst. II.xvii.2, LCC 1:530.

## Chapter 5

# Freedom as Salvation
## Reformation Insights and Their Significance and Implications for Global Christianity

SUNG WOOK CHUNG

### INTRODUCTION

The sixteenth-century European Reformation has made indelible impacts upon Europe's politics, economy, society, and culture for the past 500 years. More than anything else, the sixteenth-century European Reformation signified liberation and emancipation of numerous Europeans from the oppression of the theology and practices of the medieval church.[1] The Reformers including Martin Luther (1483–1546), Huldrych Zwingli (1484–1531), and John Calvin (1509–1564) rediscovered the authentic and apostolic gospel whose central characteristic was the good news of not only freedom from the law, sin, death, hell, and the devil, but also freedom for obedience, service, and good works. Through the recovery and restoration of the gospel

---

1. See Roland H. Bainton, *Here I Stand: A Life of Martin Luther* (London: Forgotten, 2012). Bainton argues that the Reformation was a religious revolution more than anything else. See also Timothy F. Lull & Derek R. Nelson, *Resilient Reformer: The Life and Thought of Martin Luther* (Minneapolis: Fortress, 2015).

of freedom, they endeavored to reform the church. They not only construed freedom as the integral dimension of salvation and redemption, but also attempted to ground Christian and civil ethics in the good news of freedom.

On the basis of these initial insights, this paper will explore Luther's and Calvin's ideas of freedom in relation to Christian theology of salvation and public ethics, aiming to apply their insights to global Christianity in general and Asian Christianity in particular.

## 1. LUTHER ON FREEDOM AS SALVATION IN THE FREEDOM OF A CHRISTIAN

### 1.1. Justification by Faith and Spiritual Freedom: Kingship of the Christians

Martin Luther should be viewed as a paramount theologian of freedom. Luther's theological breakthrough was catalyzed by his rediscovery of the good news of freedom. For example, Luther's epoch-making and groundbreaking treatise, *The Freedom of a Christian* (1520)[2] became a Magna Carta for the Christian idea of freedom as salvation. In this treatise, Luther articulated his doctrine of salvation as well as his moral thought based on the notion of freedom, paving the way for the future direction and shape of the Protestant discussion of freedom.

In the treatise, Luther affirms the two points: (1) "A Christian is a perfectly free lord of all, subject to none," and (2) "A Christian is a perfectly dutiful servant of all, subject to all."[3] Luther argues that a sinner is "justified by faith alone and not any works."[4] Justified by faith alone, a sinner is regarded as righteous as Jesus Christ with whom he or she is united.[5] Through this union a Christian becomes a king and priest. As a king and priest the forgiven sinner becomes a perfectly free lord of all, subject to none.[6] Thus,

---

2. Martin Luther, "The Freedom of a Christian," in Timothy F. Lull, ed., *Martin Luther's Basic Theological Writings* (Minneapolis: Fortress, 1989), 585–629.

3. Luther, "Freedom of a Christian," 596.

4. Luther, "Freedom of a Christian," 598.

5. Paul Althaus, *The Theology of Martin Luther*, trans. Robert C. Schultz (Minneapolis: Fortress, 1966), 224–45.

6. Karl Barth has also emphasized the "royal freedom" that Christians can enjoy by faith in Jesus Christ. Barth states, "The liberation of man from his misery has taken place and is a fact only in the royal freedom in which the man Jesus has accomplished it by giving up Himself, His life as very God and very man to death for us in obedience to God and as our Lord and Head and Representative" (Barth, *Church Dogmatics*, trans. G. W. Bromiley (Edinburgh: T. & T. Clark, 1956–75), IV/2, 493).

justification by faith in Christ alone brings a sinner the royal state of free lord of all. As Luther states, "First, with respect to the kingship, every Christian is by faith so exalted above all things that, by virtue of a spiritual power, he is lord of all things without exception, so that nothing can do him any harm."[7] The truth of the gospel sets sinners free perfectly from their bondage to the law,[8] sin, death, hell,[9] and the devil. This is the first dimension of the character of freedom that the faith in the gospel brings to us, that is, spiritual freedom from all negative things. As Luther states, "As you see, it is a spiritual and true freedom and makes our hearts free from all sins, laws and commands, as Paul says, 1 Tim. 1:9... It is more excellent than all other liberty, which is external, as heaven is more excellent than earth."[10]

## 1.2. Freedom for Obedience and Good Works: Servanthood of the Christians

It is important, however, to appreciate that the idea of Christian freedom has the second dimension, which is related to the servanthood of a Christian. Christians are commanded by Christ to serve one another.

> You, my brothers and sisters, were called to be free. But do not use your freedom to indulge the flesh; rather, serve one another humbly in love. (Gal 5:13)

Therefore, Luther affirms, a Christian is subject to all. In other words, a Christian is called to be a slave to all. Paradoxically, a Christian is a lord of all and a slave of all at the same time.

Only a Christian justified by faith and in Christ alone is free in an authentic and genuine sense. Thus, for Luther, freedom means salvation and vice versa. However, a Christian freed from condemnation and cursedness voluntarily subjects himself or herself to others. As Paul Althaus has argued, "Justification is the presupposition of all Christian activity and the source of all Christian activity."[11] For a Christian, freedom from all negative things means freedom for all good things. In other words, a person freed from sin,

---

7. Martin Luther, op.cit., 606.

8. Martin Luther, op.cit., 601. See Wolfhart Pannenberg, *Systematic Theology*, trans. Geoffrey W. Bromiley, Vol. 3 (Grand Rapids: Eerdmans, 1997), 88–96.

9. Martin Luther, op.cit., 604.

10. Martin Luther, op.cit., 623.

11. Paul Althaus, *The Ethics of Martin Luther*, trans. Robert C. Schultz (Minneapolis: Fortress, 1972), 3–15. See also Bernhard Lohse, *Martin Luther's Theology: Its Historical and Systematic Development*, trans. Roy A. Harrisville (Minneapolis: Fortress, 2011), 258–66.

death, and the devil, and having all good things in Christ is enabled and empowered by the Holy Spirit to live as a free man and woman in service for others.[12] "This is a truly Christian life. Here faith is truly active through love (Galatians 5:6), that is, it finds expression in works of the freest service, cheerfully and lovingly done, with which a man willingly serves another without hope of reward; and for himself he is satisfied with the fullness and wealth of his faith."[13]

Therefore, God-given and grace-given freedom is obligated freedom or freed obligation. Freedom is not a guarantee for libertinism, licentiousness, or antinomianism. This means that freedom as salvation gives birth to freedom as ethics and moral obligation, as Luther repeatedly affirms that faith is pregnant with good works and gives birth to good works.[14] For Luther, therefore, freedom encompasses both salvation and ethics as well as faith and good works. Christian ethics is always other-oriented and other-centered.[15] A Christian is freed to live voluntarily and spontaneously for others. As Luther states, "Nevertheless the works themselves do not justify him before God, but he does the works out of spontaneous love in obedience to God and considers nothing except the approval of God, whom he would most scrupulously obey in all things."[16] This voluntariness and spontaneity for others gives a Christian true happiness and joy in Christ. Or, reversely, the true happiness that a freed man and woman in Christ enjoys gives a Christian the true voluntariness for others. As Luther points out, "The inner man, who by faith is created in the image of God, is both joyful and happy because of Christ in whom so many benefits are conferred upon him; and therefore it is his one occupation to serve God joyfully and without thought of gain, in love that is not constrained."[17]

For Luther, the ultimate ideal for Christian ethics is every Christian's becoming a Christ to their neighbors.[18] "Hence, as our heavenly Father has in Christ freely come to our aid, we also ought to help our neighbor through our body and its works, and each one should become as it were a Christ

12. For an excellent discussion of the relationship between passivity and the character of freedom, see Ingolf U. Dalferth, *Creatures of Possibility: The Theological Basis of Freedom* (Grand Rapids: Baker Academic, 2016).

13. Martin Luther, op.cit., 617.

14. For a significant discussion of freedom in relation to ethics, see Donald G. Bloesch, *Freedom for Obedience: Evangelical Ethics for Contemporary Times* (Eugene, OR: Wipf & Stock, 2002).

15. See Wolfhart Pannenberg, op. cit., 182–95.

16. Martin Luther, op.cit., 611.

17. Martin Luther, op.cit., 611.

18. C. S. Lewis resonates with Luther's point and argued in his *Mere Christianity* that every Christian is to become a little Christ (San Francisco: HarperOne, 2015).

to the other that we may be Christs to one another and Christ may be the same in all, that is, that we may be truly Christians."[19] Luther continues to articulate the glories and riches of the lives of Christians based on true and authentic freedom in Christ. "Who then can comprehend the riches and the glory of the Christian life? It can do all things and has all things and lacks nothing. It is lord over sin, death, and hell, and yet at the same time it serves, ministers to, and benefits all men."[20]

## 1.3. From Personal to Public Ethics of Freedom

Luther expands his discussion of personal ethics into the public area. For example, on the incident of Christ commanding Peter to pay the tax with a shekel in the mouth of a fish (Matthew 17:24–27), Luther concludes:

> This incident fits our subject beautifully for Christ here calls himself and those who are his children sons of the king, who need nothing; and yet he freely submits and pays the tribute. Just as necessary and helpful as this work was to Christ's righteousness or salvation, just so much do all other works of his or his followers avail for righteousness, since they all follow after righteousness and are free and are done only to serve others and to give them an example of good works.[21]

Luther argues here that the Christians' fulfilling their public responsibility to pay the taxes to the government[22] is inherently connected to their call to serve others freely and with love. And this also sets an example of good works for others.

Another example is connected with Luther's explication of Romans 13:1-7 which exhorts Christians to be subject to the governing authorities. He states:

> But that in the liberty of the Spirit they shall by so doing serve others and the authorities themselves and obey their will freely

19. Martin Luther, op.cit., 619–20.
20. Martin Luther, op.cit., 620.
21. Martin Luther, op.cit., 621.

22. Assuming that the government does indeed exist to serve its people. What about situations in which the government oppresses some people in the name of service to others? Voluntary service to the government not only means voluntarily serving the people, but also voluntarily contributing to their oppression. Here, public responsibility becomes synonymous with the agenda of the state, not service to the people. The government is inherently oppressive in that it denies the Christian his or her freedom to serve voluntarily and to the fullest extent of his or her heart. No true Christian would voluntarily oppress another.

and out of love. The works of all colleges, monasteries, and priests should be of this nature. Each one should do the works of his profession and station, not that by them he may strive after righteousness, but that through them he may keep his body under control, and finally that by such works he may submit his will to that of other in the freedom of love.[23]

It is crystal clear from the above statement that Luther believed that the idea of Christian liberty has implications and significance for the Christian public ethics in relation to the government and the pursuit of common good[24] and benefit in love. For Luther, freedom and love are intrinsically connected and mutually reinforces each other.[25]

Moreover, for Luther, showing due respect for all people and setting an example for others are the rationale for the Christian public ethics of freedom. Luther continues to point out:

For a Christian, as a free man, will say, "I will fast, pray, do this and that as men command, not because it is necessary to my righteousness or salvation but that I may show due respect to the pope, the bishop, the community, a magistrate, or my neighbor, and give them an example...Although tyrants do violence or injustice in making their demands, yet it will do no harm as long as they demand nothing contrary to God.[26]

The Christian public ethics should be geared towards common good. As Luther sates, "See, according to this rule the good things we have from God should flow from one to the other and be common to all, so that everyone should 'put on' his neighbor and so conduct himself toward him as if he himself were in the other's place."[27]

In conclusion, Luther argues that both faith and love are the foundations and pillars for Christian personal and public ethics. "We conclude, therefore, that a Christian lives not in himself, but in Christ and in his neighbor. Otherwise he is not a Christian. He lives in Christ through faith, in his neighbor through love. By faith he is caught up beyond himself into God. By love he descends beneath himself into his neighbor."[28]

---

23. Martin Luther, op.cit., 621.

24. The common good in relation to the modern state is synonymous with the protection of the rich, even by means of oppression of the poor. This goes directly against Christian ethics.

25. Cf. Althaus, *Ethics of Martin Luther*, 112–54.

26. Martin Luther, op.cit., 622.

27. Martin Luther, op.cit., 623.

28. Martin Luther, op.cit., 623.

## 2. CALVIN ON FREEDOM AS SALVATION IN THE INSTITUTES OF THE CHRISTIAN RELIGION

As one of the most faithful theological disciples of Martin Luther, John Calvin described Luther as the father of his faith and the apostle of his age and appropriated Luther's profound foundational insights, presenting a theology of freedom as salvation in his masterful *Institutes of the Christian Religion*.[29] Calvin discusses the idea of Christian freedom in the 19th chapter of the third book of the *Institutes*, dividing his discussion into several parts.

### 2.1. Freedom from the Law

Calvin argues that Christian freedom is primarily related to three things, one of which is freedom from the law. Calvin states,

> Christian freedom, in my opinion, consists of three parts. The first: that the consciences of believers, in seeking assurance of their justification before God, should rise above and advance beyond the law, forgetting all low righteousness. For since, as we have elsewhere shown, the law leaves no one righteous, either it excludes from all hope of justification or we ought to be freed from it, and in such a way, indeed, that no account is taken of works.[30]

Therefore, a Christian is freed from the demand and damnation of the law because he or she is justified by faith alone apart from the works of the law. Commenting on Paul's arguments for the Christian's freedom from the law presented in Galatians, Calvin points out, "First, because the clarity of the gospel was obscured by those Jewish shadows, Paul showed that we have in Christ a perfect disclosure of all those things which were foreshadowed in the Mosaic ceremonies."[31]

However, for Calvin, this does not mean that the law's function has stopped but rather the law has a third use. Calvin continues to point out:

> Nor can any man rightly infer from this that the law is superfluous for believers, since it does not stop teaching and exhorting and urging them to good, even though before God's judgment seat it has no place in their consciences. . .The whole life of Christians ought to be a sort of practice of godliness, for we have

---

29. John Calvin, *Institutes of the Christian Religion*, trans. Ford L. Battles (Louisville: Westminster, 1960)

30. *Institutes*, 3.19.2.

31. *Institutes*, 3.19.3.

been called to sanctification. Here it is the function of the law, by warning men of their duty, to arouse them to a zeal for holiness and innocence.[32]

There is a major difference between Luther and Calvin in terms of the third use of the law. As Paul Althaus has argued, "Luther does not use the expression 'the third function of the law (*tertius usus legis*),' Melanchthon did use this expression and it was when adopted in the Formula of Concord, in Lutheran orthodoxy, and by nineteenth century theology."[33] However, it is undeniable that they concur that one of the central dimensions of the Christian freedom is their freedom from the law. This is what Luther called "spiritual freedom."

## 2.2. Freedom for Obedience

Like Luther, Calvin believes that Christians freed from the law's condemnation by faith in Christ are empowered and enabled to obey the law freely and willingly. In other words, freedom from the law leads Christians to live in accordance with the principle of the law, that is, love with the power of the Holy Spirit. Calvin states:

> The second part is that consciences observe the law, not as if constrained by the necessity of the law, but that freed from the law's yoke they willingly obey God's will. . .But sons, who are more generously and candidly treated by their fathers, do not hesitate to offer them incomplete and half-done and even defective works, trusting that their obedience and readiness of mind will be accepted by their fathers, even though they have not quite achieved what their fathers intended. Such children ought we to be, firmly trusting that our services will be approved by our most merciful Father, however small, rude, and imperfect these may be.[34]

Calvin also says that when Christians are empowered to obey the law after experiencing freedom from the law by faith and justification, "they will cheerfully and with great eagerness answer, and [follow] his (God's) leading."[35] For Calvin, even though Christians have the remnants of sin, "there is still no reason to be afraid and cast down in mind as if God were continually offended by the remnants of sin, seeing that they have

---

32. *Institutes*, 3.19.2.
33. Althaus, *Theology of Martin Luther*, 273.
34. *Institutes*, 3.19.4–5.
35. *Institutes*, 3.19.5.

been emancipated from the law by grace, so that their works are not to be measured according to its rules."[36]

## 2.3. Freedom in Things Indifferent

For Calvin, "the third part of Christian freedom lies in this: regarding outward things that are of themselves 'indifferent,' we are not bound before God by any religious obligation preventing us from sometimes using them and other times not using them, indifferently."[37] This demonstrates that Calvin goes beyond Luther in his discussion of freedom by delving into the relationship between Christian freedom and indifferent things, namely, *adiaphora*. Calvin believes that Christians can enjoy absolute freedom in relation to indifferent things, saying "With these words (Romans 14:14) Paul subjects all outward things to our freedom."[38]

Calvin also argues that Christians have true freedom in the use of God's gifts for his purposes. It is important to appreciate, however, that Calvin does not endorse the abuse of Christian freedom in using God's gifts for gluttony and luxury because Calvin views Christian freedom as "a spiritual thing in all its parts."[39] He continues to point out:

> And we have never been forbidden to laugh, or to be filled, or to join new possessions to old or ancestral ones, or to delight in musical harmony, or to drink wine. Ture indeed. But where there is plenty, to wallow in delights, to gorge oneself, to intoxicate mind and heart with present pleasures and be always panting after new ones—such are very far removed from a lawful use of God's gifts. Away, then with uncontrolled desire, away with immoderate prodigality, away with vanity and arrogance—in order that men may with a clean conscience cleanly use God's gifts.[40]

It is clear from the above statement that Calvin connects Christian freedom with the clear consciences of the Christians. Thus, for him, Christian freedom of conscience must be upheld in relation to everything whether doctrinally and morally essential or nonessential and indifferent.

---

36. *Institutes*, 3.19.6.
37. *Institutes*, 3.19.7.
38. *Institutes*, 3.19.8.
39. *Institutes*, 3.19.9.
40. *Institutes*, 3.19.9.

## 3. CRITICAL ENGAGEMENT WITH THE REFORMERS' INSIGHTS INTO THE IDEA OF FREEDOM

More than anything else, for Luther, the idea of freedom is of soteriological character. Luther identifies freedom with soteriological concepts such as justification and salvation. Luther believes that by faith alone sinners are justified and when they are justified, they are freed from the law, sin, death and hell. For him, salvation simply means freedom from sinners' spiritual bondage to sin and death. This means, for Luther, freedom is primarily of a spiritual category rather than political or social one.

Calvin would totally agree with Luther's insights. For Calvin, the first dimension of Christian freedom is freedom from the demand and damnation of the law. This spiritual freedom is given to believers as God's gift of grace through faith alone. There is no conflict between Luther and Calvin in their understanding of the spiritual and soteriological character of Christian freedom.

Moreover, Luther believes that Christian spiritual freedom gives birth to Christian ethical freedom, which is closely connected with joyful voluntariness and happy spontaneity in responding to God's will. Christians justified and freed by faith alone are empowered and enabled by the Holy Spirit to obey God and live for others. And this personal ethical freedom, for Luther, is expanded into public ethical freedom that leads Christians to subject themselves for the common good of society and community which they belong to.

Calvin would have no issues with Luther's argument that Christian spiritual freedom gives birth to Christian ethical freedom. In a sense, however, Calvin goes beyond Luther when he argues for the third use of the law. Luther has never used the term and emphasized it explicitly. It is still undeniable that Luther had some incipient ideas of the third use of the law in his mind. As Paul Althaus has argued persuasively, Luther believed that the law has a function for Christians even after their justification.[41]

But it is undeniable that Calvin was so emphatic upon the third use of the law that he claimed it to be the principal function of the law.[42] Furthermore, he believed that Christians are called to live according to the exhortations of the law with the power of the Holy Spirit.[43] Paradoxically,

---

41. Althaus, *Theology of Martin Luther*, 266–73. See Bernhard Lohse, op.cit., 267–76.

42. *Institutes*, 2.7.12. In terms of Calvin's understanding of the function of the law, it is very important to note that Calvin was in total agreement with Luther that the law reveals human sinfulness and thus leads them to Christ as their savior.

43. Cf. I. John Hesselink, *Calvin's Concept of the Law* (Eugene, OR: Wipf & Stock, 1992).

for Calvin, freedom from the law is pregnant with freedom for the law. So it is not an overstatement that in spite of the differences in terms of emphases, Luther and Calvin had similar thoughts in relation to the idea of Christian spiritual and soteriological freedom and Christian ethical freedom as its corollary.[44]

However, there might be a difference in their approaches to the idea of Christian freedom. Whereas Luther makes an intrinsic connection between personal ethical freedom and public ethical freedom, Calvin seems to focus more on Christian freedom in relation to indifferent things and God's gifts. Of course, it is undeniable that Calvin did pay attention to the issue of public ethical freedom. Calvin discusses Christian freedom in relation to public matters of civil government and magistracy.[45] Nevertheless, Calvin did not follow Luther in his discussion of Christian freedom by not explicitly focusing upon Christian freedom in relation to public ethics.

## 4. SIGNIFICANCE AND IMPLICATIONS FOR GLOBAL CHRISTIANITY

Then, what are significance and implication of the Reformers' insights into the idea of freedom for global Christianity? I would respond to this question in terms of the following two categories—global theology and global public ethics.

### 4.1. Global Theology

In terms of global theology, Luther's and Calvin's insights into the idea of freedom have profound significance and implications. More than anything else, it is important to appreciate that in the global South the idea of freedom has been misused, misunderstood, misinterpreted, misrepresented and miscommunicated. For example, in Latin American liberation theology the idea of freedom has been almost unilaterally identified with horizontal liberation from unjust social and economic structure and system.[46] As a result, the soteriological and vertical dimension of spiritual freedom from the

---

44. Althaus, op.cit., 272–73. Althaus agrees with my point.

45. *Institutes*, 4.20.14–32.

46. For an important survey of Latin American liberation theology and its character, see David Tombs, *Latin American Liberation Theology: Religions in the Americas* (Leiden: Brill, 2003). Also for an excellent discussion of a variety of liberation theologies, see Christopher Rowland, ed., *The Cambridge Companion to Liberation Theology* (New York: Cambridge University Press, 1999).

law, sin, death, hell and the devil has been deemphasized and dismissed. It is high time that the idea of spiritual freedom should be restored and the balance between the vertical and the horizontal dimensions of salvation should be recovered in Latin American Christianity where liberation theology has been deeply influencing.

In addition, in the Asian context including China and South Korea, the idea of spiritual freedom has been misrepresented and miscommunicated. For example, in South Korea the idea of spiritual freedom has been associated with antinomian tendencies in some Christian circles including orthodox churches and sectarian groups. Some Christians have misunderstood the idea of spiritual freedom to mean that they are allowed to indulge in licentiousness and lust in the name of liberty.[47] However, it is important to appreciate that Luther and Calvin never endorsed such an antinomian attitude in relation to the idea of spiritual freedom but rather they emphasized that spiritual freedom gives birth to ethical freedom in both personal and public dimensions. South Korean Christianity should strive to retrieve the wisdom and insights of the Reformers in order to renew orthodox churches and to remedy sectarian groups. In so doing, they should recover an appropriate and balanced construal of the relationship between spiritual freedom and ethical life as its corollary.

## 4.2. Global Public Ethics

In terms of global public ethics the Reformers' insights into the idea of freedom possess tremendous significance and fascinating implications. For example, in China, Christianity has been growing drastically for the past thirty years[48] but most Chinese Christians have never been educated in relation to their social and public responsibility. Of course, it is understandable that it would have been very difficult for Chinese Christians to focus on developing their public ethics in the context of severe persecutions by the government. Many Chinese Christians have been endeavoring to survive

---

47. In South Korea, the so-called Salvation Sect has been promoting antinomian ethos. The Salvation Sect has more than 100,000 followers. Evangelical Christians in South Korea are concerned that the negative impact of the Salvation Sect is growing. The Salvation Sect has been manifesting gnostic tendencies by arguing that salvation is not about personal trust in Jesus Christ, but rather about intellectual enlightenment that salvation is a free gift. The Salvation Sect also does not properly emphasize that Christians should continue to repent of their sins in the process of sanctification.

48. For a significant discussion of the rise of Chinese Christianity, see Rodney Stark & Xiuhua Wang, *A Star in the East: The Rise of Christianity in China* (West Conshohocken, PA: Templeton, 2016).

those persecutions and to evangelize as many individuals as possible. The numerical growth of the churches have been the major focus for many Chinese churches whether official three-self churches or unofficial house churches.

However, it is important to appreciate that Chinese churches and Christians need to develop their public ethics which is geared toward making positive contributions to the Chinese society and nation.[49] For this purpose the Reformers' insights, especially Luther's can provide Chinese churches and Christians with invaluable guidance. For example, Luther emphasized that Christians freed from the law, sin, death, hell and the devil can be servants of all others, pursuing their benefits wholeheartedly. By seeking others' benefits joyfully and voluntarily, Chinese churches and Christians can set up a model that even nonbelievers can emulate for the realization of the common good for Chinese society.

With the encroachment of global capitalism into Chinese society, many negative symptoms and effects of inhumane mammonism are increasingly manifesting.[50] In this context, Chinese churches and Christians should take the responsibility to provide a good example of genuine altruism and sacrificial generosity by seeking to be servants in order to bless general public in the name of the gospel. Furthermore, in the long run Chinese churches and Christians should strive to develop a strategy with which they can engage with the Chinese government productively and constructively.

## 5. CONCLUSION

Last year we celebrate the quincentennial of the sixteenth century European Reformation. It is crystal clear that the Reformers including Luther and Calvin left a profound legacy for the future of global Christianity. In particular, both Luther and Calvin provide tremendous theological resources to the

---

49. See J. Carpenter, et al., *Christianity in Chinese Public Life: Religion, Society, and the Rule of Law* (London: Palgrave Pivot, 2014).

50. For discussions of capitalism in China, see Andrew Collier, *Shadow Banking and the Rise of Capitalism in China* (Singapore: Palgrave Macmillan, 2017); Kellee S. Tsai, *Capitalism without Democracy: The Private Sector in Contemporary China* (Ithaca, NY: Cornell University Press, 2007); Arif Dirlik, *Complicities: The People's Republic of China and Global Capitalism* (Chicago: Prickly Paradigm, 2017); Xiaoshuo Hou, *Community Capitalism in China: The State, the Market and Collectivism* (New York: Cambridge University Press, 2014); and Minxin Pei, *China's Crony Capitalism: The Dynamics of Regime Decay* (Cambridge, MA: Harvard University Press, 2016). For a discussion of crony capitalism in Korea, see David C. Kang, *Crony Capitalism: Corruption and Development in South Korea and the Philippines* (New York: Cambridge University Press, 2002).

idea of Christian freedom in relation to both private and public dimensions. When global churches and Christians endeavor to retrieve their wisdom and insights in their own contexts, their effort will bear beautiful fruits. The Reformation has not ended but rather it is still going on. I hope and pray that the Reformation's theological legacy will be faithfully handed down to next generations, and this will make a significant contribution to the healthy future of global Christianity.

Chapter 6

# An Edwardsian Quandary Concerning the Atonement

OLIVER D. CRISP

IN THE COURSE OF one of his "Miscellanies" notebook entries on the atonement, the great New England divine, Jonathan Edwards, asks "how can it be a fit and becoming thing in Christ, thus to love and unite himself to those that are infinitely ill-deserving, and when justice requires that they be the objects of eternal hatred and indignation? Is not the [sic] thus taking their part and uniting himself to them a making himself guilty of their sin?"[1] His answer to this quandary is intriguing, "Christ does as it were hereby bring their guilt upon himself, but not in any blameable sense."[2] He goes on to elaborate on this point, "It was not esteemed a fit thing for Christ thus by love to unite himself to such guilty ones, unless he had manifested a readiness to bear their guilt himself and suffer their punishment."[3] That is, it is because Christ takes upon himself the guilt of sinners, acting as their penal

---

1. "Miscellanies" entry, "No. 483. Righteousness and Satisfaction of Christ," in *The "Miscellanies": Nos. a-z, aa-zz, 1–500, The Works of Jonathan Edwards Vol. 13*, ed. Thomas A. Schafer (New Haven: Yale University Press, 1994), 526. Hereinafter, all references are to the Yale edition of Edwards's Works, cited as "WJE" followed by volume number and page reference.

2. "Miscellanies" entry, "No. 483. Righteousness and Satisfaction of Christ," 526.

3. "Miscellanies" entry, "No. 483. Righteousness and Satisfaction of Christ," 526.

substitute, that this arrangement is a just and fitting one, rather than being unjust and inappropriate:

> It was but fair, and what justice required, that seeing Christ would so unite himself by love to sinners that had deserved wrath, that they might be partakers of the Father's love to him and so they be screened and sheltered, that he himself should receive the Father's wrath to them. That love of Christ which united him to sinners, assumed their guilt upon himself. So that Christ's death and sufferings were absolutely necessary, in order [to] our being delivered from destruction for the sake of Christ's worthiness and excellency, and through the love of God to him that loved us.[4]

However, there is a lacuna in Edwards's thinking here, one that, to my knowledge, he never adequately addresses. It is this: even if Christ does take upon himself the work of a penal substitute for fallen human beings, such an arrangement in and of itself, and without further elaboration, does not explain *how* in uniting himself to those guilty of sin, he remains without guilt for sin, and is not besmirched or contaminated by that sin. To say, as Edwards does in this "Miscellanies" entry, that "Christ does as it were hereby bring their guilt upon himself, but not in any blameable sense" simply asserts without argument that atonement for human guilt doesn't compromise Christ's integrity. Let us call this apparently unresolved issue in Edwards's account of the atonement, *the Edwardsian Quandary concerning the atonement*, or just *the Edwardsian Quandary* for short.

Edwards's doctrine of atonement is an interesting one, and the subject of ongoing scholarly discussion.[5] There are important ways in which what

---

4. "Miscellanies" entry, "No. 483. Righteousness and Satisfaction of Christ," 526. This "Miscellanies" No. 483 is discussed at greater length by Kyle Strobel in Oliver D. Crisp and Kyle Strobel, *Jonathan Edwards: An Introduction to His Thought* (Grand Rapids: Eerdmans, 2018), ch. 5, and Oliver D. Crisp, *Jonathan Edwards and the Metaphysics of Sin* (New York: Routledge, 2016), *Appendix: The Imputation of Christ's Righteousness*.

5. Recent examples include Brandon James Crawford, *Jonathan Edwards on the Atonement: Understanding the Legacy of America's Greatest Theologian* (Eugene, OR: Wipf & Stock, 2017); Oliver D. Crisp, *Jonathan Edwards Among the Theologians* (Grand Rapids: Eerdmans, 2015), ch. 7; S. Mark Hamilton, "Jonathan Edwards on the Atonement," *International Journal of Systematic Theology* 15.4 (2013) 394–415; S. Mark Hamilton, "Jonathan Edwards, Anselmic Satisfaction and God's Moral Government," *International Journal of Systematic Theology* 17.1 (2015) 46–67; S. Mark Hamilton, "Rethinking Atonement in Jonathan Edwards and New England Theology," *Perichoresis* 15.1 (2017) 85–99; Peter Leithart, "New Science of Sacrifice," in Kyle C. Strobel, ed., *The Ecumenical Edwards: Jonathan Edwards and the Theologians* (New York: Routledge, 2016), 51–66; and Garry Williams, "Jonathan Edwards," in Adam J. Johnson, ed., *T&T Clark Companion to Atonement* (London: Bloomsbury, 2017), 467–72.

he says about both salvation and atonement resonate with broader themes in soteriology—having to do with participation in the divine life by means of *theosis*—that I think are important contributions to our understanding of Christ's reconciling work.[6] However, rather than focusing on these wider themes in Edwards's thought in particular, in this essay I want to use Edwards's question as a way of framing a more narrow concern about whether Christ can be said to be guilty of the sin of fallen human beings as their representative. For the relationship between culpability or blameworthiness, guilt, and punishment, as well as notions of representation and substitution, are at the heart of a number of traditional accounts of the atonement such as that articulated by Edwards.[7] So getting a clearer picture of the relationship between this cluster of concepts is a task that should be of help to those for whom such notions are important, load-bearing structures in their doctrines of atonement—particularly those sympathetic to a version of penal substitution, as Edwards appears to have been.

Thus, this essay is an attempt to address a kind of theological puzzle that is helpfully illustrated for us by Edwards, and one that he in particular doesn't seem to have resolved satisfactorily. Although the focus of attention is not on Edwards's theology *per se*, but upon the quandary that he raises, we shall circle back to Edwards at the end of the essay to see whether our rumination may help to plug the lacuna in his thought. This, then, is a kind of exercise in Edwards*ian* theologizing—that is, theology done in the spirit (but not necessarily according to the letter) of Edward himself.[8] We proceed as follows.

The first section considers the question of human guilt for sin. In this connection, a key distinction with which Edwards would have been familiar

---

6. See, e.g., the discussion in W. Ross Hastings, *Jonathan Edwards and the Life of God: Toward an Evangelical Theology of Participation* (Minneapolis: Fortress, 2015); Michael J. McClymond, "Salvation as Divinization: Jonathan Edwards, Gregory Palamas and the Theological Uses of Neoplatonism," in Paul Helm and Oliver D. Crisp, eds., *Jonathan Edwards: Philosophical Theologian* (Aldershot, UK: Ashgate, 2003), 139–60; Kyle C. Strobel, "Jonathan Edwards and the Polemics of Theosis," *Harvard Theological Review* 105.3 (2012) 259–79; Strobel, "Jonathan Edwards's Reformed Doctrine of Theosis," *Harvard Theological Review* 109.3 (2016) 371–99; Oliver D. Crisp and Kyle C. Strobel, *Jonathan Edwards: An Introduction to His Thought* (Grand Rapids: Eerdmans, 2018), ch. 6; and Brandon G. Withrow, *Becoming Divine: Jonathan Edwards's Incarnational Spirituality within the Christian Tradition* (Eugene, OR: Wipf & Stock, 2011).

7. This is true of versions of penal substitution. It is also true of closely related doctrines like satisfaction, the governmental view of atonement, and John McLeod Campbell's understanding of Christ's vicarious penitence.

8. Hence, our focus is on the theological issues Edwards helpfully raises, not upon finding some solution to these issues from within Edwards's work (in part because Edwards doesn't appear to have addressed them himself).

is that between culpability and punishment in relation to guilt.[9] In the second section, I apply this discussion of guilt and culpability to the atonement. A third section deals with the complication of original sin in relation to guilt and atonement. And in the final section I draw together the threads of the foregoing reasoning to make clear the theological upshot of this proposed solution to the Edwardsian Quandary.

## GUILT AND CULPABILITY

Normally, we tend to think that a person's guilt is inalienable. That is, it cannot be removed from the possessor of that guilt, and it cannot be transferred to another person innocent of the crime committed. An example will make the point.

Consider someone on trial for first-degree murder. Assume for the sake of simplicity that the evidence in favor of the defendant's guilt is overwhelming, and that the defendant has confessed to the crime. Now, normally we presume that where culpability can be shown beyond reasonable doubt, punishment should follow. Were we to prize these two things apart so that punishment did not necessarily follow on the heels of culpability, I suggest—other things being equal[10]—that this would be thought of as a potentially serious problem with any judgment reached. For instance, suppose the judge in passing sentence upon the accused said, "despite the overwhelming evidence of your culpability for this crime, it is the judgment of this court that your nominated penal substitute should take your place, so that you may not be punished; your substitute will take upon himself or herself the penal consequences for your actions." Normally, this would be thought a travesty of justice rather than an instance of it. The reason for this is that we think that under normal conditions there must be a fit between punishment and crime, one that has to do with this question of the moral link between culpability and desert.

I suggest that part of this matter of "fit" between crime and punishment has to do with a presumed deep moral connection between the crime itself (especially if it is a heinous crime, like a felony), and the blameworthiness of the person who committed the crime. This presumed moral connection is what pumps the intuition that punishment must be served upon the guilty party, rather than upon someone else. Other things being equal,

---

9. See, WJE3, IV. III.

10. This *ceteris paribus* clause stands in for various conditions that would bear upon strict culpability such as whether the defendant was *compos mentis* when committing the crime, whether it was committed under duress, and so on.

it is normally the guilty party that is regarded as culpable. It would not normally be thought just for the punishment to be served upon some penal substitute innocent of the crime committed if it is a felony. (And, of course, this is an important traditional objection to theological accounts of penal substitution that goes back to the work of Faustus Socinus in the sixteenth century.[11]) This is the case for at least three reasons.

First, the penal substitute is not the person who committed the crime. She or he is innocent. So (on this way of thinking) it would be improper to treat a penal substitute *as if* she or he were the guilty party, visiting harsh treatment upon him or her. This would involve a kind of moral fiction that is insupportable.

Second, and closely related to this, it seems to me that—strictly speaking—it is not possible to punish an innocent person. This is just a category mistake, like saying the number 2 is green. Punishment can only be meted out to one who is culpable for a crime. By definition the innocent person is not the culpable party; so it makes no moral sense to say that the penal substitute is "punished" in place of the guilty person. The penal substitute could take upon himself the harsh treatment that in the case of the guilty person would constitute punishment. However, if this harsh treatment were meted out to the innocent substitute it would still be merely unmerited harsh treatment, rather than punishment (strictly speaking) precisely because it is an innocent person suffering, not one guilty of a crime.[12]

Third, and following on the heels of the previous two points, guilt seems to be an inalienable quality. That is, it seems that guilt is a property that in principle cannot be transferred from one person to another. The murderer is the one who committed the crime, not his brother or mother or

---

11. For discussion of this matter, see William Lane Craig, "Is Penal Substitution Incoherent? An Examination of Mark Murphy's Criticisms," *Religious Studies* (2018), forthcoming; Oliver D. Crisp, "The Logic of Penal Substitution Revisited," in Derek Tidball et al., eds., *The Atonement Debate: Papers from the London Symposium on the Atonement* (Grand Rapids: Zondervan, 2008), 208–27; Stephen R. Holmes, "Penal Substitution," in Adam J. Johnson, ed., *T&T Clark Companion to Atonement* (London: Bloomsbury, 2017), 295–314; and David Lewis, "Do We Believe in Penal Substitution?," in Oliver D. Crisp, ed., *A Reader in Contemporary Philosophical Theology* (London: T. & T. Clark, 2009), 328–34.

12. I am not denying that innocent people are "punished" in modern legal systems. My point is just that when an innocent person is treated harshly in this way, it is not in fact a punishment, and cannot in fact be a punishment because the notion of punishment is inextricably linked to the notion of desert and culpability—neither of which pertain to someone innocent of the crime committed. For an attempt to show that the innocent cannot be punished, see A. M. Quinton, "On Punishment," *Analysis* 14.6 (1954) 133–42.

daughter or anyone else; only him.[13] What is more, the murderer is the one *guilty* of having committed the crime, not his brother or mother or daughter or anyone else; only him. His guilt cannot be parceled out to another. It cannot be transferred like money from one bank account to another. It remains the property of the one who has committed the crime. Now, the punishable aspect of guilt can be met, so that the one guilty of the crime is no longer liable for punishment. If the murderer serves a life sentence in prison, say, then upon being released we would say that although he is the one guilty of having committed the murder, he is no longer punishable for that crime because he has paid his debt to society. So what we might call the punishable aspect of guilt can be expunged through appropriate harsh treatment such as a custodial sentence. But the fact that this person committed the crime in question—that this person is the one culpable or blameworthy for having committed the crime—*that* fact cannot be removed by any form of punishment. In scholastic theology this difference was marked by the distinction between the *reatus culpae* (the culpability aspect of guilt), and the *reatus poenae* (the punishable aspect of guilt). The *reatus poenae* can be met through punishment, but the *reatus culpae* remains. I am simply reiterating substantially the same point here.[14]

With these three things made tolerably clear we can see that the reason why it would not normally be thought just for some crime or sin to be served upon a penal substitute innocent of the crime committed has to do with the fact that morally suitable candidates for punishment must be blameworthy. Because they bear guilt they are culpable, and because they are culpable they are (in principle) punishable. Plausibly, guilt has a double-aspect. There is the punishable aspect of guilt as well as the culpability aspect that is inalienable. This is the lesson of the scholastic distinction between *reatus culpae* and the *reatus poenae*. The punishable aspect of guilt is not inalienable because it can be expunged through some suitable penalty. Nevertheless, the punishable aspect of guilt cannot be transferred to another because a substitute is innocent and as a consequence is not a suitable moral candidate for punishment. The perpetrator alone is the one who must bear punishment

---

13. Presuming he had no accomplice; and presuming no other parties were involved.

14. At one point Stephen Holmes suggests that this distinction between the *reatus culpae* and *reatus poenae*, as it is taken up in the work of the nineteenth-century Princeton theologian, Charles Hodge, is a puzzling one. He says, "This seems to me counterintuitive; Hodge's argument for it is essentially that in the atonement it happened, so it must be possible" (Holmes, "Penal Substitution," 298). This is an odd thing to say, for Hodge is simply reiterating an older, scholastic distinction, one which seems to track with our moral intuitions about punishment, not about atonement.

in order to deal with the punishable aspect of guilt. And this cannot be transferred to an innocent party. Even if it were in principle transferrable, it wouldn't be punishment in the case of the innocent party precisely because she or he is innocent and therefore not a morally appropriate candidate for punishment. So the link between culpability and punishability is lost in the case of standard accounts of penal substitution that think of Christ's work as a substitute punishment for human sin.

Much more would need to be said on this subject in order to provide an air-tight argument for the connection between culpability, guilt, and punishment, and there is a sophisticated literature in jurisprudence on this topic.[15] However, I suggest that this brief foray provides some reason for thinking that the culpability aspect of guilt is *normally* thought to be the inalienable property of the person who has committed the crime. ("Normally" here functions as a kind of *ceteris paribus* condition, that is, "other things being equal." The "other things" here include conditions like the person guilty of the crime being a morally responsible agent, being *compos mentis* when committing the crime or sin, and so on.) Moreover, although the punishment aspect of guilt may be met by the application of an appropriate penalty, it is *normally* met by the one guilty of having committed the crime, not by some penal substitute who is innocent of the crime and therefore ineligible for consideration as a suitable target-candidate for the harsh treatment of punishment.[16]

---

15. For instance, see R. A. Duff and David Garland, eds., *Punishment: A Reader. Oxford Readings in Socio-Legal Studies* (Oxford: Oxford University Press, 1994); and Thomas A. Nadelhoffer, ed., *The Future of Punishment. Oxford Series in Neuroscience, Law, and Philosophy* (Oxford: Oxford University Press, 2013). An important rebuttal of the sort of intuitions I am trading on here can be found in David Boonin, *The Problem of Punishment* (Cambridge: Cambridge University Press, 2008).

16. This is not true of fines, which may be paid by a party other than the guilty party. (This includes significant fines, such as those obtained in convictions for serious fraud.) Fines incur what David Lewis calls a "debt of punishment" (See Lewis, "Do We Believe in Penal Substitution?," reprinted in Oliver Crisp, ed., *A Reader in Philosophical Theology* [London: T. & T. Clark, 2009], 328–34.) They are a special case of crimes where we do allow penal substitution of a sort. So, Lewis avers, we are all—religious and nonreligious alike—in two minds about penal substitution because we all allow it on at least some occasions (e.g., in the case of Christ for theologians like Edwards, and in the case of fines in society at large). Granted. Hence, the *ceteris paribus* usage of "normally" in the formulation above should be taken to mean something like, "normally, except in the case of fines . . ." I would imagine many Christian theologians, like Edwards, for whom human sin requires the death of Christ, would think of sin as being closer to a felony than a "debt of punishment" like a fine (*pace* Anselm). For an interesting recent theological discussion of some of these things, see Joshua Farris and S. Mark Hamilton, "The Logic of Reparative Substitution: Contemporary Restitution Models of Atonement, Divine Justice, and Somatic Death," *Irish Theological Quarterly*

## THE TRANSFER OF GUILT IN ATONEMENT[17]

We turn to the question of the transfer of guilt from one person to another, and, more specifically, from fallen human beings to Christ who (according to the sort of penal substitutionary arrangement familiar to theologians like Edwards) takes upon himself the penalty due for sin. Recall that our target here is to provide some reason that may motivate Edwards's claim that "Christ does as it were hereby bring their guilt upon himself, *but not in any blameable sense.*"

In his recent essay on penal substitution, the British theologian Stephen Holmes offers three traditional ways in which the worry about transference of guilt has been addressed by defenders of penal substitution.[18] I will take them in the reverse order to which they appear in his essay. First, there is the notion of legal relaxation so that the strict demands of the law may be relaxed in order that a "vicarious equivalent punishment"[19] may be accepted in place of the one legally demanded. This is an odd arrangement, and one that Holmes finds insufficient because "it is not clear why Jesus had to suffer such humiliation and agony" if "there is not absolute legal requirement for the penalty of death to be inflicted."[20] However, the defender of this view can surely reply that the issue is not the relaxation of the penalty, but the relaxation of the question of who suffers the penalty. The full force of the penalty is still in place, for the wages of sin is death (Rom 6:23).[21] But on this

---

17. This issue is also dealt with in Oliver D. Crisp, *The Word Enfleshed: Exploring the Person and Work of Christ* (Grand Rapids: Baker Academic, 2016); Oliver D. Crisp, "Scholastic Theology, Augustinian Realism and Original Guilt," *European Journal of Theology* 13.1 (2004) 17–28; and Oliver D. Crisp, "Federalism vs. Realism: Charles Hodge, Augustus Strong and William Shedd on The Imputation of Sin," *International Journal of Systematic Theology* 8 (2006) 1–17. The discussion here follows the shape of these other treatments of the topic.

18. Holmes, "Penal Substitution," 297–99.

19. Holmes, "Penal Substitution," 299.

20. Holmes, "Penal Substitution," 299.

21. It could be argued that Christ's death is not a strict equivalent to the death pursuant to the wages of sin in Romans 6:23 because the death in view in Romans is spiritual death that involves being cut off from God everlastingly. Christ is not cut off from God's presence everlastingly, so his death is not a strict equivalent to the wages of sin. I think this must be granted to the objector, in which case, Holmes's point may be rephrased as an objection about strict equivalence, and defenders of penal substitution may fall back on a weaker notion of suitable equivalence in order to bolster their argument. For discussion of this and other related matters to do with the value of the atonement, see Oliver D. Crisp, "Salvation and Atonement: On the Value and Necessity of the Work of Jesus Christ," in Ivor J. Davidson and Murray A. Rae, eds., *God of Salvation: Soteriology in Theological Perspective* (Aldershot, UK: Ashgate, 2011), ch. 7.

view Christ may act as a penal substitute taking upon himself the penalty if the requisite legal relaxation obtains.

Nevertheless, there is still a real problem with this view. The problem is this: the legal arrangement envisaged is a kind of fiction, where God allows an exception to a legal norm so that Christ may be treated as if he is the one guilty of the sin, and can suffer the penal consequences of that sin in place of the guilty sinner. Consequently, no guilt is really transferred to Christ on this view. Rather, God imputes our guilt to Christ, treating him as if he were guilty. But we have already seen that a standard objection to this line of reasoning is that it is not morally appropriate. Christ is not guilty of any sin and it is not morally acceptable to make an innocent person suffer the penalty of the guilty. Even if such an arrangement were tolerated, it would not be the right sort of moral arrangement for atonement to take place because Christ, as an innocent party, cannot in principle be punished. Since the retributive exercise of divine justice is usually in view in penal substitutionary doctrines of atonement, the fit between crime and punishment, and, more specifically, between culpability and guilt, is legally salient. But Christ is not culpable (he is not a sinner); he is not guilty (the legal relaxation arrangement presumes that he is not guilty, hence the need for relaxation of the demands of the law); and, therefore by definition he is not punishable.

The second way in which defenders of penal substitution have tried to provide some reason for thinking guilt is transferred from fallen human beings to Christ in atonement has to do with the distinction between the culpability and punishable aspects of guilt referred to earlier. Taking up Charles Hodge's way of construing these things, Holmes says that the distinction itself somehow provides a basis for distinguishing an aspect of guilt that is transferrable in principle because it is separable from culpability, namely, the punishable aspect of guilt.[22] But we have already noted that the distinction itself does no work in explaining how guilt can be transferred from one party to another. It merely helps us to see that there is an aspect of guilt that is inalienable (culpability), and another aspect that is not inalienable, and may be met by a penalty served (the punishable aspect). However, because an innocent person cannot in principle suffer punishment, and because it would be immoral to serve the harsh treatment for sin upon an innocent substitute like Christ, this does not explain how guilt can be transferred from fallen human beings to Christ.[23]

---

22. Holmes, "Penal Substitution," 298.

23. Holmes thinks this distinction "counterintuitive," but I do not understand why, and he doesn't really explain his thinking. Nor am I entirely clear that he has been as charitable to Hodge as he might have been. But I shall pass over that for now.

This brings us to the third way of making good on the transfer of guilt according to historic defenders of penal substitution. This depends on a strong doctrine of union with Christ that can be found in the work of some Reformed theologians such as John Calvin.[24] In his debate with Osiander, Calvin writes:

> Now, lest Osiander deceive the unlearned by his cavils, I confess that we are deprived of this utterly incomparable good [i.e., righteousness] until Christ is made ours. Therefore, that joining together of Head and members, that indwelling of Christ in our hearts—in short, that mystical union—are accorded by us the highest degree of importance, so that Christ, having been made ours, makes us sharers with him in the gifts with which he has been endowed. We do not, therefore, contemplate him outside ourselves from afar in order that his righteousness may be imputed to us but because we put on Christ and are engrafted into his body—in short because he deigns to make us one with him.[25]

Commenting on Calvin's position in particular, Holmes writes, "The union of the believer with Christ results in 'Christ-and-the-church' being a single moral agent" so that there "is not transference of guilt . . . the head being held responsible for the sins of the body."[26] Calvin does use such concrete, Pauline imagery in his account of union with Christ, although I am not clear that he thinks of Christ-and-the-church as one moral agent. But, in any case, to my way of thinking this sort of approach to the question of the transfer of guilt is by far the most promising way forward. Holmes thinks it is "difficult to hold . . . in the face of conceptions of personhood as unassailable interiority that arose at the beginning of the nineteenth century."[27] But that seems an odd judgment to make.[28] Notions of par-

24. Holmes also names William Ames in this regard, but the relevant section in his *Marrow of Theology* (trans. John Dykstra Eusden [Grand Rapids: Baker, 1968]) makes clear that although he is willing to talk of the mystical union of the church with Christ (I.xxxi.15) his understanding of union with Christ in justification (I.xxvii.1) is to be construed in terms of "the pronouncing of a sentence," which "does not denote in the Holy Scriptures a real or physical change. There is rather a judicial or moral change which takes shape in the pronouncing of the sentence and in the reckoning" (I.xxvii.7, 161 in Eusden trans.).

25. John Calvin, *Institutes of the Christian Religion, Vol 1*, trans. Ford Lewis Battles, ed. John T. McNeil (Philadelphia: Westminster, 1960), 3.11.10.

26. Holmes, "Penal Substitution," 297.

27. Holmes, "Penal Substitution," 298.

28. For an account of the atonement that draws on such a notion of union with Christ, see Crisp, *Word Enfleshed*, ch. 7.

ticipation in the divine and of some strong doctrine of union with Christ, are familiar enough in Reformed theology, with analogous doctrines to be found in other branches of the Christian tradition as well going back to the patristic period.[29] Such doctrines are not merely of historical interest, but are invoked in contemporary constructive theological discussion of the topic as well.[30]

Nevertheless, providing some plausible metaphysical story according to which Christ-and-the-church may somehow constitute one entity so that God may "transfer" the sin of fallen humanity to Christ as "head" of the body is a tall order; but perhaps not insuperable. Let us sketch out one such scenario. First, let us distinguish substitution, representation, and participation. In substitution, one thing stands in for another, taking the place of the first thing. Thus, if Christ is a substitute for fallen human beings in his act of atonement, then he stands in the place of fallen human beings, substituting for them in some way (as he does in penal substitution—taking upon himself the punishment, or penal consequences, of human sin). In representation, one entity stands in for another as a member of the *same group*.[31] Christ may be our representative provided he is like us in relevant ways—he is a member of the same group (humanity) as those whose interests he represents in atonement. Participation connotes the sharing of something held in common between two parties, as when two people participate together in an act of worship. Both people are included in the expression of the liturgy; they participate together. If one of those people is the minister and

---

29. The literature on this topic is large. A good place to begin in Reformed thought is Julie Canlis, *Calvin's Ladder: A Spiritual Theology of Ascent and Ascension* (Grand Rapids: Eerdmans, 2010). Also of note are J. Todd Billings, *Calvin, Participation, and the Gift: The Activity of Believers in Union with Christ* (Changing Paradigms in Historical and Systematic Theology) (Oxford: Oxford University Press, 2007), and William B. Evans, *Imputation and Impartation: Union with Christ in American Reformed Theology* (Studies in Christian History and Thought) (Milton Keynes, UK: Paternoster, 2007).

30. See Crisp, *Word Enfleshed*; Kathryn Tanner, *Christ the Key* (Cambridge: Cambridge University Press, 2009); Thomas Torrance, *The Mediation of Christ* (Grand Rapids: Eerdmans, 1984), and, amongst New Testament scholars, Michael J. Gorman, *The Death of the Messiah and the Birth of the New Covenant: A (Not So) New Model of the Atonement* (Eugene: Wipf & Stock, 2014); and Grant Macaskill, *Union with Christ in the New Testament* (Oxford: Oxford University Press, 2013). There are other recent "participation" accounts of the atonement in the recent literature, including works by philosophers Tim Bayne and Greg Restall, "A Participatory Model of the Atonement," in Yujin Nagasawa and Eric I. Wielenberg, eds., *New Waves in Philosophy of Religion* (London: Palgrave Macmillan, 2009), 150–66. If Holmes's point is that modern notions of personhood make "union" accounts of atonement difficult to motivate, these recent works should at least demonstrate that such a judgment is not a foregone conclusion.

31. This point is made by Simon Gathercole in *Defending Substitution: An Essay on Atonement in Paul* (Grand Rapids: Baker Academic, 2015), 20.

the other a member of the congregation then the minister may be said to inaugurate and undertake the liturgy as the celebrant, though the member of the congregation also participates in the liturgy enacted by the celebrant. In a similar manner, Christ brings about atonement and (on this way of thinking) fallen human beings may participate in the benefits that act brings about by means of union with Christ secured through the secret interior working of the Holy Spirit. As the New Testament scholar Morna Hooker puts it in commenting on Paul's theology of union with Christ in atonement:

> If Christ shares our death, it is in order that we might share his resurrection life. Paul's understanding of the process [of reconciliation with God via atonement] is therefore one of participation, not of substitution; it is a sharing of experience, not an exchange. Christ is identified with us in order that—in him—we might share in what he is.[32]

Hooker seems to think that this aspect of Paul's theology is aptly summed up by the Irenaean (and Athanasian) adage, "Christ became what we are in order that we might become what he is."[33] Similar sentiments have been expressed in several recent philosophical accounts of the atonement, which draw on New Testament Pauline scholarship like that of Hooker. In an essay that is indebted to the work of Douglas Campbell in particular, philosophers Tim Bayne and Greg Restall argue that Paul's use of the "Second Adam" motif (e.g., Rom 5: 12–19) "is code for Paul's conception of Christ's death as inaugurating a new human nature (Rom 8: 19–22; Col. 1: 15–20). In Paul's eyes there is a deep sense in which we really are new creatures (Gal 2:20). This new identity, grounded in the Christian's participation in the death and resurrection of Christ is symbolized—and perhaps constituted—by the rites of baptism and the Eucharist"[34] which are also participatory acts, in an institution (the church) that is itself said to be the "body of Christ" in Pauline theology.[35]

That said, *how* such participation language should be spelt out metaphysically-speaking, is somewhat less clear in Hooker's work, as well as in Bayne and Restall's essay. Bayne and Restall even admit that their view may be thought to be just a poor gloss on a jumble of biblical metaphors that are

---

32. Morna D. Hooker, *From Adam to Christ: Essays on Paul* (Cambridge: Cambridge University Press, 1990), 26–27.

33. Hooker, *From Adam to Christ*, 26. Compare Athanasius: "He, indeed, assumed humanity that we might become God" (*On the Incarnation* §54).

34. Bayne and Restall, "Participatory Model of the Atonement," 160.

35. Bayne and Restall, "Participatory Model of the Atonement," 160.

not supposed to be taken with metaphysical seriousness.[36] Their response to this worry is to claim that there are two ways in which participation language in the Pauline understanding of atonement has real bite. The first is the moral change involved in becoming united to Christ. To be in Christ is to have a moral center in Christ—to be morally reoriented so that one's moral identity is now located in Christ, and in participation in Christ's life, not in life apart from Christ. "To be in Christ is for one's identity as a moral agent—as a moral self—to be centered on Christ."[37] Second, this involves a change from an "old" state to a "new" one, which "Paul regards . . . as a work in progress."[38] They link this change to moral identity, which is not always determinate. "One and the same person can be caught between two or more moral identities, as they endorse and affirm different sets of relations, values and commitments."[39]

The idea seems to be that the moral change to the individual believer brought about via union with Christ and participation in the benefits of his reconciling work is a real change that takes time, and that remains incomplete in the individual believer this side of the grave. Yet there is a real sense in which this redemptive action involves the believer in being identified with Christ, participation in his benefits, and moral change that this brings about. Christ represents us, becoming one of us as a human being, and identifying with us, in order that we might become what he is. This is not an exchange, but an act of representation. The language of participation expresses the mysterious way in which, by the secret working of the Holy Spirit, the believer is united to Christ and his benefits—benefits that have tangible results in moral transformation, even if this transformation is incomplete in this life.

## ORIGINAL SIN, GUILT, AND ATONEMENT

Having dealt with the question of guilt and its transfer in the case of the atonement, it is worth turning to a closely related issue in systematic theology, namely, original sin. In much of the Reformed tradition, original sin is said to be a moral corruption that affects human beings post-Fall, and that includes the notion of original guilt. This is the idea that I am not merely the bearer of the moral corruption of sin bequeathed to me by the first ancestral pair. I am also said to be guilty of the sin of the first ancestral pair. Both the

---

36. Bayne and Restall, "Participatory Model of the Atonement," 161–62.
37. Bayne and Restall, "Participatory Model of the Atonement," 163.
38. Bayne and Restall, "Participatory Model of the Atonement," 163.
39. Bayne and Restall, "Participatory Model of the Atonement," 163.

primal sin committed by Adam and Eve and the guilt of that sin, are somehow transmitted or imputed to all subsequent human beings. But original guilt is subject to the same sort of worries about the transfer of guilt as we saw obtain in the case of the atonement. That is, if guilt is not a transferable property, then it is not clear how I can be said to be guilty of Adam's sin.

It could be argued that original guilt is a distinct and separable part of the doctrine of original sin.[40] Perhaps human beings do bear the corruption of original sin, but do not also bear original guilt. This is consistent with a strand of early Reformed thought, exemplified by the theology of Huldrych Zwingli. It also reflects the teaching of several important early confessions in the Reformed tradition. So there is some support for this view in the Reformed tradition, even if later Reformed theology tended to include a doctrine of original guilt as well.

Suppose this view is right. Then, the guilt that Smith bears for her sin is not original guilt, as such, but the guilt accruing to the actual sins she performs because she bears the corruption of original sin. The condition of original sin will yield actual sin if a person lives long enough to commit actual sin (and is a moral agent capable of sinning). That is true of Smith, let us say. Nevertheless, this does not mean that Smith has no guilt. It only means that Smith does not bear the guilt of being generated with original sin (i.e., original guilt) *plus* the guilt for her own actual sins. Instead, she merely bears the guilt incurred for her own (actual) sins. This guilt for actual sins committed by Smith still requires atonement, of course, and that is one of the things that Christ's reconciling work seeks to address. Nevertheless, it is important to note that the issue of guilt here is rather different if we construe it in terms of actual guilt for actual sins committed by fallen individuals and not also in term of a doctrine of original guilt.

How then can the actual guilt for actual sins that Smith has committed be dealt with by Christ on this way of thinking? Well, if we take the option of conceiving of the transference of guilt in terms of some strong doctrine of union with Christ, coupled with our scholastic distinction between the culpability aspect of guilt and its punishable aspect, then we have a scenario in which Christ's atonement deals with the punishable aspect of Smith's actual guilt for her actual sin. (It does more than this, of course. For instance, Christ's atonement heals Smith of the corruption of original sin, and it brings her into renewed relationship with God by the power of the

---

40. I have argued for this in Oliver D. Crisp, "On Original Sin," *International Journal of Systematic Theology* 17.3 (2015) 252–66; Oliver D. Crisp, "Retrieving Zwingli's Doctrine of Original Sin," *Journal of Reformed Theology* 10.4 (2016) 1–21; Oliver D. Crisp, "Sin," in Michael Allen and Scott R. Swain, eds., *Christian Dogmatics: Reformed Theology for the Church Catholic* (Grand Rapids: Baker Academic, 2016), 194–215.

Holy Spirit who unites her to Christ, and it begins her on a trajectory "into" the divine life, so to speak, in the process of *theosis*—but we do not need to complicate matters by considering all these additional details here.) But this only makes our original question more pressing. How can Christ's reconciling work deal with the punishable aspect of Smith's guilt when Christ is innocent of Smith's sin and is an agent distinct from Smith? In other words, even if original guilt is removed from our account of original sin there is still a problem concerning the transfer of the punishable aspect of Smith's guilt (that is, the guilt for Smith's actual sin) from Smith to Christ.

At this juncture the defender of penal substitution runs into real difficulties if she wants to continue to maintain that Christ is *punished* in the place of fallen human beings. One way to meet this worry is to deny that Christ is, in fact, punished for fallen human beings, opting instead for the view that Christ suffers the *penal consequences* of human sin. In this connection, the penal consequences of human sin is the harsh treatment that in the case of mere human beings would be punishment, but in the case of Christ is not. Opting for the idea that Christ's atonement involves him suffering the penal consequences of human sin but not punishment for human sin is a weaker version of the doctrine of penal substitution.[41] But it may be a more defensible version of the doctrine as well. For it does mean that Christ can be said to represent fallen human beings without having to incorporate the idea that the punishable aspect of Smith's guilt for her actual sin is transferred to Christ in the act of atonement. Instead, Christ may be said to suffer the penal consequences of human sin, including the penal consequences for the guilt of Smith's actual sin, without thereby being made guilty of Smith's sin, or being treated as if he were guilty of Smith's sin, and so on.

## TAKING STOCK

We are now in a position to take stock. To this end, I will set out a series of numbered statements that synthesize the foregoing reasoning into one constructive account:

1. Original sin renders human beings incapable of being united to Christ without some act of atonement. This original sin comprises a moral corruption that means all human beings born in the state of sin will in due course commit actual sins for which they are guilty. Though fallen

---

41. For a recent discussion of this version of penal substitution, see Christopher Woznicki, "Do We Believe in Consequences? Revisiting the 'Incoherence Objection' to Penal Substitution," forthcoming in *Neue Zeitschrift für Systematische Theologie und Religionsphilosophie* 60.2 (2018).

human beings are not guilty for being born with the moral stain of original sin, they are culpable for the actual sins they commit on the basis of this moral corruption.

2. Guilt for sin normally renders human beings culpable. There is the inalienable aspect of guilt (*reatus culpae*) that is the property of the person who has committed the actual sin. It is not transferrable to another. The person who is guilty of a particular sin remains the one guilty of that particular sin irrespective of punishment. Then there is the punishable aspect of guilt (*reatus poenae*) that may be met by suitable harsh treatment of the sinner. In an act of legal relaxation, it is possible that some other individual suffers the harsh treatment that would have been suffered by the guilty party without such an act of substitution. In that case, the harsh treatment undergone by a penal substitute is not punishment, strictly speaking, because the penal substitute is innocent of the sin committed. Instead, such harsh treatment visited upon a penal substitute is the suffering of the penal consequences that should be visited upon the sin of the guilty party without the interposition of an act of penal substitution on the basis of legal relaxation.

3. Christ is an appropriate candidate for such an act of penal substitution because he is God incarnate. He has a complete and sinless human nature (so that he does not have sin or guilt himself, which would render him incapable of acting as a penal substitute because he would then be in a state of sin requiring salvation himself). And this human nature is united to a divine person such that the act of atonement is suitably equivalent to the sort of harsh treatment that would be visited upon fallen human beings in the absence of atonement.

4. In taking upon himself the penal consequences of human sin, Christ suffers the harsh treatment that would be visited upon fallen humans absent atonement. This is an appropriate substitutionary act because Christ is a suitable representative of fallen humanity (being fully human himself). So Christ can be treated as a representative standing in for fallen human beings.

5. This act of representation may be fictional. That is, it may be such that the act is morally and legally appropriate because God ordains that it is so (a view that finds some support in Edwards's work, for example[42]), treating Christ as a suitable representative and penal substitute. But it may be that God brings about a union between Christ and those he

---

42. See WJE3, IV. III.

comes to reconcile such that Christ's action is predicated on a mystical union between himself and those he represents so that he is in some sense really united to them and really capable of representing their interests. (Compare a situation in which a person may really represent the interests of her spouse because she is united to her spouse in matrimony. There is a legal union between the two, but there is also a real union between the two. This twofold union is the reason why one spouse may represent the other. Were a friend to offer to represent one of the spouses it would not be appropriate precisely because the friend is not legally and really united like the two espoused partners in a marriage union. Such language is familiar to readers of the Pauline corpus in the New Testament.)[43]

6. Christ's atonement is an act of penal substitution on the basis of legal relaxation for the actual sin and guilt accrued by fallen human beings. It is also a means by which fallen human beings are restored to fellowship with God by removing the stain of original sin. This latter action is brought about by the renewing work of the Holy Spirit in regeneration who brings moral order to the corrupt soul in the course of sanctification, and who unites the human soul to Christ.

The Edwardsian Quandary with which we began this essay had to do with how in atoning for human sin "Christ does as it were hereby bring their guilt upon himself, but not in any blameable sense." This, as we saw, is not an issue Edwards himself finally resolves—it is a kind of lacuna in his thinking. I have argued that, strictly speaking, Christ does not bring upon himself the guilt of fallen humanity. Indeed, he cannot do so because he is innocent of sin. Nevertheless, in acting as a representative and a penal substitute he may be said to take upon himself the penal consequences of the sin of fallen human beings. Although this is not a matter of taking on the guilt of fallen human beings, it is still a vicarious act of representation that involves suffering the penal consequences for human sin. So, if Edwards thought

---

43. An aside: as a matter of interest, Edwards thinks that the real union between Christ and his church is the basis of the legal union between them. He writes, "what is real in the union between Christ and his people, is the foundation of what is legal; that is, it is something really in them, and between them, uniting them, that is the ground of the suitableness of their being accounted as one by the Judge" (WJE19, 158). For discussion of this point see, e.g., Brandon Withrow, *Becoming Divine*, 163–68. But the reverse might be the case as is true in a marriage: one partner is legally joined to another whereupon they may consummate their legal union in a real union of bodies. This is an important theological difference, but for our purposes we do not need to make a judgment about which of these is right. For on either way of thinking, Christ represents those with whom he is united legally and really on the basis of which he is able to atone for human sin and reconcile fallen human beings to God

that Christ really does take upon himself human guilt in atonement, then it seems he was mistaken for the reasons we have given here. However, Edwards was a canny theologian who often used phrases like "as it were" in order to guard against the application of too strict a relation between one thing and another. He clearly saw the difference between the inalienable and punishable aspect of human guilt for sin. And he also thought that a real union with Christ is the foundation of the legal union with Christ in atonement. I have argued that the application of a doctrine of legal relaxation in penal substitution is able to deal with the problem of punishment that some versions of the doctrine yield. Applied to the Edwardsian Quandary, we may say this: though Christ did not suffer the punishment for human sin and guilt, he did suffer the penal consequences of that sin and guilt. Whether that representative act is fundamentally legal or real, this milder version of penal substitution does, I think, have promise as a way of addressing the worry that the Edwardsian Quandary raises for defenders of account of atonement that involve an act of representative substitution, such as the doctrine of penal substitution.[44]

---

44. My thanks to Christopher Woznicki and S. Mark Hamilton for very helpful comments on a previous draft of this essay.

# Chapter 7

# Reality?

Jonathan R. Wilson

Alister McGrath's three-volume *A Scientific Theology* is a stunning achievement. *Nature, Reality,* and *Doctrine* require all of McGrath's historical, theological, philosophical, and scientific erudition to provide a congruent and coherent proposal for a scientific theology.[1] In this essay, I will focus on the second volume, *Reality.* For McGrath, the question "What is real?" largely focuses on epistemological questions. In keeping with his scientific theology project, he initially frames his investigation within the natural sciences. His aim in this volume is to develop and defend an account of epistemological realism that will fund a scientific theology.[2]

McGrath develops this epistemological realism in several steps. First, he notes several challenges to epistemological realism; chief among these

---

1. See my reviews of these volumes: *A Scientific Theology, Volume 1: Nature* by Alister E. McGrath, *Journal of the American Academy of Religion* 71.4 (Winter 2003) 955–58; *A Scientific Theology, Volume 2: Reality* by Alister E. McGrath, *Christian Scholar's Review* 33.2 (Winter 2004) 282–85; *A Scientific Theology, Volume 3: Theory* by Alister E. McGrath, *Christian Scholar's Review* 33.3 (Spring 2004) 417–19.

2. McGrath's consideration of reality and epistemological questions is not confined to this volume. However, due to space limitations and the focus of my essay, I will not consider those other sources. Suffice it to say that McGrath is admirably consistent even as he develops his scientific theology in other places. See especially Alister E. McGrath, *The Open Secret: A New Vision for Natural Theology* (Malden, MA: Blackwell, 2008), and *A Fine-Tuned Universe: The Quest for God in Science and Theology* (Louisville: Westminster/John Knox, 2009).

are the new historicism and postliberal theology. Second, he gives an account of realism in natural theology and the natural sciences, while also noting their limitations. This leads him thirdly to the critical realism of Roy Bhaskar as the means for correcting and strengthening previous accounts of epistemological realism. Then, fourthly, he builds upon all of these steps to describe our "encounter with reality" in order to propose "the contours of a scientific theology."[3]

In this essay I will engage with McGrath's argument by means of four thinkers: Richard Rorty, T. F. Torrance, Roy Bhaskar, and McGrath himself. I will show that the epistemological framing of the question, "What is real?" is mistaken, given the practices and convictions that form Christians in the gospel. I will also argue that it is a mistake to frame the work of theology by first giving an account of natural theology and natural sciences because the "object" in question in these three spheres (or practices) is categorically incommensurable. Finally, I will propose that the answer to "What is real?" is found in the practice of discipleship, which at its core is the disciple community gathered in worship.

## IS ANYTHING REAL?

Challenging the "realism" of the natural sciences is the "new historicism." Although the "new historicism" has been around long enough to no longer warrant the "new," it continues to exert significant influence in many fields, including philosophy, literary criticism, and science and theology.[4] The seminal work of Richard Rorty has been absorbed and (arguably) marginalized in philosophy, but his arguments continue to shape some theological projects.

In *A Scientific Theology, Volume 2: Reality*, McGrath takes on Rorty and others, including postliberal theologians, by drawing on the work of Roy Bhaskar.[5] McGrath's argument draws on the epistemology and practices of the sciences as a means of response and as a guide for theological work. In this essay, I will draw on the epistemology and practices of the church in

---

3. Here I have taken apart the title of McGrath's chapter 11 in *Reality*.

4. The mood that I have labelled "the new historicism" also goes by other names. In using "new historicism," I am following William Dean, "The Challenge of the New Historicism," *Journal of Religion*, 66.3 (July 1986) 261–81. There Dean identifies Richard Rorty, Nelson Goodman, Hilary Putnam, Richard Bernstein, and Frank Lentricchia as new historicists (261).

5. Alister E. McGrath, *Scientific Theology*, 2:5–11 for the consideration of Rorty, and 2:209–26 for the work of Bhaskar. I will set aside McGrath's controversy with postliberal theology until the final section of this essay.

response to Rorty and the new historicism, especially as some theologians continue to look to that movement as a guide to their own work. The work of T. F. Torrance will be appropriated critically and appreciatively to accomplish this goal.

The new historicism often carries with it implicit and explicit critiques of theology. Richard Rorty, in particular, represents this aspect to the point of dismissing theology as irrelevant and trivial.[6] This essay seeks to take Rorty's critique seriously, considering its import from Christian theology and how theology may, without betraying itself, take its place as a conversation partner in this intellectual climate. Eventually this essay attempts to enter this conversation by considering the implications of Christian practices, especially worship, for the task of theology.

Although the "new" historicism provides a strong account of antirealism, I do not see the position advanced here as a retreat in the face of Rorty's critique, nor as simply a coping strategy—a reduction of the faith which attempts to make it acceptable to its cultured despisers. Rather, Rorty and his kin enable us to see what, perhaps, has always been there, but has been forgotten or obscured in recent times. Indeed, I will conclude with a challenge to the new historicism from theology.

## THE NEW HISTORICIST CHALLENGE TO THEOLOGY

Since Rorty dismisses theology as passé, and does not mount a direct critique, we will have to read his challenge to theology off his critique of philosophy. This is a proper procedure, I believe, because Rorty clearly indicates that if he thought a critique of theology were necessary it would proceed along the same lines as his critique of philosophy.[7]

In order to present Rorty's critique, I must first identify his distinguishing Philosophy from philosophy. To Rorty "Philosophy" refers to the intellectual tradition stretching from Plato to Nietzsche.[8] This "Philosophy" has a particular set of problems and certain methods for dealing with those problems: it is an academic discipline. In contrast, "philosophy" refers not to a proscribed discipline with a set of problems peculiar to it, but to hard thinking about whatever comes along—literature, history, politics, science,

---

6. Richard Rorty, *Consequences of Pragmatism: Essays, 1972–1980* (Minneapolis: University of Minnesota Press, 1982), xiv, xxii.

7. This is particularly evident in his treatment of Kierkegaard in his essay, "Overcoming the Tradition," in *Consequences of Pragmatism*, 37–59.

8. Rorty, *Consequences of Pragmatism*, 52–53; also xv, 91.

etc. (religion?). The former view sees Philosophy finding a home among the sciences, the latter views it at home among the humanities.[9]

Rorty rejects, or at least trivializes, Philosophy in favor of philosophy on two related but distinct grounds. First, Philosophy's conscious preoccupation with the "Real" (which is true of both realism and idealism) turns out to be a concern for something that is either trivial and innocuous or ineffable.[10] Secondly, Philosophy's quest for metaphysical comfort distracts us from the evident and immediate problems of our times.[11] Thus, this dead-end and even dangerous quest must be replaced by philosophy.

To round out our understanding of Rorty's critique we will consider his proposal regarding philosophy. Rorty's philosophy springs from certain aspects of American pragmatism: (1) it is anti-essentialist;[12] (2) it acknowledges "no epistemological difference between truth about what ought to be and truth about what is, nor any metaphysical difference between facts and values, nor any methodological difference between morality and science;"[13] and (3) "there are no constraints on inquiry save conversational ones."[14] Rorty underscores the radical historicity and contingency of his suggestion by rejecting the "metaphysical turn" in William James's philosophy and the "misleading" Dewey of *Experience and Nature*.[15] As one commentator says, the new historicists "have argued that actual truths are entirely historical creatures, conceived within history, directed at history, and grown in a historical chain, as interpretation refers to interpretation refers to interpretation throughout history."[16]

We may now apply this critique of Philosophy to Theology (transposing Rorty's distinction between philosophy and Philosophy into a distinction between theology and Theology). Traditionally, we must admit, Theology and Philosophy have been companions. Theology, too, has been concerned with the "real." It has been essentialist, has perpetuated epistemological, metaphysical, and methodological differences, and has acknowledged many constraints. In short, the theological tradition has been everything that Philosophy, in Rorty's account, has been.

---

9. Rorty, *Consequences of Pragmatism*, 19–36, 60–71.
10. Rorty, *Consequences of Pragmatism*, 3–18, especially 15.
11. Rorty, *Consequences of Pragmatism*, 166.
12. Rorty, *Consequences of Pragmatism*, 162.
13. Rorty, *Consequences of Pragmatism*, 163.
14. Rorty, *Consequences of Pragmatism*, 165.
15. Rorty, *Consequences of Pragmatism*, 72–89, 214–15.
16. Dean, "Challenge of the New Historicism," 261.

Rorty's account and his rejection of Philosophy may very well be flawed; some have thought so.[17] But the stature of his companions and critics demonstrates the force of his proposal. Our purpose here, then, is not to consider the accuracy of Rorty's account, but rather to enter into the conversation from the theological side.

In fact, it might be helpful to think of this essay as three conversations. We have just completed the first conversation in which Richard Rorty described to a group of theologians his rejection of Philosophy and, thus, of Theology. Now we will excuse Rorty from the room while the theologians discuss among themselves the work of theology in the light of Rorty's critique. Then, in a final conversation, we will engage in a conversation with Rorty in the light of the second conversation.

## TOWARD A DOXOLOGICAL TURN IN THEOLOGY

In this section we turn to theological concerns. That is, given Rorty's claims, what should theologians be doing? Of course, one might argue that the new historicism presents no challenge or problem for theology. This essay suggests, however, that the challenge of the new historicism provokes a clarification of the task of theology in the church. This clarification occurs as worship informs and transforms theology. The case for this assertion will be advanced by explaining the appropriateness and effectiveness of worship in the task of theology.

First, let me define worship as used here. Good reasons exist for taking worship in a very broad sense: the service of God in all of life. But here we will think of worship in a more restricted sense: what most of the gathered Christian community does, in North America, on Sunday morning, and what some do at other times on other days. We do not need, for our purposes here, to establish some normative account of Christian worship. We are simply asking what theology would look like if it were approached from the standpoint of worship.

The impact of worship on theology can be seen at several points in the past: the early Christological debates, the Trinitarian controversy, some aspects of the Reformation. Today, worship is the pressure point for the reopening of some of those debates, as well as for the use of inclusive language. Several theologians have recently provided accounts of the relationship

---

17. See Cornel West's criticisms in his review of Rorty's earlier work, *Philosophy and the Mirror of Nature*, in *Union Seminary Quarterly Review* 37.2 (Fall/Winter, 1981–1982) 179–85, and his chapter in Cornel West, ed., *Post-Analytic Philosophy*, 269–75.

between theology and worship.[18] And the *Blackwell Companion to Christian Ethics* is shaped entirely by worship.[19]

Thomas Torrance is one theologian who engages the natural sciences and for whom worship provides a significant source for method in theology. Although Torrance still talks about realism, it is not a Kantian or critical realism. Thus, Torrance also describes "a transition away from cosmological and epistemological dualisms that have had, as we now realize, a damaging effect on human culture, in science and philosophy, and not least upon religion and theology."[20] Moreover he describes the universe as "utterly contingent even in the kind of intelligibility intrinsic to it."[21] Even more important is Torrance's persistent engagement with the natural sciences. This engagement brings McGrath's work into the same broad stream as Torrance's and is reflected in McGrath's use of Torrance in *Reality*.[22]

Perhaps, then, there might be some help for question, "What is real?," in a theologian with such an outlook. What do we find? In *The Ground and Grammar of Theology*, after a thorough discussion relating developments in contemporary science to the possibility of theology in a unitary outlook, Torrance presents "the Basic Grammar of Theology." Here, I believe, we find considerable help in Torrance's examination of the stratified structure of theology.[23]

The stratification that Torrance describes is very much embedded in his whole account. To remove it from that account here may do his thought

---

18. Among them, Theodore Jennings, *Introduction to Theology*, and Geoffrey Wainwright, *Doxology*.

19. Stanley Hauerwas and Samuel Wells, *The Blackwell Companion to Christian Ethics*, 2nd ed. (Malden, MA: Wiley-Blackwell, 2011).

20. Thomas F. Torrance, *The Ground and Grammar of Theology*, ix. This book offers a concise statement of the position that Torrance also argues in *Theological Science* (London: Oxford University Press, 1969), which is based on the Hewett Lectures of 1959 entitled "The Nature of Theology and Scientific Method."

21. Torrance, *Ground and Grammar of Theology*, 127, cf. 86.

22. McGrath's engagement with Torrance is scattered throughout the text; see especially 81–82 and 234–38. See also Alister E. McGrath, *T. F. Torrance: An Intellectual Biography* (Edinburgh: T. & T. Clark, 1999).

23. Torrance, *Ground and Grammar of Theology*, 151–71; see also McGrath's very different appropriation of Torrance's work, *Reality*, 266–68, where he accepts Torrance's construction and concludes that "[t]he key assumptions and working methods that the empirical sciences bring to the study of nature, seen as creation, are to be brought by a scientific theology to the study of Jesus Christ, seen as God incarnate" (268). The move from nature to creation and the connection between creation and God incarnate in Jesus Christ are significant, important moves. But the overall claim to import the methods of the empirical sciences into the work of theology puts the matter exactly backwards, so I argue in this essay.

a disservice. Furthermore, I will argue that at one crucial point Torrance takes a wrong turn. So the reader is warned that rejecting my account may not be the same as rejecting Torrance's position. Nevertheless, with these caveats in mind, I believe that Torrance's thinking provides a basis for pursuing the issue at hand.

Torrance presents three strata of theology. First, there is "the basic level of experience and worship, in which we encounter God's revealing and reconciling activity in the Gospel." This Torrance calls "the evangelical and doxological level."[24] Secondly, there is the "theological level" in which "we direct our inquiries to God in this field of evangelical and doxological experience."[25] Thirdly, there is "a higher theological and scientific level, in which we penetrate more deeply into the self-communication of God in the saving and revealing activity of Christ and his Spirit. At this level we are explicitly concerned with the epistemological and ontological structure of our knowledge of God."[26]

Torrance's specific concern in this passage is the development of the doctrine of the Trinity; this, along with some of his language, will lead us to suggest some modifications in his account. But first, let us note some characteristics of his sketch. Torrance begins with experience and worship, moves through an economic, ordering level, and only then to ontology (given his later discussion, one could say "metaphysics"). Although he speaks of this last level as a "higher" level, he has recognized, through his study of Chalcedon and Nicaea, that the experience of worship energizes the best theological reflection.[27] Torrance also cautions that "any formulation we make in a movement from the second to the third epistemological level. . .can be done only at the expense of substituting highly attenuated relations for the concrete relations of God's self-revealing and self-giving through Christ and in the Spirit. Hence, we may engage in this movement of thought if we allow the concepts and relations we employ to suppost for real relations, or, more simply, if we steadily hold to the identity of the Ontological Trinity with the Economic Trinity."[28] In the midst of this, Torrance's language remains personal and relational. Ontological language, for him, always seeks "to reproduce in thought and speech the ultimate constitutive relations in God."[29] This maintaining of the personal and relational contributes to his incorporation of a disclosure model of theological inquiry. Ear-

---

24. Torrance, *Ground and Grammar of Theology*, 156.
25. Torrance, *Ground and Grammar of Theology*, 157.
26. Torrance, *Ground and Grammar of Theology*, 158.
27. Torrance, *Ground and Grammar of Theology*, 126–27, 159.
28. Torrance, *Ground and Grammar of Theology*, 168.
29. Torrance, *Ground and Grammar of Theology*, 168.

lier, regarding Christology, Torrance described this model: "Far from being a picturing model then, a disclosure model of Christ is one in which, not the representative, but the referential element is primary, for it functions only as an instrument for the progressive self-revelation of Christ to us."[30] Likewise, when speaking of the Trinity at the third level of theological language, Torrance confesses, "it would be sheer theological sin to think of identifying the Trinitarian structures of our thought and speech of God with the constitutive relations in the Being of the Godhead. All true theological concepts and statements inevitably fall short of the God to whom they refer. . . The Triune God is more to be adored than expressed."[31] Finally, following on this last quote, there is still a strong element of doxology in the third level of theology. For even here "the sheer rationality, as well as the majesty of God's self-revelation. . .summons us to respond. . .in rational thought and speech in ways that are *worthy* of God."[32] That, of course, is worship.

There are points at which we may wish to quibble over Torrance's choice of words, particularly where his vocabulary is not fully integrated with his own account. And he gives us warrant for this by admitting that this new way of thinking conflicts with his "habits of mind."[33] Nevertheless, the characteristics of his thought which we have noted provide us with some building blocks for an understanding of theology which may be very productive. Before turning to that constructive task I want to propose one corrective to Torrance's presentation.

There is an early hint in Torrance's account that the third level of theological language is the most important. It is, after all, the "higher" and "scientific" level. As he pursues parallels between theological and scientific thought, Torrance makes this hint explicit. Scientific thought, at the ontological level, is a grand and glorious achievement where

> we reach the ultimate theoretic structure characterized by logical economy and simplicity (i.e. with a minimum of conceptual relations), through which we grasp reality in its depth as faithfully as we can, and which we use as the unitary basis for simplifying and unifying the whole body of our knowledge in the field in question, in the course of which not a little of it will disappear, as of only a temporary nature and finally irrelevant.[34]

---

30. Torrance, *Ground and Grammar of Theology*, 126.
31. Torrance, *Ground and Grammar of Theology*, 167.
32. Torrance, *Ground and Grammar of Theology*, 167; his emphasis.
33. Torrance, *Ground and Grammar of Theology*, 178.
34. Torrance, *Ground and Grammar of Theology*, 171. Torrance's other work tends to go in the same direction as this quote.

When Torrance develops a theological account grounded in this scientific model, theology takes on all the characteristics of science just described—and becomes Theology. In Torrance's account this Theology bears fruit for physics.[35] But it seems to me that this development is in serious tension with, perhaps in contradiction to, Torrance's earlier presentation. Earlier in his account, the ontological level of theology was dependent on the doxological and evangelical. Is he now suggesting that the ontological is more important? Would he now argue that being a theologian (at this ontological level) is more important than being a worshiper? These are the inferences I read out of his later account.

But, as already indicated, this ontological emphasis is in tension with the earlier account of the strata of theological language. Torrance goes wrong, I think, in turning aside to develop a scientific model which he then applies to theology. He is on surer ground when he concerns himself solely with the strata of theology. Thus, in my judgment, Torrance's later account tends toward a view susceptible to Rorty's critique and to a critique that could be developed from Torrance's earlier account. But perhaps Torrance gives us some pointers toward answering the question, "What is real?"

## FROM KNOWING TO BEING?

After finding considerable help from Torrance, McGrath turns to the "critical realism" of Roy Bhaskar for a significant turn in his quest for Reality. In contradistinction to Torrance's stratified theology, Bhaskar posits stratified *reality*.[36] For Bhaskar and others who follow his lead, this stratification of reality explains the various levels of explanation that may be given for scientific phenomena. But it also means that the method(s) by which one arrives at theories and explanations must be scaled, even determined by the particular stratum that one is dealing with. McGrath adopts this proposal for a scientific theology, arguing that Torrance's three levels of theological reflection correspond to three strata of reality.[37]

When McGrath brings together, Torrance, Bhaskar, and his own arguments and insights, he presents a scientific theology that

1. takes the form of a coherent response to an existing reality;

2. is an *a posteriori* discipline;

---

35. Torrance, *Ground and Grammar of Theology*, 175–77.
36. McGrath, *Reality*, 218–26.
37. McGrath, *Reality*, 234–38.

3. takes account of the unique character of its object;

4. offers an explanation of reality.[38]

At this point, we are ready to subject McGrath's proposal to careful examination and critique.

## REALITY TURNS ON THEOLOGY

The presumption running through McGrath's commitment to a scientific theology, Torrance's ascending scale of theological reflection, and even Bhaskar's stratified reality, is that reality is to be judged, engaged, analyzed, and even dissected—*anthropocentrically*. It may seem strange and counterintuitive to make this assertion, but our examination of each of these thinkers exposes this presumption. McGrath's language sometimes points away from anthropocentrism,[39] but those occasional pointers are overwhelmed by his reliance on the natural sciences and his framing of the problem of reality as an epistemological question. Likewise, Torrance begins well with worship as the fundamental level of theological reflection, but he then develops an ascending scale of theological reflection as engagement with reality in which the ontological is the highest form of engagement. Finally, Bhaskar, while he does not have God in view, begins well with his stratification of reality but this quickly takes an anthropocentric turn.

But if reality is the concern for McGrath and these other thinkers, if "What is real?" is the question that haunts us, then Christian theology must frame our quest not epistemologically but *doxologically*. A lot of McGrath's account comes very close to this insight, this proclamation, but it always turns away just before reaching this doxological end. If the "object" of theology is God, then worship is the central means of participation in and with God. If Reality is the creative-redemptive God: Father, Son, and Holy Spirit, then worship is our participation in the fullness of that reality. If this Reality creates a people for God, then worship joins us in communion with one another.

We may now explore what worship means for theology. In doing so, we engage with two basic convictions. First, setting theology within the practice of worship means that Reality has turned on us. McGrath's account, while coming very close to this, nevertheless, keeps reality at distance. In

---

38. McGrath, *Reality*, 246.

39. For example, "The proper role of theology is to posit that *the creative and redemptive being of God is the most fundamental of all strata of reality*" (*Reality*, 228; italics his).

contrast, if the God of Jesus Christ is Reality, if the incarnation is Reality, if the Spirit's gift of life is Reality, then it is we and *all creation*, which is caught up into reality. We are enraptured by God.[40] Thus, to participate in Reality is to worship; to worship properly is to participate in Reality.

Second, if theology takes place within the practice of worship, it also takes place within the context of other practices of the church.[41] Prophetic passages in the OT and the gospels as well as Paul's didactic passages tell us that "worship" is a practice of the community of God's people, Jesus' disciples, set within and properly congruent with those other practices. Isaiah 1 and Jesus' condemnation of the Pharisees (for example, Matthew 23:23) reveal to us the full Reality of being enraptured by the Father, Son, and Holy Spirit. Worship does not stand alone. Nevertheless, worship is the crux of this Reality where our idolatries and illusions are exposed so that we may participate ever more fully in the Life of God.[42]

Worship, then, places theology within a community. "Community" can be used in a vague, catch-all, cure-all way. To specify the community as a worshipping community gathered by the Spirit, through Jesus Christ, to the glory of the Father, makes the community concrete. Of course Christian worship may be solitary but the authority and norm for solitary, worship derives from communal worship.[43]

Setting theology within the worshipping community makes possible the overcoming of the individualism of the western liberal tradition. So often theology has partaken of this tradition, alienating rather than reconciling. Elevating the role of the community forces upon it its proper task as a community of reconciliation. Theology is understood, then, not as the work of a solitary, heroic thinker, but as the work of the community.

Worship also provides theology with a focal point in the community. Various analyses of religion have been suggested — Newman's three

---

40. I was set on this way of thinking by reading Reinhard Hütter, *Suffering Divine Things: Theology as Church Practice* (Grand Rapids: Eerdmans, 2000).

41. In addition to my exposition, see again Hütter on church practice, as well as Hauerwas and Wells, *Blackwell Companion to Christian Ethics*. This notion of church practices is almost entirely missing from McGrath. He seems caught up in the project of a scientific theology such that there is little place for the church as a countercommunity to the scientific community.

42. Although Torrance has a fundamental place for worship in his account, it is not set within other practices of discipleship. Perhaps we have a hint as to why this is so in McGrath's observation that "Barth addressed some issues on which Torrance has not chosen to focus in depth, such as the foundations and structure of Christian ethics" (McGrath, *T. F. Torrance*, 112n1).

43. See Ninian Smart, *The Concept of Worship* (London: Macmillan, 1972). Smart's book presents a closely argued case supportive of the views advanced here.

aspects and Smart's six dimensions being among the most prominent.[44] The language—"aspect," "dimension"—emphasizes the organic unity of religion (Smart in fact calls religion a "six-dimensional organism"), but what I want to emphasize is that the worship of the community provides these dimensions or aspects with a focal moment. It is in worship that the community brings together the devotional, doctrinal and practical aspects, the dimensions of doctrine, myth, ritual, social institution, ethical teachings, and experience. Here tensions and contradictions between these various elements arise and are identified. These tensions and contradictions are the proper grist for the theological mill. That the concerns of theology most often arise from other contexts serves only to isolate it from the concerns of the community which it supposedly serves.

By placing theology within a worshiping community we also provide theology with an orientation toward practice. As an intellectual activity theology has often elevated the concerns of *theoria* far above the concerns of *praxis*. To place it within a community's worship, however, forces upon theology a strong practical element and a pragmatic concern. Thus worship sites within the predominantly intellectual activity of theology a hedge against the dominance of *theoria*.

Secondly, granting worship a central role re-places metaphysics in the work of theology. Thus, metaphysics and ontology become glosses or commentaries on the first and second levels of theology. This change may be clarified by contrast with the traditional use of metaphysics.

Metaphysics has traditionally been seen as a meta-theological foundation for a theology or a theological system. While it might not be explicitly stated, some metaphysical position was supposed to lay behind any Theology, whether the metaphysics was Absolute Idealism, Personalism, or some other option. If the metaphysics was criticized or discredited so was the Theology.

The re-placing of metaphysics in the work of theology transforms it from something of primary, crucial importance to something of tertiary importance. Metaphysics and ontology become a kind of language which may at times prove helpful in theological discussions, like Nicea and Chalcedon, and perhaps in other discussion, such as Torrance's exchange with Fritjof Capra.[45] But neither metaphysics nor ontology is essential to this account of theology. Further, previous metaphysical accounts in the history of theology are made contingent and mutable. No longer is the language of metaphysics

---

44. See a discussion of these positions in Wainwright, *Doxology*, 8–10, and Stephen Sykes, *The Identity of Christianity* (Minneapolis: Fortress, 1984), 27–34.

45. Torrance, *Ground and Grammar of Theology*, 175–77.

the purest, most accurate account of theology; nor do one's metaphysical commitments exercise a controlling interest in one's theology.[46]

If a full defense of the position suggested here were developed, it might draw on a biblical argument from the importance of doxology in the Christian Scriptures; a historical argument from the dynamics behind the early councils; a theological argument from the very nature of theology; and a philosophical argument similar to Rorty's. Unlike Rorty's argument, however, my suggestion allows metaphysics a limited role. To this difference we will later return.

It is not clear, however, that this re-placing of metaphysics is faithful to the position developed by Torrance or McGrath. In fact, Torrance's use of the third level of theology indicates otherwise. There he discovers the concept of *ousios* in the Nicean discussions. This term, he suggests, was initially shorthand for the doxological and economic levels of theology. He develops it, however, into a firm ontological principle with which to grasp and interpret reality.[47] Likewise, McGrath's casting the question of reality as an epistemological one and his turn to *Theory* in the third volume of his scientific theology indicates a more traditional role for metaphysics. However, this must be qualified by McGrath's insistence that Bhaskar's critical realism prohibits any reductionism—the various strata of reality cannot be reduced to one ontology that is matched by one methodology for all levels.

With Rorty and against what I infer from Torrance's account, I would argue that Torrance is wrong to consider ontology an ultimate or foundational principle. It may very well be useful to the new physics (and here I may stand against Rorty), but what happens when the new physics becomes the old physics? And it may express very well the doxological and economic theology of Nicea, but what would count for its universal validity? So a theology based in the worship of a particular community assigns metaphysics a much restrained and contingent role in its work.

But we must be careful not to give away too much; we must not give away the persistent claims of the worshipping community that it is truly caught up in Reality. So now we will turn to the language of worship as a guide for us in considering this claim within our present concerns.

Our third consideration, then, in granting to worship a central role in theology is the very language of worship. The linguistic turn in philosophy has been matched in theology. has shown this same interest in religious

---

46. My willingness to retain even a restrained metaphysics runs counter to Rorty. On this difference see below, 15–16. See my further development of this re-placement of metaphysics in Jonathan R. Wilson, *Theology as Cultural Critique: The Achievement of Julian Hartt* (Macon, GA: Mercer University Press, 1966), 158–61.

47. Torrance, *Ground and Grammar of Theology*, 160–67.

language generally and more particularly, in the language of worship.[48] The debate is far ranging and offers many distractions from our present concerns. Two specific aspects of the language of worship, however, advance our discussion.

The first aspect of the language of worship which we will find instructive is its self-involving character. Ninian Smart argues this (and much more) very thoroughly in the first section of *The Concept of Worship*. And Anthony Thiselton's nuanced description of performative language in worship makes the same point.[49]

So the self-involving character of Torrance's first level of theology is clearly evident. But is the same true of the second and third levels? I suggest that it is. To reflect on the economy and "ontology" (as qualified above) of doxological and evangelical theology requires self-involvement.

Of course, we may allow varying degrees of understanding by observers: the ideal objective observer stands far away, if such a person exists at all. The empathetic participant-observer of cultural anthropology approaches much closer; the "passing over and coming back" exemplified by John Dunne yields many insights.[50] But only the self-involved could do that which is truly theology. One has not worshipped if one is not self-involved, and one cannot provide a theological ordering or interpretation of worship apart from that self-involvement.

One way the church expresses this conviction is through the language of conversion. Here is how Stephen Sykes describes it:

> Worship, as the surrender of the whole of the self, itself contextualizes the work of the theologian. The discussion of methodological questions…do (*sic*) not take place on a level above that of commitment. The identity of Christianity is not, therefore, reshaped by the activity of theologians acting externally to the principal source of its continuous perpetuation. Their activity, indeed, is set in context by the continuous offering of the community's worship; and as a member of the community the theologian is challenged to see what she or he does as itself an act of self-surrender.[51]

48. Theodore Jennings, *Beyond Theism*, 186–208. Jennings's work is provocative, but to my mind retains too much of the flavor of foundationalism in seeking to establish a metatheological argument. Also see Smart, *Concept of Worship*; and Anthony Thiselton, *Language, Liturgy, and Meaning*. Wainwright, *Doxology*, 467n26 provides a good bibliography.

49. Smart, *Concept of Worship*, 26–27; Thiselton, *Language, Liturgy, and Meaning*.

50. The fullest account of Dunne's method is found in a note appended to *Reasons of the Heart*.

51. Sykes, *Idea of Christianity*, 274–75.

Thus this emphasis on the self-involving character of the language of worship leads back to a restatement of the place of the theologian in the worshipping community.

But this emphasis on self-involvement also advances the discussion by bringing the language of Theology into the cross-hairs of Rorty's critique. That language has traditionally been cast in the garb of objectivity—what the theologian was doing could be done by anyone with similar education and ability. There was supposedly some object and some problems which defined Theology as a discipline. If one took the time and trouble to learn what these were, one could be a Theologian without involving oneself. The account of theological language offered here runs counter to that tradition by emphasizing the self-involvement required of the theologian.[52]

The second aspect of the language of worship which is useful in our present discussion is its reality-depicting nature. Janet Martin Soskice develops this claim in *Metaphor and Religious Language*.[53] After an extensive discussion of metaphor and how metaphors work, she turns to "the cognitive potentialities of metaphor, especially when speaking of God."[54] Her hope is to "support the Christian in his seemingly paradoxical conviction that, despite his utter inability to comprehend God, he is justified in speaking of God and that metaphor is the principal means by which he does so."[55] The crux of her argument is a distinction between referring and defining:

> It is, hence, of the utmost importance to keep in mind the distinction, never remote in the writings of Anselm or of Aquinas, between referring to God and defining Him. This is the fine edge at which negative theology and positive theology meet, for the apophatic insight that we say nothing of God, but only point towards him, is the basis for the tentative and avowedly inadequate stammerings by which we attempt to speak of God and His acts. And, as we have argued, this separation of referring and defining is at the very heart of metaphorical speaking

---

52. Another source for moving theology into a response to its being captured by the reality of the gospel is through the work of James Wm. McClendon Jr. See especially James Wm. McClendon Jr., and James M. Smith, *Convictions: Defusing Religious Relativism*, revised edition (Valley Forge, PA: Trinity, 1994), and the three volumes of his *Collected Works*, eds. Ryan Anderson Newson and Andrew C. Wright (Waco, TX: Baylor University Press, 2016).

53. Janet Martin Soskice, *Metaphor and Religious Language* (Oxford: Clarendon, 1985). The term "reality-depicting" is Soskice's term for her position. While I support Soskice's argument in general, "reality-depicting" seems problematic to me since it retains a form of "picture," the term that Soskice desire to avoid.

54. Soskice, *Metaphor and Religious Language*, x.

55. Soskice, *Metaphor and Religious Language*, x.

and is what makes it not only possible but necessary that in our stammering after a transcendent God we must speak, for the most part, metaphorically or not at all.[56]

Applying Soskice's view to the language of worship, we would say that language does not define or describe God; but it is more than merely performative or descriptive of the dispositions and attitudes of the speaker. The language of worship does, indeed, refer to God.

But we must pursue this one step further. To what do we point when we point to God? In the context of worship do we point to Jesus, through the Scriptures, or do we point to the experience and activity of the worshipping community or individual, which we claim reflects the presence of God? And so, while our conviction is that we have to do with Someone from beyond history, we nevertheless point to that transcendence by pointing to these historical entities, but also by pointing through them to God.[57] So we are chastened by Rorty's critique, but we are not dismayed or silenced.

The theology we have described would take seriously its responsibility to a community characterized by worship. Thus, the questions and issues of theology would be those arising as the many dimensions of the Christian life are brought together in worship. The predominant responsibility of this theology would be to provide the worshipping community with an account of the God in whose life we participate most fully and deeply when we worship. The methods and content of this theology would be disciplined by worship. At the same time, theologians are bound to keep the worship of the community in faithful congruence with the other practices of the disciple community. These practices would be the primary orienting guides for the community's theologians. Metaphysics would only be a concern if it were shown to be useful—and if it was kept in its place. The theologian doing this work would be a member of and worshipping participant in the community. Finally, this theology would walk a fine line between claiming too much and claiming too little for its language of God.

## THEOLOGY TURNS ON ANTI-REALISM

"What is real?" During the course of this essay we have been carrying on two conversations: a primary conversation with Alister McGrath's scientific theology project and its critical realism and a secondary conversation with Richard Rorty's anti-realism. I have argued that McGrath's project is erudite

56. Soskice, *Metaphor and Religious Language*, 140.
57. Cf. Soskice's use of similar language in *Metaphor and Religious Language,* 140.

and insightful with many promising paths and outlooks on Reality. But ultimately it falls short because the question of reality is framed epistemologically rather than doxologically. After a brief introduction, Rorty's work has faded into the background. It is time to bring it to the fore to see how a doxological participation in reality challenges Rorty's anti-realism.

We have sought to take seriously Rorty's implicit critique of Theology in it affinities with Philosophy. But I have suggested that there is theology after Theology. This theology poses three challenges to Rorty and his kin that correspond to the three emphases growing out of our stress on worship.

First, emphasis on the worshipping community challenges Rorty's imprecise notions of community. To Rorty community is "our society, our political tradition, our intellectual heritage."[58] But this is a very weak, thin description of human community, incapable, it seems to me, of replacing "metaphysical comfort." The worshipping community, on the other hand, embodies a strong, thick human community. This community of practice participates in a living tradition marked, formed, and extended in time by the arguments that deepen our participation in the reality of the gospel: arguments over the proper use of Trinitarian language, Eucharistic and Baptismal practices, and much more. The worshipping community is thick with people from many tribes, tongues, and nations, living and dead.

Our emphasis on the worshipping community also contrasts sharply, as a full-orbed community, with Rorty's merely intellectual community. Cornel West Identifies this weakness in Rorty's thought:

> Yet, ironically, his project, though pregnant with rich possibilities, remains polemical and hence barren. It refuses to give birth to the offspring it conceives. Rorty leads philosophy to the complex world of politics and culture, but confines his engagement to transformation in the academy and apologetics for the modern West.[59]

West supplies the needed "political community" in *Prophesy Deliverance*. I am suggesting that he is right, and am identifying "worshiping community" as the concept which will travel from West's black Baptist Marxism into other strands of the Christian community. The point is to be as concrete as possible. The reality of the gospel is made visible by the Spirit in the concrete lives of communities of practice—not in ideas or ideals—though there is a place for ideas in these communities of practice as we will see.

The second emphasis which challenges Rorty is our re-placing metaphysics. Rorty can only suggest two things to do with metaphysics:

---

58. Rorty, *Consequences of Pragmatism*, 166; cf. xxx.
59. West, *Post-Analytic Philosophy*, 268.

(1) trivialize metaphysical notions of reality;[60] (2) suppress metaphysical intuitions. So he urges that "we develop a *new* intellectual tradition."[61] Although I agree with the call for a new intellectual tradition, his suggestions for dealing with metaphysical notions seem to me to be special pleading. Therefore, I suggest that Metaphysics is relative to a historic community and, concomitantly, to a tradition. This allows for the continuation of metaphysics, neither trivializing its notions of reality nor suppressing metaphysical intuitions, while at the same time avoiding the unrevisable, ahistorical, foundational claims traditionally made for metaphysics. This, I believe, is a more useful approach than Rorty's. But I agree with him that history will be the judge of our claims.

Our emphasis on the language of worship brings us into direct conflict with Rorty. Rorty's philosopher longs for a home, perhaps in the humanities, but effectively remains a free-lance consultant, applying philosophical analysis and hard thinking to all sorts of things.[62] Thus, the philosopher is parasitic, at most symbiotic. But this perpetuates the very kind of dichotomy and alienation Rorty wishes to overcome. What Rorty is missing is an account of the philosopher that places him within a community and tradition. The self-involving language of worship does this for the theologian—her work incorporates her into the community or worship; she is part of the organism.

This emphasis on the language of worship also points us toward a way of becoming free from the picture theory of language without falling into the radical skepticism of Rorty. Some theologians have joined Rorty in rejecting the view that language can define and describe reality — or God.[63] But in doing so they join Rorty, not only in dissent, but also in captivity to a picture theory of language. That is, they reject the possibility of defining and describing a transcendent reality; moreover, they may present a coherent alternative. But they are so captive to the picture theory of language that they exhaust their critique on these notions. They do not confront a critical realism which, in Soskice's words, "is not to say that any one account could ever be regarded as ultimately privileged, nor even does it entail 'the realism of its primary entities and their properties as described in any given theory,' and in this sense it is not a metaphysical realism.' On the contrary, it is part of the critical realism we have been discussing that it need not

60. Rorty, *Consequences of Pragmatism*, 15.
61. Rorty, *Consequences of Pragmatism*, xxx.
62. Rorty, *Consequences of Pragmatism*, 227.
63. I am thinking particularly of the contributors of *The Myth of God Incarnate*, both there and in some of their other writings.

hold that the terms of a mature science mirror the world in an unrevisable fashion. Its terms are seen as representing reality without claiming to be representationally privileged."[64] The placing together of the language of worship and Soskice's theory provides a coherent, credible alternative to this denial of any speech about God by moving us beyond a "critical realism" to a participatory realism. This alternative, along with the persistent claim of the Christian community to be able to speak of a transcendent God, is a challenge not yet answered by those who would deny that claim.[65]

## CONCLUSION

"What is real?" The question is to be answered doxologically, by the practice of worship set in proper relation to the other practices of the disciple community. By these practices we participate in the life into which we are enraptured by the Spirit through the work of Christ by the will and purpose of the Father. To these practices rightly caught up in the Real, theology is servant, humbly bowing before God and aiding the people of God in confidently proclaiming in word and deed the gospel of the redemption of creation in, through, and for Christ.

---

64. Soskice, *Metaphor and Religious Language*, 132.

65. There are other issues in which theology would confront the new historicism. Perhaps the most divisive would be the concept of truth—an issue which this essay has essentially ignored. We have, however, laid the groundwork for conversation on this point.

# Chapter 8

# A Christian Vision of the "End" of Cosmos and Life
Towards a Constructive Eschatology for the Contemporary World[1]

VELI-MATTI KÄRKKÄINEN

## INTRODUCTION

The Omnipresence of the Visions of "End" in Society, Religions, and Sciences

AS PROBLEMATIC AND CONTESTED as the role of eschatology, the doctrine of last things, may be in contemporary mainstream Christian theology, the visions of "end" and consummation are not missing either in cultural, scientific, or religious conjectures. Call it "eschatology" or not, the "end" seems to be of high interest everywhere.

1. This essay is based on and directly draws from Veli-Matti Kärkkäinen, *Hope and Community. A Constructive Christian Theology for the Pluralistic World*, vol. 5 (Grand Rapids: Eerdmans, 2017), ch. 1. The publisher has kindly granted the permission to use the materials for this essay.

In the general sense of the term, it can be said that "eschatology" is not limited exclusively to the religious sphere. Just think of the growing concern, at times anxiety, in secular culture over the impending "end"—either of our planet or of human life.[2] Indeed, it seems obvious that "[e]very culture has an eschatology; it is part of our inescapable human attempt to make sense of the world."[3] Although these secular visions are not distinctively religious, they tend to feature structural similarities with religions, as is evident, for example, in the Marxist tripartite outline of the world's history: "A primal state of innocence, followed by a period of social tension, which is, in turn, supplanted by a new era of harmony, the communist society of the future."[4]

Some kind of eschatological outlook can be discerned in many recent predictions of the future of human civilization in sociopolitical thought. How else to think of the (in)famous proposal of Francis Fukuyama at the time of the collapse of Soviet Communism, ominously titled *The End of History and the Last Man*? With a neoconservative confidence in the final victory of free-market capitalism and its version of democracy over other political ideologies, Fukuyama took it as the most developed and final stage of evolution, finally leading into peace as democracy's supremacy is discerned by all.[5] Not surprisingly, this "right-wing" vision of the inevitable progress of history toward freedom was harshly contested by the ideological left. In *Empire*, the neo-Marxist manifesto of Michael Hardt and Antonio Negri, freedom is defeated by the empire, which replaces nation-states and even national conflicts with a new transnational global order, indeed an absolute and violent one. The new combined world rulers are international agencies and organizations from the UN to the World Bank and the alliance of rich nations, along with the "superpower" (USA).[6] The sequel by the same authors, written after 9/11, titled *Multitude: War and Democracy in the Age of Empire* (2004), further diagnoses reasons for the failure of the dream of progress. In sum: whatever one thinks of these various scenarios for the future, it appears that "eschatology" dies hard even in the secular realm.[7]

2. See Ulrich Körtner, *The End of the World: A Theological Interpretation* (Louisville: Westminster John Knox, 1995), 1–22.

3. Neil Gillman, *The Death of Death: Resurrection and Immortality in Jewish Thought* (Woodstock, VT: Jewish Lights, 1997), 21.

4 Gillman, *Death of Death*, 21, attributing the idea to Will Herberg, *Judaism and Modern Man* (New York: Farrar, Straus, and Young, 1951), 230–31.

5. Francis Fukuyama, *The End of History and the Last Man* (New York: Free Press, 1992).

6. Michael Hardt and Antonio Negri, *Empire* (Cambridge, MA: Harvard University Press, 2000).

7. Michael Hardt and Antonio Negri, *Multitude: War and Democracy in the Age of Empire* (New York: Penguin, 2004).

Back to religions. Although the Christian theologian has to be careful when speaking of "eschatology" as a panreligious theme, it is true that all world religions express a concern over mortality, and all of them also envision some form of life after death. Furthermore, religions embrace beliefs not only about the origins but also about the "end" (or at least cycles of beginning and ending) of the whole of the cosmos. As diverse as these beliefs and symbols may be, it is clear that some kind of common denominator exists. That said, insofar as eschatology is "the study of the final end of things, the ultimate resolution of the entire creation," then it applies much more easily to "theistic religions that hold to a doctrine of creation and a linear view of history and that believe that creation will come to a final end than to nontheistic traditions, particularly Buddhism."[8] Recall that

> Buddhist Scriptures regularly refer to 'beginningless saṁsāra,' a cycle of birth and death of the universe (as well as of the individual) for which no starting point can be discerned. Nor is there an end, for Buddhists share with members of other Indian religions (notably the Hindus and the Jains) the idea that the universe passes through an unending series of cycles of manifestation and nonmanifestation.[9]

Add to that the general observation that "[c]ultures that view time as an endless succession of repetitive cycles . . . develop only 'relative eschatologies,' because the concept of an ultimate consummation of history is alien to them."[10] Again, Buddhism is a grand example; this principle applies also to Hinduism. All that said, eschatology persists among religions in one form or another.

Nor are sciences immune to eschatological conjectures. Indeed, the picture painted of the "end" in sciences is not complicated: it leads to eventual decay and annihilation.[11] As is well known, three basic options are available on the basis of Einstein's theory: if an open universe, then the process of expanding eventually leads to "freeze"; if "closed," the expansion will reach the culmination point and eventually "contract" until it results in "fry,"

---

8. Jerry L. Walls, introduction to *Oxford Handbook of Eschatology*, ed. Jerry L. Walls (New York: Oxford University Press, 2009), 4. The now-classic study is Mircea Eliade, *The Myth of the Eternal Return, or Cosmos and History,* trans. W. R. Trask (Princeton: Princeton University Press, 1971).

9. Jan Nattier, "Buddhist Eschatology," in *Oxford Handbook of Eschatology*, ed. Jerry L. Walls (New York: Oxford University Press, 2009), 151.

10. R. J. Zwi Werblowsky, "Eschatology: An Overview," in *Encyclopedia of Religion*, ed. Lindsay Jones, 15 vols., 2nd ed., (Detroit: Macmillan Reference USA, 2005) 2834.

11. For details, see chapter 2 in my *Hope and Community*, with detailed documentation.

the big crunch; and if a "flat" curvature, as in the first scenario, it will expand (forever) and finally reach "freeze."[12] Most all scientists in recent years have become convinced that the open universe is the correct guess and that its expansion is accelerating ever and ever more rapidly.[13]

In light of omnipresence of the visions of the "end" in cultural, religious, and scientific consciousness, the gradual eclipse of eschatology as a stated doctrine in Christian theology is counterintuitive. It calls for some critical assessment.

## THE RISE AND ECLIPSE OF ESCHATOLOGY IN CHRISTIAN TRADITION

In distinctively Christian forms of eschatology, marked shifts have taken place in history. For the earliest followers of Christ, the intense expectation of the imminent return of their Lord was just that — *intense*; the (early) patristic church continued this focus.[14] Apocalyptic enthusiasm flourished in diverse forms. Even such intellectually oriented writers as the apologists of the second century employed urgent eschatological warnings and visions in their defense of the faith before the unbelieving world.[15] Although the eschatological hope waned some after the establishment of Christendom and its amillennialism, in no way did it die out. Indeed, more often than not, particularly in the Middle Ages and all way to the Reformation era, eschatological-apocalyptic imagination fueled spirituality.

By the time of modernity, eschatological "hope" had lost its meaning among the intelligentsia.[16] Kant's focus on religion's effect on morality undoubtedly helped the nineteenth-century liberal Protestants and others to reduce faith to the subjective and moral dimensions. And even the "rediscovery" of eschatology at the turn of the twentieth century in liberal New Testament scholarship (Johannes Weiss, Albert Schweitzer, and others) hardly signaled a robust interest in the *theological* significance of the end times. Not only did these scholars not believe the content of the

---

12. Robert J. Russell, *Time in Eternity: Pannenberg, Physics, and Eschatology in Creative Mutual Interaction* (Notre Dame, IN: Notre Dame University Press, 2012), 56-59 (and the extensive documentation therein).

13. See Russell, *Time in Eternity*, 59-60 (59).

14. A massive resource is Brian E. Daley, *The Hope of the Early Church: A Handbook of Patristic Eschatology*, rev. ed. (Peabody, MA: Hendrickson, 2003).

15. Just consider the influential early second-century writings, the *Apocalypse of Peter* and *Epistle of the Apostles*, which discuss extensively end-time events.

16. See further Wolfhart Pannenberg, *Systematic Theology*, trans. Geoffrey W. Bromiley (Grand Rapids: Eerdmans, 1998), 3:532-45.

New Testament claims regarding eschatology, but they were more keen on apocalypticism and, most ironically, its naive but totally mistaken application by Jesus and the disciples!

Simultaneously, though for different reasons, dismissal — or even an aggressive disavowal — of eschatological hope was funded by other leading philosophical and cultural figures. As is well known, L. Feuerbach took the human desire for life after death as a form of egotism.[17] He completely misunderstood the essence of Christian eschatological hope, as he took it as the denial of true human existence, particularly physicality.[18] The Freudian rejection of (religious) imagination of the afterlife merely as a (neurotic, or at least immature) form of an illusion attracted many followers.[19]

The Freudian interpretation sticks well with the contemporary naturalist worldview. The famed early twentieth-century British atheist philosopher Bertrand Russell opined that "[a]ll the evidence goes to show that what we regard as our mental life is bound up with brain structure and organized bodily energy. Therefore it is rational to suppose that mental life ceases when body ceases."[20] Philosophers such as Anthony Flew continued their persistent critique, targeting any belief in an afterlife and personal survival after death. He found logically and rationally failing the attempts by ancient philosophers, Christians and other believers, as well as those who consider near-death experiences, to establish the possibility of personal survival.[21]

No wonder that in much of post-Enlightenment theology any talk in the line of tradition about the "end" lacked content and became marginalized. The work begun by A. Schweitzer and other liberals was picked up in the latter part of the twentieth century by the (in)famous American Jesus Seminar. The late Marcus J. Borg advocated a totally noneschatological interpretation of Jesus and took the kingdom of God as merely a this-worldly entity.[22]

---

17. Ludwig Feuerbach, *The Essence of Christianity*, trans. George Eliot (New York: Harper and Brothers, 1957), particularly 170-84.

18. For details and sources, see Hans Schwarz, *Eschatology* (Grand Rapids: Eerdmans, 2000), 176-77.

19. Sigmund Freud, *Reflections on War and Death*, trans. A. A. Brill and Alfred B. Kuttner (New York: Moffat, Yard, 1918), 19.

20. Bertrand Russell, *Why I Am Not a Christian, and Other Essays on Religion and Related Subjects* (London: Allen and Unwin, 1957), 45.

21. For an accessible account, see Anthony Flew, "The Logic of Mortality," in *Death and Immortality in the Religions of the World*, ed. Paul Badham and Linda Badham (New York: Paragon, 1987), 171-87.

22 See Marcus J. Borg, *Jesus, A New Vision: Spirit, Culture, and the Life of Discipleship* (San Francisco: Harper & Row, 1987); for criticism, see Ben Witherington III, *Jesus, Paul, and the End of the World* (Downers Grove, IL: InterVarsity, 1992).

Some leading systematic theologians similarly dismissed or radically revised eschatology. There is almost no mention of eschatological themes in Gordon Kaufman's *In Face of Mystery: A Constructive Theology*, with the exception of a few unnuanced, hasty rebuttals of what he considers the traditional view of the judgment of God.[23] The *Cambridge Companion to Postmodern Theology* contains no entry on eschatology — the index does not even list the term! Virtual opposition to traditional eschatology comes from many quarters of women's, particularly feminist, green, and other liberation theologians. Some leading feminist pioneers have charged the (Christian) hope for afterlife (or "personal immortality," as it is sometimes put) to be "a patriarchal concept arising predominantly from the male psyche," while others argue that it necessarily neglects the destiny of the nonhuman creation and the cosmos.[24]

Similarly, consistent opposition to all notions of the consummation of God's kingdom after the book of Revelation has come from various types of postmodern philosophers, particularly on the more deconstructionist side on the old continent. If for Derrida "eschatology" is endless postponement without any arrival of the "Messiah,"[25] for his (former) colleague Gilles Deleuze and those like-minded, eschatology signals the threat of totality and homogenization.[26]

## SOME ATTEMPTS AT REDISCOVERY AND RECONCEIVING OF ESCHATOLOGY

It is not that all twentieth-century theological movements are willing to ignore eschatology. There is also the desire to reconceive it. Some nuanced and creative contemporary alternatives have been put forth to construct a viable eschatological vision. One of the most sophisticated revisions comes from the soil of process theology's deeply panentheistic and in many ways immanentist conception of God: therein God (in his two "dimensions," the

23. See Gordon Kaufman, *In Face of Mystery: A Constructive Theology* (Cambridge, MA: Harvard University Press, 1993), 409.

24. Valerie A. Karras, "Eschatology," in *Cambridge Companion to Feminist Theology*, ed. Susan Frank Parsons (Cambridge: Cambridge University Press, 2002), 243-44 (244).

25. Jacques Derrida, "Hospitality, Justice, and Responsibility: A Dialogue with Jacques Derrida," in *Questioning Ethics: Contemporary Debates in Continental Philosophy*, ed. Richard Kearney and Mark Dooley (London: Routledge, 1999), 70.

26. Gilles Deleuze, with Fanny Deleuze, "Nietzsche and Saint Paul, Lawrence and John of Patmos," in *Essays Critical and Clinical*, ed. Gilles Deleuze, trans. D. W. Smith and M. A. Greco (Minneapolis: University of Minnesota Press, 1997), 36-53.

consequent and primordial)[27] provides the "lure" for the future events but is not the one who guarantees an eschatological solution in any certainty.[28] There is neither an *ex nihilo* beginning (as God emerges with the cosmos) nor a final eschaton. Furthermore, rather than resurrection hope for humanity, there is (in the original Whiteheadian process philosophy) an idea of "objective immortality," that is, some kind of nonpersonal recollection of us in divine memory. Even the post-Whiteheadian attempts by some recent process theologians (Marjorie Hewitt Suchocki and others) to frame that "memory" in terms of "subjective immortality" are a far cry from the personal resurrection of the body of classical Christianity.[29]

Another marked reorientation of eschatology is the feminist theologian Kathryn Tanner's "Eschatology without a Future" proposal, which resonates with the this-worldly approach of much of New Testament scholarship, although Tanner's reasons are theological and scientific. The main reason has to do with the obvious fact that the natural sciences' bleak picture of all life, and the cosmos itself, seems to be heading eventually toward annihilation; hence, these scientific "end-time scenarios conflict with the future-oriented, this-worldly eschatology"[30] of traditional Christianity.

Yet another highly important — as revisionist as it may be — eschatological restatement is the late John Hick's 1976 magnum opus, *Death and Eternal Life*. Mapping a huge domain of ideas among various religious traditions and in the tradition of Christian theology, he sets forth a creative synthesis between some living Asiatic faiths and a Judeo-Christian vision. He also staunchly opposes the prevailing naturalistic rebuttal of religious eschatologies: "In contrast to it," Hick states, "it seems to me that the claim of the religions that this life is part of a much larger existence that transcends our lifespan as animal organisms, whether through the continuation of individual consciousness or through participation in a greater transpersonal life, is very likely to be true." He further argues, "this is not ruled out by established scientific findings or by any agreed philosophical arguments."[31]

27. David Ray Griffin, "Process Eschatology," in *Oxford Handbook of Eschatology*, ed. Jerry L. Walls (New York: Oxford University Press, 2009), 297, with the citation from Alfred North Whitehead, *Process and Reality: An Essay in Cosmology*, ed. David R. Griffin and Donald W. Sherburn, (New York: Free Press, 1978), 527.

28 See John B. Cobb Jr., *Christ in a Pluralistic Age* (Philadelphia: Westminster, 1975), chs. 15–16.

29. See Griffin, "Process Eschatology," 295–307.

30. Kathryn E. Tanner, "Eschatology Without a Future," in *The End of the World and the Ends of God: Science and Theology on Eschatology*, ed. John Polkinghorne and Michael Welker (Harrisburg, PA: Trinity, 2000), 222.

31. John Hick, *Death and Eternal Life: With a New Preface by the Author* (Louisville: Westminster John Knox, 1994), 15.

Although the present essay cannot follow the material proposals of these and related revisionist eschatologies, it acknowledges their desire not to leave behind the theology of the "end." Coming closest to the current proposal's intuitions are the many contemporary proposals that stay closely linked with the best of Christian tradition even when they seek to challenge and revise them. To a brief presentation of those we turn next before outlining our own constructive vision.

## THE RISE OF CONSTRUCTIVE CHRISTIAN ESCHATOLOGIES

In the midst of the dismissal and radical reworking of the doctrine of last things, some leading contemporary theologians have helped rediscover eschatology and even put it at the center of theological conversations. Barth's classic rediscovery of eschatology is routinely mentioned as the clarion call: he claimed that without eschatology, no theology is worth its salt. That he was not able to materially deliver the promise does not make his initial call any less valuable.

The publication of German Reformed theologian J. Moltmann's *Theology of Hope* in the mid-1960s launched a new movement called "theology of hope."[32] For him, eschatology is the "first" chapter of Christian theology. Another German, the Lutheran W. Pannenberg, talks about the "causal priority of the future"[33] and makes the surprising and counterintuitive claim of "the present as an effect of the future, in contrast to the conventional assumption that past and present are the cause of the future."[34] Because of that, for Pannenberg, the concept of anticipation of the future became a leading theme: the historical resurrection of Jesus Christ as a "proleptic" event makes Christian hope confident (albeit not yet fully determined) of the coming eschatological consummation on which ultimately hinges the truth of the Christian message.[35]

Several Americans have joined the turn to the future, including the two Lutherans, Ted Peters, with his concept of "retroactive ontology" materially repeating Pannenberg's futuristic causality,[36] and Robert W. Jenson, to

---

32. Jürgen Moltmann, *Theology of Hope: On the Ground and the Implications of a Christian Eschatology* (London: SCM, 1967).

33. So named by Russell, *Time in Eternity*, 117-19.

34. Wolfhart Pannenberg, *Theology and the Kingdom of God*, trans. Richard John Neuhaus (Philadelphia: Westminster, 1969), 54, cited in Russell, *Time in Eternity*, 118.

35. For a fine synopsis, see Russell, *Time in Eternity*, 119-22.

36. Ted Peters, *Anticipating Omega: Science, Faith, and Our Ultimate Future* (Göttingen: Vandenhoeck & Ruprecht, 2006).

whom God's true "triune identity" can be known in the course of history's unfolding toward consummation, in which process God shows his faithfulness.[37] Yet another American, the Anabaptist Thomas N. Finger, not only makes room for eschatology in his doctrinal presentation but even gives it the primary place by making it the leading theme.[38]

The British Anglican New Testament scholar N. T. Wright has labored for decades not only with issues such as resurrection but also, more recently, with the biblical basis of future hope. That I have had to critique him for a less than satisfactory vision of the "ultimate" consummation does not mean that his proposal would not have made a significant contribution.[39] He has been recently joined by another senior New Testament expert, A. Thiselton.[40]

Some leading science-religion experts, particularly the British physicist-priest John Polkinghorne and the American physicist-theologian Robert J. Russell, in collaboration with systematicians such as the German Michael Welker, have done groundbreaking work in helping rediscover the centrality of eschatology after the advent of modern science. And so forth. This is to say that with all the push toward ignoring eschatology in some theological quarters, in others it is alive and well.

Now, if there is a call and place for a constructive Christian eschatology for the third millennium—in a world plagued with secularism, religious enthusiasm, and the power of sciences—what might that doctrine look like? To our constructive vision we turn next.

## ON THE CONDITIONS OF A COMPREHENSIVE CHRISTIAN ESCHATOLOGY

Although the equivalent of the term "eschatology," the Latin *de novissimis* ("the last things"), was used much earlier, only at the time of Protestant orthodoxy, in the *Loci theologici* (1610–1621) of the Lutheran Johann Gerhard, did the topic receive a full-scale treatment.[41] A few decades later the

---

37. Robert W. Jenson, *The Triune Identity: God According to the Gospel* (Philadelphia: Fortress, 1982).

38. Thomas N. Finger, *Christian Theology: An Eschatological Approach* (Scottdale, PA: Herald, 1985).

39. See my *Hope and Community*, particularly chapter 10.

40. Anthony C. Thiselton, *Life after Death: A New Approach to the Last Things* (Grand Rapids: Eerdmans, 2012).

41. Johann Gerhard, in *Loci theologici* (1610–1621), devotes no fewer than two of nine books to the detailed discussion of eschatological topics (books eight and nine).

term *eschatologia* itself was used in the last volume of another Lutheran scholastic, Abraham Calov's *Systema locorum theologicorum* (1655–1677).

But what is the "end" eschatology speaks of? A notoriously polyvalent term, "end" can mean both completion (that is, coming or bringing to an end)[42] and fulfillment (as in the Greek term *telos*). Both meanings are present in the Christian eschatological expectation.[43] Paul Tillich saw this in his highly nuanced discussion of "the kingdom of God as the end of history," minding the dual nature of the term "end" as completion and fulfillment.[44] Stating that although "[p]ast and present meet in the present, and both are included in the eternal 'now,' . . . they are not swallowed by the present," he added that the future reference is not thereby ignored.[45] This sounds good and correct. Where Tillich goes astray, however, is when he argues that "the fulfillment of history lies in the permanently present end of history," leading to the disappointing thesis that, therefore, ultimately "[t]he eternal is not a future state of things; it is always present."[46] To say that the eternal is not a future state of things is of course true in one sense; eternity is "much more" than a temporal state of things; however, to say that alone (in Tillich's system) means that there is not a future in the sense that traditional eschatology intuits.[47] Tillich's abandonment of the future, final fulfillment of God's kingdom is but an example of the wide trend in the twentieth-century eclipse of future-oriented eschatology.[48]

Contemporary eschatology has to try to strike a radical balance between the New Testament type of enthusiastic hope for the coming of God's righteous rule and the fact that, simply put, "we are no longer a young religion looking forward to the imminent coming of Christ, as the members of the nascent church did in the first centuries."[49] As the German Lutheran theologian Hans Schwarz puts it, "we must guard against two frequent temptations: undue restraint and a travelogue eschatology."[50] It is instructive

---

42. Immanuel Kant famously problematized the idea of "end" in this sense and rightly intuited that the idea of time coming to an end greatly challenges our mental powers. See his "The End of All Things," in *Religion and Rational Theology*, trans. and ed. Allen W. Wood and George di Giovanni (Cambridge: Cambridge University Press, 2001), 221–22.

43. See Pannenberg, *Systematic Theology*, 3:586–87.

44. Paul Tillich, *Systematic Theology*, 3 vols. (Chicago: University Press of Chicago, 1963), 3:394.

45. Tillich, *Systematic Theology*, 3:395–96 (395).

46. Tillich, *Systematic Theology*, 3:396, 400.

47. So also Pannenberg, *Systematic Theology*, 3:587.

48. For details, see Pannenberg, *Systematic Theology*, 3:588–89.

49. Schwarz, *Eschatology*, xii.

50. Schwarz, *Eschatology*, 247.

to note that while on the one hand the Christian Bible has eschatological-apocalyptic sections, and even a whole book devoted to the topic in the New Testament, the church also wisely left out from its canon such wildly speculative and fantasy-oriented pieces of literature as the *Book of Enoch* and the *Apocalypse of Paul*.[51]

Seeking for a middle path between the two extremes, however, should not frustrate or push into the margins the radical nature of eschatological hope: "Eschatological faith has about it an undeniable defiance of common-sense appearances. In the face of suffering, violence, and seemingly hopeless injustice and tragedy, it is bold to believe that these are not the deepest and truest realities."[52] Particularly resurrection

> requires of faith something even more terrible than submission before the violence of being and acceptance of fate, and forbids faith the consolations of tragic wisdom; it places all hope and consolation upon the insane expectation that what is lost will be given back, not as heroic wisdom (death has been robbed of its tragic beauty) but as the gift it always was.[53]

When negotiating a radical middle path towards the dynamic vision of the "end" in its two-fold sense explicated above, three essential aspects should be integrated tightly into any constructive eschatology:

- first, the hope not only for the human future but also for the transformation and renewal of all creatures and the cosmos itself;
- second, hope for both persons and communities, including the whole of humanity; and third,
- hope for both the afterlife and the life-before-afterlife.

## THE DOMAIN AND HORIZON OF A CONSTRUCTIVE ESCHATOLOGY FOR THE PLURALISTIC WORLD

At the very center of Christian hope, Pannenberg rightly reminds us, is "participation in the eternal life of God. . . . [And all] else that is related to

---

51. Schwarz, *Eschatology*, 247.

52. Jerry L. Walls, introduction to *Oxford Handbook of Eschatology*, ed. Jerry L. Walls (New York: Oxford University Press, 2009), 5.

53. David Bentley Hart, *The Beauty of the Infinite: The Aesthetics of Christian Truth* (Grand Rapids: Eerdmans, 2003), 392, as cited in Jerry L. Walls, introduction to *Oxford Handbook of Eschatology*, ed. Jerry L. Walls (New York: Oxford University Press, 2009), 6.

it, including the resurrection of the dead and the last judgment, is a consequence of God's own coming to consummate his rule over his creation." This "future of God's kingdom," the "epitome of Christian hope,"[54] encompasses all of creation, not only humans, nor merely Earth — but the whole vast cosmos. This is the proper framework for eschatology. This widest horizon, however, has not been at the center of Christian eschatology. Indeed, what happened early in Christian theology was that personal eschatology became the focus of the Christian hope. And the concept of the kingdom of God was soon marginalized. Even worse, when employed, its meaning was reduced mainly to hope for the personal resurrection of the body. Communal and cosmic horizons were marginalized. A telling example can be found in the eighth-century (Eastern) doctrinal manual *The Orthodox Faith* by John of Damascus, in which the whole concept of the kingdom is missing and individual resurrection is made the defining theme. The same is true of Western doctrinal presentations from Lombard's *Distinctions* all the way to the Reformation and Protestant Scholasticism. Even classical liberalism's rediscovery of the kingdom of God ended in an immanentist and personalist interpretation.[55]

Only in twentieth-century theology have the centrality and comprehensive nature of eschatology been rediscovered, including not only the personal but also the communal. But even here, a key weakness can still be discerned: the lack of a cosmic orientation. Whereas Barth succeeded in helping rediscover the centrality of eschatology to theology, only in the theologies of Rahner, Moltmann, and Pannenberg, among others, have the implications of what we know of the vastness of the cosmos — in terms of size, "age," and expansion — begun to emerge as integral themes. But even in them the *cosmic* orientation is still by and large in the making.

The development of a viable constructive eschatology for the sake of the religiously pluralistic and secular culture of the globalizing world, as already mentioned above, has to encompass the following spheres: personal and communal hope, human and cosmic destiny, and present and future hope.

## PERSONAL AND COMMUNAL HOPE

A systematically crucial problem for constructive eschatology is negotiating personal and communal hopes (ultimately relating to the whole human race) not only as parallel with each other but also as mutually linked. Only

---

54. Pannenberg, *Systematic Theology*, 3:527.
55. For details and sources, see Pannenberg, *Systematic Theology*, 3:527-30.

such an eschatology that can successfully envision "the perfecting of individual life after death . . . with the consummation of humanity and world in the kingdom of God" will suffice.[56] Unless one is willing to go with the idea of physical death as an immediate entrance to God's eternity (without any "intermediate time"), a way has to be found to link one's own death and bodily resurrection with the rest of humanity. The theological options are these: "*Either* we expect full and real personal salvation at death even though this minimizes what takes place at the end, allowing for it nothing decisive for individual fulfillment and giving it the significance of an addition, since everything decisive has taken place already; *or* we expect the real decision and salvation to come only at the last day, though this is to play down death as access to Christ, as decision, as purifying, and as transformation."[57]

In the Old Testament and Jewish tradition, the communal hope lay in the forefront and the individual emerged only later gradually. Even when the hope for individuals developed, it was not divorced from but rather integrated into the hope for all of humanity. The Christian church adopted this view and faced the task of even expanding it with the inclusion of Gentiles into the hope for a common destiny. In comparison, the pagan hope of the immortality of the soul (as in Plato) has no reference to the whole of humanity, only to the individual. Nor is the contemporary secular hope for the completion of human dreams in an ideal society, as expressed particularly in Marxism, successful in conceiving this utopia as for the whole of humanity; it only deals with those currently living; those who have passed away will totally miss it. The idealist philosopher Gotthold Lessing clearly understood that in his *Education of the Human Race* and was led to the idea of reincarnation for its solution.[58]

The solution of Christian tradition to this dilemma is based on the Trinitarian faith, particularly on pneumatological resources. Similarly to the related locus of soteriology and ecclesiology, it is the Spirit's work to "lift us" up in filial relationship with Jesus Christ, the Savior, but not only as individuals without an integral link with others, but rather as members of the same "body" whose "head" is Christ. This "ecstatic" (as in "standing outside one's self") work of the Spirit is of course already at work in a different manner in creation, linking all creatures to the rest of creation.[59]

---

56. Pannenberg, *Systematic Theology*, 3:546.
57. Pannenberg, *Systematic Theology*, 3:547, emphasis in original.
58. See Pannenberg, *Systematic Theology*, 3:546–50.
59. Pannenberg, *Systematic Theology*, 3:551–52.

## HUMAN AND COSMIC DESTINY

Although he himself failed to carry out the program, Tillich's demand that the basic dilemma of any eschatology — the relationship between the individual and collective hope — should not be "separated from the destiny of the universe"[60] is definitely pointing in the right direction. Christian hope of the eschatological consummation includes the whole of God's creation, "the integration of the real history of human beings with the nature of the earth."[61] This holistic and "earthly" eschatological vision is masterfully expressed by the American Anabaptist theologian Thomas A. Finger: "Since the new creation arrives through God's Spirit, and since it reshapes the physical world, every theological locus is informed by the Spirit's transformation of matter-energy."[62] Christ's resurrection through the life-giving Spirit is already a foretaste of the "transformation of matter-energy" in new creation, "a transformation of the present nature beyond what emergence refers to."[63] The pneumatologically loaded eschatological openness of creation points to the final consummation in which matter and physicality — no more than time — are not so much "deleted" as transformed, made transcendent, so to speak.[64]

## PRESENT AND FUTURE HOPE

The present and future are linked tightly with each other through the presence of the Spirit: "By the Spirit the eschatological future is present already in the hearts of believers. His dynamic is the basis of anticipations of eschatological salvation already in the as yet incomplete history of the world."[65] This is a corrective to merely this-worldly "eschatologies," whether those of classical liberalism and other Enlightenment-driven traditions or contemporary eco-feminist (and some liberationist) views. It is also a defeat of those fundamentalist and other otherworldly eschatological visions that end up being escapist and dismissive of work toward improving the current world. The "already" and "not yet" (of the arrival of the kingdom of God)

---

60. Tillich, *Systematic Theology*, 3:418.

61. Jürgen Moltmann, *God in Creation: A New Theology of Creation and the Spirit of God*, trans. Margaret Kohl (Minneapolis: Fortress, 1993), xi.

62. Finger, *Contemporary Anabaptist Theology*, 563.

63. Robert J. Russell, *Cosmology: From Alpha to Omega: The Creative Mutual Interaction of Theology and Science* (Minneapolis: Fortress, 2008), 37.

64. Russell, *Cosmology*, 37-38.

65. Pannenberg, *Systematic Theology*, 3:552.

and the "continuity" versus "discontinuity" (between new creation and this world) templates hold the present and future in dynamic tension and mutual conditioning. Russell summarizes it succinctly: "Eschatologies such as these view the new creation not as a replacement of the present creation — i.e., not as a second *ex nihilo* — nor as the mere working out of the natural processes of the world. Instead eschatology involves the complete transformation of the world by a radically new act of God beginning at Easter and continuing into the future."[66]

## FINAL REFLECTIONS: ON THE DIFFICULTY AND CHALLENGES OF DOING ESCHATOLOGY

This essay has argued that eschatology, a proper vision of the "end," *telos* of cosmos, life, and humanity is an essential part of a constructive Christian theology for the sake of the pluralistic world in which secularism, religions, and sciences compete and rule. To its own detriment, modern theology abandoned this robust biblically-based vision for an elusive, mainly this-worldly account of Christian hope.

The limited space of the essay has only allowed the sketching of a rough outline of a comprehensive Christian vision of future for all aspects of God's vast, (almost) infinite creation. In keeping with the nature of an *essai*, a sketch rather than an overly schematized system, this one main point has been repeated: a new kind of vision for the doctrine of the "last things" is needed. In addition to its comprehensive nature, it has to deal with a number of complicated and complex issues, including the cosmic, communal, and personal implications of Christ's resurrection; the proper conception of the transition from "here" to "there," that is, how to imagine the continuity-*versus*-discontinuity between the conditions of the current world and the world-to-come particularly in light of the Christian embodied hope of the resurrected body; and so forth.[67]

While doing that intellectually demanding work, the constructive theologian would do well to heed to Moltmann's brilliant, although obvious observation. Any claim for *logos*, "teaching," "doctrine," "principle" about eschaton, events yet-to-happen, is quite a precarious assertion![68] Therefore, he

---

66. Robert J. Russell, "Cosmology and Eschatology," in *Oxford Handbook of Eschatology*, ed. Jerry L. Walls (New York: Oxford University Press, 2009), 567.

67. In my *Community and Hope*, Part 1, such a comprehensive Christian vision has been set forth in a critical-sympathetic dialogue with the whole of Christian tradition, past and present, natural sciences, and four living faith traditions.

68. Moltmann, *Theology of Hope*, 16–17.

recommends, we should instead speak of "the believing hope."[69] That kind of discourse cannot be merely—and not always even primarily—analytic and doctrinal as much as that goal should be kept in mind. To speak of eschatology is to employ also suggestive, metaphorical, and testimonial resources. No wonder much of the New Testament teaching on eschatology, as the late American Baptist theologian James McClendon put it, comes to us in the form of "word pictures," "words that present visual scenes."[70] Hence, McClendon recommends "eschatological picture thinking" as a methodological guide: therein the theologian engages various biblical-theological (and historical) pictures of God's eschatological rule to show that eschatology is both an image of the end and a directive for the church's present: eschatology is concerned "with what lasts and with what comes last."[71] Similarly, the Jewish theologian Neil Gillman says: "All eschatologies are imaginative constructs. They must be imaginative not only because they deal with events that no human has ever beheld, but even more because these events will inaugurate an age which is properly timeless."[72]

Add to those caveats yet another obvious one, namely, the vast size of the observed cosmos as we now know it. Speaking of its "end" and "destiny" — which we must attempt in contrast to earlier anthropocentric (and our-planet-centered) approaches — in light of its immensity should lead us into humble, tentative, and suggestive concepts. Not only that, but there is yet another layer of challenges to any serious talk about eschatology, what the Italian liberationist Vítor Westhelle names as its liminality, in three interrelated senses of the term — ontologically, ethically, and epistemologically:

> Eschatology is a discourse on liminality, on that which is different in an ontological, ethical and also epistemological sense. Ontologically, because it addresses the question of an Other reality, as different as the reality of God is from this world; ethically, because it pertains to a different code for morality, as different as the Sermon on the Mount is from all our ethical systems and moral prescriptions; epistemologically, because eschatology is also about the liminality of our accepted epistemic régimes, i.e.,

---

69. Moltmann, *Theology of Hope*, 19–22.

70. James McClendon, *Doctrine*, vol. 2 of *Systematic Theology* (Nashville: Abingdon, 1994), 75–77, 92; the latter quoted phrase is from Nancey Murphy, "The Resurrection Body and Personal Identity: Possibilities and Limits of Eschatological Knowledge," in *Resurrection: Theological and Scientific Assessments*, ed. T. Peters et al. (Grand Rapids: Eerdmans, 2002), 205.

71 McClendon, *Doctrine*, 44, 75.

72. Gillman, *Death of Death*, 25.

that there are other, often-suppressed "knowledges" beyond the commonly accepted noetic realm of the academy.[73]

These words of caution, however, are not to be taken in terms of stifling the theology of the "end." They are meant to be a constant reminder of the extreme caution the eschatologist should exercise when proposing constructive ideas. Although theologians should be quick to acknowledge the limits of human language and intellectual powers, they should also not capitulate before the bar of reason. Consider what A. McGrath, a leading expert on religion-science dialogue, states: "From a Christian perspective, the horizons defined by the parameters of our human existence merely limit what we can see; they do not define what there is to be seen."[74] Theological imagination, as much as it has to be anchored in the wider human pursuit of truth, should bravely, though also carefully, rush in where angels fear to tread. Modern and contemporary theologians have so much feared the fame of the fool that they also often lacked the rewards of the discovery of the radically new and unanticipated.

---

73. Vitor Westhelle, "Liberation Theology: A Latitudinal Perspective," in *Oxford Handbook of Eschatology*, ed. Jerry L. Walls (New York: Oxford University Press, 2009), 312–13.

74. Alister E. McGrath, *A Brief History of Heaven* (Oxford: Blackwell, 2003), 1–7 (1).

## Chapter 9

# Christology and Creation
## Another Kind of Naturalism

Graham Ward

### SO WHAT IS NATURE IN NATURAL THEOLOGY?

In the concluding chapter of his book *Re-Imagining Nature*, entitled (like the volume's subtitle) "The Promise of a Christian Natural Theology," Alister McGrath writes: "The Christian *imaginarium* breaks this rationalist imprisonment by offering an alternative which captures the imagination and prompts a more critical and radical reassessment of possibilities."[1] By "this rationalist imprisonment" McGrath intends both the instrumentalism of scientism and the rational proof for the existence of God furnished by the design argument championed by certain philosophers of religion. Both these camps struggle to find a positive role for the imagination and thus operate on the bases of highly reductive understandings of reason, belief, and nature.[2] In his own reimagined account of Christian natural theology,

---

1. Alister McGrath, *Re-Imagining Nature: The Promise of a Christian Natural Theology* (Oxford: Wiley Blackwell, 2017), 158.

2. See Graham Ward, *Unbelievable: Why We Believe and Why We Don't* (London: I. B. Tauris, 2016), and Graham Ward, *Unimaginable: What We Imagine and What We Can't* (London: I. B. Tauris, 2018).

McGrath emphasizes that there is no pure "nature" as such as an object out there; there is only the "nature" we see and imagine. And for the Christian that means seeing in through the Christian *imaginarium*.[3]

McGrath goes on to point out how this Christian *theoria* of nature needs to be related far more closely to systematic theology—something he doesn't undertake in his own volume. The Christian *imaginarium* is founded upon the revelation of God in Christ, but as Augustine points out in *De Trinitate*—each person of the Triune Godhead is involved in creation and all the acts of Christ (including the incarnation).[4] This essay, in honor of Alister McGrath's work, undertakes something of that necessary finessing of a Christian natural theology with systematic theology by examining the equivocations and ambiguities of "nature" (and therefore both our understanding of the natural world and being human) with respect to Jesus Christ. It pursues the imaginative and radical possibilities of another kind of natural, intending (like McGrath) to displace "scientism" through exploring a deeper incarnational materialism.

## CONTEMPORARY CONTEXT

The pursuit of alternative possibilities I am proposing is Christian in its conception, as "incarnational" suggests. But it is not just Christian. The Christian *imaginarium* does not exist in a cultural vacuum, and recognition of this is as forceful a driver of faith seeking understanding as any apologetics of evangelical intent. What I am proposing emerges at a time when new approaches to our material conditions as embodied are also on the rise. The rejection of a scientism that treats the world as an object out there that we can catalogue and vivisect finds a number of advocates involved in new interdisciplinary projects. An argument could be made that it is scientific research (which is not the same as "scientism") that has laid the foundation for such projects—particularly quantum physics, molecular biology, the connections in AI between neuroscience and cosmology's string theory, and a host of quasi-mythemes that have entered scientific discourse around dark energy and dark matter, plasticity and emergence. These projects would include: interesting analyses of embodiment along the lines of Bruno Latour's

---

3. For what McGrath understands by "*imaginarium*," see, op.cit., 2–3, 41–68.

4. In Book IV of *De Trinitate*, he makes one and two, the single and the double, a principle of the Trinitarian operations in creation, incarnation, and our enlightenment as participation in the word, *Inluminatio quippe nostra participatio uerbi est* (IV.4). References throughout are to Edmund Hill's translation, *The Trinity* (New York: New City, 1991), here to 154–55. The Latin text used can be found at http://www.thelatinlibrary.com/august.html.

Actor Network Theory in the work of Annemarie Mol;[5] the late entry of Eve Kosofsky Sedgwick's work into affect theory and the investigations into the somatic nature of emotion;[6] the philosophical turn towards neuroscience by Catherine Malabou;[7] and the engagement with evolution by Elizabeth Grosz in her attempt to construct an ontoethics of the "incorporeal."[8] With a reimagining of Stoic philosophy, these projects are developing new materialisms that take full consideration of co-evolution (where the circular and top-down causations of the natural world affect the way we behave, and the way we behave affects, in turn, the structures of the natural world) and new animisms that treat protomentality at the level of the single cell and sentience.

In what follows I wish to reopen a discussion on how we are to understand our own embodiment as participating in the embodiment of Christ; Christ, that is, through whom all things were created. A full-blown exposition cannot be undertaken here, but a start can be made by examining being, in Paul's phrase, *en Christō* and the church's deliberations (across two very different languages) on the embodiment of God as a human being. Elsewhere I have attempted an investigation into the body of Christ as it offers itself to us in the Scriptures.[9] This is the first, primary level in developing a theology of corporeality and embodiment that is christological in its orientation. But the second level composes an examination of the church's reflections upon the body of Christ in what became the cornerstone of Christian orthodoxy: the hypostatic union. I return then to the body of Jesus Christ that the question of "nature" installs. And the obvious place for the inception of such an exploration is the Chalcedon *symbolum* in which the "hypostatic union" is formulated.

## THREE PRELIMINARY NOTES

I say "formulated" because the words "hypostatic union" themselves do not appear in the "definition," though they were Cyril of Jerusalem's ultimate

---

5. *The Body Multiple: Ontology in Medical Practice* (Durham, NC: Duke University Press, 2002).

6. Eve Kosofsky Sedgwick, *Touching Feeling: Affect, Pedagogy, Performativity* (Durham, NC: Duke University Press, 2003).

7. Catherine Malabou, with Adrian Johnston, *Self and Emotional Life: Philosophy, Psychoanalysis, and Neuroscience* (New York: Columbia University Press, 2013).

8. See Elizabeth Grosz, *The Incorporeal: Ontology, Ethics, and the Limits of Materialism* (New York: Columbia University Press, 2017).

9. See Graham Ward, *Cites of God* (London: Routledge, 2001), 97–116.

defense against Nestorianism[10]—of which many non-Chalcedonian Christians in the years following the Council made much. Secondly, because although we often translate the Greek *horos* (a description of what the Council of Chalcedon formulated, debated and acclaimed over Sessions V and VI of the Council) as "definition," as Sarah Coakley has pointed out this word does not mean "definition" in anything like the way we understand the word. Unless, that is, we return to the Latin *finis* from which "definition" is derived: meaning "boundary" and, in the plural, "country" or "territory." These geographical associations will be important in what follows. Coakley translates the Greek *horos* as "horizon," because "horizon" is derived from *horos*. This fits with her overall argument that the Chalcedon *symbolum* should be understood apophatically; a "horizon" being infinitely extendible.[11] But, the geographical associations accumulating, *horos* can also mean "land-mark." It's a Greek masculine word. The same word in the neuter means "mountain-range." When, then, we ask what the Chalcedon *symbolum* is, I venture to propose that it's a signpost, a trig point, that does two things: a) orientates any orthodox understanding of the union of two natures (*phuses*) in Christ, and b) acts as "a common monument erected against heretics"—to cite Leo the Great's *Tome*, a document very much in mind in the deliberations at Chalcedon.

Before I start what is a rather technical exegesis, a further note about "orthodoxy." This was something that was made.[12] It bears a relation to truth, the way God sees and understands things, but it is a human product of inference on the basis of *sacra pagina* or Holy Scriptures. In its production, orthodoxy is governed by soteriology. If we understand Christ is to be X then can that X-Christ save us? So although Chalcedon was very much a working through of various schools of Christological thought—the Antiochene two natures (Apollinarius and a certain extreme Nestorianism) and the Alexandria moves towards monophysitism (Clement)[13]—what each school and

---

10. "The Word, having united to himself in his own hypostasis" ("2nd Letter to Nestorius," in *Patrologia Graeca* lxxvii, 45BC, trans. E. F. Bindley, *Oecumenical Documents of the Faith* [London: Methuen, 1950], 210).

11. Sarah Coakley, "What Does Chalcedon Solve and What Does It Not? Some Reflections on the Status and Meaning of the Chalcedonian 'Definition,'" in *The Incarnation: An International Symposium on the Son of God*, eds. Stephen T. Davis et al. (Oxford: Oxford University Press, 2003), 143–63. As my argument will suggest, *pace* Coakley, I doubt the *symbolum* is an expression of *apophasis*.

12. For a more detailed treatment of this "making," see Rowan Williams, ed., *The Making of Orthodoxy: Essays in Honor of Henry Chadwick* (Cambridge: Cambridge University Press, 1989).

13. On the instability of the conception that there were two monolithic "schools," see Andrew Louth, "Why Did the Syrians Reject the Council?," in *Chalcedon in Context:*

the subsequent resolution at Chalcedon was attempting was soteriological: how can Christ as the God-Man save us. Heresy was only the by-product of this thinking: that if Christ was the impassible and omnipotent God in a human body; that if Christ the Logos as the soul and spirit of the human being one formed nature: neither of these positions could fully redeem the human as such because a *deus ex machina* model of the incarnation denied the full humanity of Christ. And only the full humanity of Christ could save human beings.

Finally, we have to make a distinction in these early forms of Christology between description and explanation. In his seminal essay "Christological Models in Cyril of Alexandria," R. A. Norris takes the distinction between Antiochene (two natures) and Alexandrine (monophysite) traditions to task as being too geographical and inaccurate. He proposes in its place two models—a physical model focused on the notion of "composition" and a logical model focused on a subject-attribute structure.[14] He draws attention to the way the logical model in particular follows from the narrative structure of the kenotic hymn in *Philippians* 2.5ff. and how complexities in understanding the coherence of Cyril's Christology arise because of "groups of expressions and concepts, which are associated with his usage because in different ways, or for different purposes, . . . articulate a particular way of envisaging the Incarnation—or perhaps explaining it."[15] But he does not develop this distinction between "envisaging" and "explaining," or what I am calling the descriptive and the explanatory. And there is a distinction: between representation and diagnosis. Both are ways of talking about Christ. The Pauline hymn and the Johannine Prologue are both descriptive, narrative based accounts; but they are not forms of theological analysis: they show *that* this was the case (the incarnation of God); they are not attempts at showing *how* this was the case. Even Luke's Annunciation scene does not encroach upon *how* the Holy Spirit was the come upon the Virgin Mary such that she would conceive a child and what the divine-human make-up of that child would be. Any account of *how* this was the case has to treat, if it can indeed be treated, what Cyril describes as "an ineffable and inconceivable manner [αφρατῶς τε και απερινοητῶς]."[16] Now accepting that there is a descriptive

---

Church Councils 400–700, eds. Richard Price and Mary Whitby (Liverpool: Liverpool University Press, 2009), 107–16.

14. R. A. Norris, "Christological Models in Cyril of Alexandria," in *Studia Patristica, Papers Presented to the Sixth International Conference on Patristic Studies* (Berlin: Akademie-Verlag, 1975), XIII:255–68.

15. Norris, "Christological Models," XIII:257.

16. "2nd Letter to Nestorius" in *Patrologia Graeca* lxxvii, 23 BC, 45. I am drawing attention to the use of the alpha-privative as a figure of the transcendent here that I will return to later.

element in all diagnosis, nevertheless we can distinguish between different intentions governing the discourse. Preoccupations with the *how* impact upon soteriology—that certainly emerges with the early Christian debates on the "nature" of Christ. This goes back to the point a made above: If we understand Christ is to be X then can that X-Christ save us? Soteriologies *are* explanatory because they are accounts of *how* salvation comes about.

## CHALCEDON

With these three notes we can now turn to the Chalcedon "formulation."

> Following, then, the holy Fathers, we all unanimously teach that our Lord Jesus Christ is to us One and the same Son, the Self-same Perfect in Godhead, the Self-same Perfect in Manhood; truly God and truly Man; the Self-same of a rational soul and body; co-essential with the Father according to the Godhead, the Self-same co-essential with us according to the Manhood; like us in all things, sin apart; before the ages begotten of the Father as to the Godhead, but in the last days, the Self-same, for us and for our salvation (born) of Mary the Virgin *Theotokos* as to the Manhood; One and the Same Christ, Son, Lord, Only-begotten; acknowledged in Two Natures unconfusedly, unchangeably, indivisibly, inseparably; the difference of the Natures being in no way removed because of the Union, but rather the properties of each Nature being preserved, and (both) concurring into One Person and One *Hypostasis*; not as though He were parted or divided into Two Persons, but One and the Self-same Son and Only-begotten God, Word, Lord, Jesus Christ; even as from the beginning the prophets have taught concerning Him, and as the Lord Jesus Christ Himself hath taught us, and as the Symbol of the Fathers hath handed down to us.[17]

What the Council of Chalcedon did was to acknowledge that we human beings would never be able to understand the incarnation as God understands and lived it. That seems rather negative, but as I'll go on to point out it is negative in a positive way. Chalcedon also separated three terms related to an understanding of the incarnation: nature, *hypostasis* and person (προσωπον). These terms were being used before this time, along with ουσια with respect to nature and *hypostasis*, in ways that confused or used them interchangeably. But, and this is significant, for us today and for

---

17. T. Herbert Bindley, ed., trans., *The Oecumenical Documents of the Faith*, 297, available at https://archive.org/stream/MN41552ucmf_1/MN41552ucmf_1_djvu.txt.

all subsequent reflection in the tradition that was to follow, the terms were "placeholders." That is, although they were distinguished from each other none of them were given any content; they were coming to be used and defined theologically throughout the debates. Chalcedon did not define what nature, hypostasis or person was. In fact, it problematized any reductive understanding of them. In that problematization, as I shall show, "nature" becomes emphatically aporetic and multiple. Let's look at the text.

In a pair of balanced clauses, we are told at the beginning that Christ is "perfect in Godhead" [τέλειον τὸν αὐτὸν ἐν θεότητι] and "perfect in humanity" [τέλειον τὸν αὐτὸν ἐν ἀνθρωπότητι]. "Perfect" is right, but τέλειον is also the summit and completion, the final and absolute statement of divinity and humanity. The phrase doesn't tell us what either defined this divinity or this humanity. Though we might have to acknowledge that τέλειος with respect to humanity may carry a sense of "coming to perfection through time" (related to τελος and teleology) and so the word used both of God and human being has to be understood analogically. We'll leave this to one side for further consideration. A second pairing restates this, θεὸν ἀληθῶς καὶ ἄνθρωπον ἀληθῶς, truly God and truly human, adding ἐκ ψυχῆς λογικῆς καὶ σώματος with respect to being human. So human beings are rational souls and physical bodies. There is no sense that the rational soul can be divorced from the physical body, but the nature of being a rational soul already associates human beings with the Godhead, for later we are informed that the Lord Jesus Christ is God the Word [θεὸν λόγον]. The relationship between human rationality [λογικος] and the Logos is not defined, but in a *symbolum* very much concerned with a doctrine of creation and the relationship between creator and creation there is a verbal association, participation, that means human beings are not totally alien from their creator; nor creation alienated by its creator. But a proviso is delivered emphatically: "in all things like unto us, but without sin" [πάντα ὅμοιον ἡμῖν χωρὶς ἁμαρτίας]. The very phrasing is, grammatically, a positive statement abruptly qualified in its conclusion χωρὶς ἁμαρτίας. The qualification is essential if the work of salvation, freedom from and forgiveness of sin, is to be accomplished. But the phrase χωρὶς ἁμαρτίας does render more complex what it is we understand as human nature. For we only understand being human under the condition of sin. God understands our nature better than we do ourselves. Christ's humanity is a more perfect (τέλειος) humanity than ours. Sin must affect both the rationality of our souls and the physicality of our bodies, but we have no grasp as to exactly how—and the Chalcedon *symbolum* doesn't assist us here.

An aporia is evident between the natural order as God understands it as its creator, and human accounts of the natural under the conditions of sin.

And that aporia deepens in what follows. In part, this is because what "sin" is needs to be disclosed to humankind—αμαρτας or αμαρτια or αμαρτημα is error, wrong direction, failure to do, deprivation. It can only be recognized when what is the right, the true, direction, is shown. What is lacking can only be recognized in and through the advent of that which is complete (τέλειος). Human beings cannot know this apart from being shown it, from another, more perfect, perspective. We cannot read our humanity into Jesus Christ's humanity, then, because ours is an errant humanity. We can only understand Jesus Christ's humanity through those writings that attest to it and in which *that* nature reveals itself as "without sin." As Cyril infers, in Christ there is a complete human nature κατ' ιδιον λογον. This isn't a different human nature to ours. We cannot translate κατ' ιδιον λογον as "according to his distinctive species or kind." To do so would effect whether Christ could save our human condition. But κατ' ιδιον λογον means Christ's human nature is not identical to ours, because ours is sinful.

Leo the Great's *Letter XXVII* to Flavian, known as "The Tome," had an influential bearing upon the debates at Chalcedon. In this letter, Leo gives his own version of Cyril's Christ's nature as κατ' ιδιον λογον. Writing in Latin (and that will be important), Leo speaks of a wondrous and unique nature that "is not to be understood in such wise that the properties of His kind were removed through the novelty of His creation [*non. . .proprietas remota sic genens*].[18] So "Without detriment therefore to the properties of either nature or substance [*proprietate utrisque naturae at substantiae*], Christ "partook of man's weaknesses [but He did not] therefore share our faults."[19]

The Latin introduces a new ambivalence; and, again, it is the ambivalences our theologies of Christ's "nature" inherited. Leo's model of nature is Aristotelian: the language of substance, genus and properties.[20] *Substantia* (that is a synonym for *natura*), bears all the semantic possibilities of πυσις: nature, every living thing (*omnem*) or substance. In Aristotle, substance is "this thing" with its individual and essential properties, and the Greek

18. Leo the Great, *Letter XXVIII* (hereafter, *Tome*) in *Nicene and Post-Nicene Fathers*, Volume 12: *Leo the Great*, 14 vols., trans. Charles Lett Feltoe, eds. Philip Schaff and Henry Wace (Peabody, MA: Hendrickson, 1994), 39. Latin text T. H. Bindley available at https://archive.org/stream/MN41552ucmf_1/MN41552ucmf_1_djvu.txt.

19. Leo the Great, *Tome*, 12:40.

20. The language of properties, developed by the Stoics, finds its way (via Leo?) into the Chalcedon *symbolum*, but what these properties are is not defined. The Stoics would not admit of "divine" properties, since "properties" belonged to bodies—such as shape, three-dimensionality, the ability to act and be acted upon, etc. See Jean-Baptiste Gourinat, "The Stoics on Matter and Prime Matter: 'Corporealism' and the Imprint of Plato's *Timaeus*," in Richardo Salles, *God and the Cosmos in Stoicism* (Oxford: Oxford University Press, 2009), 46–70.

used is ουσια. On this basis the Stoics developed their own understanding of "nature," with influential implications for early Christian thinking. Hence in early Christological debates in the Greek speaking world ουσια, πυσις and *hupostasis* were frequently conflated, as Basil of Caesarea attests in his letter to Gregory of Nyssa with respect to his own conflation of ουσια and *hypostasis*.[21] But what Leo intends by *substantia* is what Cyril understood by *hypostasis*, not πυσις. And this seems to have had an impact of their different models of Christology. To return to Norris's two models: Leo's physical model is "compositional"—there are distinct divine properties and distinct human properties and in Christ they came together in one person. Cyril's model is more a logical model of subject-attribute, although he also plays with the compositional model.[22] As Mark Edwards has recently pointed out, Cyril was concerned about the "compositional model," particularly when it came to how Christ as a human being suffered and yet by nature remained impassible.[23] In his "Tome" Leo had written how each "form does what is proper to it with the co-operation of the other [*agit enim utraque form cum alterius communion quod propriun est*]; that is the word performing what appertains to the word, and the flesh carrying out what appertains to the flesh."[24] Again the notion owes something to Aristotle, who, like Plato, understood "that in incorporeal entities there is nothing but form."[25] But this can invite awkward and textually unsupported distinctions in the life of Christ recorded in the Gospels—in walking on water he is divine, in weeping over Lazarus he is human, for example. Much weight falls on the ambiguous "with the co-operation [*communione*] of the other." As Edwards explains: "Cyril's scruples are no doubt reinforced by his awareness that there is no

21. *Letter XXXVIII* in *Basil: Letters and Selected Works*, 14 vols., trans. Rev. Blomfield Jackson, in the *Nicene and Post-Nicene Fathers*, vol. 8, eds. Philip Schaff and Henry Wace (Peabody, MA: Hendrickson, 1994), 137–41.

22. In *De Recta Fide ad Theodosium Imperatorem* (ed. Philip Edward Pusey, Cyrilli Archiepiscopi Alexandrini, 10 vols. [Oxford: James Parker & Co, 1877], VII, 50), Cyril accentuates the intellectual in terms of a "concurrence [*sundpomēn*] into union of unequal [*anisōn*] and unlike [*anomoiōn*] natures." Of course, the phrase "two natures" is not original to the Acts of Chalcedon. The formula occurs in documents that were incorporated into the Chalcedon deliberations. It is found in the *Formulary of Reunion* (431) drawn up by the Antiochene School to help pave the way for peace with Cyril of Alexandria. When that peace was secured and John of Antioch preached twice (in 432–33) in Alexandria at Cyril's bequest, he used the phrase on each occasion, speaking of the "concurrence of two perfect natures." See R. V. Sellers, *The Council of Chalcedon: A Historical and Doctrinal Survey* (London: SPCK, 1953), 17–18.

23. Mark Edwards, "One Nature of the Word Enfleshed," *Harvard Theological Review*, 108.2 (2015) 289–306 (300).

24. Leo the Great, *Tome*, 12:40.

25. Edwards, "One Nature of the Word," 302.

allusion to human nature anywhere in the Scriptures; on the other hand, the one reference in the Scriptures to "divine nature" [*theia phusis*], at 2 Pet.1:4, is quoted by Cyril more frequently than any other theologian before him. This is not to deny that human beings have a nature, but only that what is nature *in us* can be allotted as a nature *to the Word*."[26] And, again, we have to recall that "nature *in us*," should it be explicated, is a fallen, sinful nature. Leo's model is confident it can identify the "properties" of human nature, irrespective of its fallenness ("our faults"); the Chalcedon *symbolum* does not share this confidence and neither does Cyril.

The aporetics of nature as πυσις proliferate. The word is employed in four different ways by Cyril. We have examined divine "nature," human "nature" as Christ exemplifies it and human "nature" as we sinful creatures might understand it. But fourth use becomes apparent with respect to Christ's union; since that "union," while being an *exemplum* of what human being should be, is a unique condition pertaining to Christ alone: we are not divine, Christ is. Even in our perfected and redeemed state human "nature" is not identical with the "nature" of hypostatic union. In Cyril's *Letter to Eulogius*, the presbyter at Constantinople who agreed with Nestorius, he writes that "for the nature of the Word is one nature and the nature of the flesh another."[27] Then, in distinction he adds, "we. . . when asserting their union. . . confess one incarnate *phusis* of God."[28] In the third anathema appended to his *Third Letter to Nestorius*, he speaks of this as a "natural union" [*enōsis phusikē*].[29] His successor Dioscuros, at Chalcedon, reaffirmed Cyril in a way which shows the paradoxical character of talk about "two natures" and the aporetics of *phusis*, while pointing out why the monophysite "confusion" of natures was such a threat: "after the Incarnation there are not two natures, but one incarnate nature of the divine Logos:"[30] the nature of the

---

26. Edwards, "One Nature of the Word," 301.

27. Cyril of Alexandria, *Letters 1–50*, Fathers of the Church Patristic Series, trans. John I. McEnerney, (Washington, DC: The Catholic University of America Press, 1987), 186.

28. Cyril of Alexandria, *Letters 1–50*, 186.

29. This phrase caused so much confusion such later that Cyril had to redefine it as "true union"—a phrase he had used in his *Second Letter to Nestorius*. For a detailed discussion of the phrase, see *The Dyophysite Christology of Cyril of Alexandria*, Hans von Loon (Leiden: Brill, 2009), 519–20. Loon concludes: "The logic of a 'natural union' is not that it results in 'one nature'" (520).

30. Cited in Sellers, *Council of Chalcedon*, 33. The importance of the preposition *ek* in ἐκ δύο φύσεων cannot be overstated here. The *ek* delivers a third understanding of *phusis* perhaps in a way that the other Chalcedon phrase ἐν δύο φύσεσιν does not, since *en*, understood as a dative locative, suggests "a place of containment" and Jesus Christ as a vessel for the two natures—though it might be argued that this *en* should be related

Logos, the nature of human embodiment and then the "incarnate nature" in which there is union. The "union" is not a *tertium quid*, though—that would be a "confusion" that would compromise divine simplicity.

## SOMETHING BEYOND PARADOX

So when, in the Chalcedon *symbolum* we are told "one and the same Christ" has "two natures" [ἕνα καὶ τὸν αὐτὸν Χριστόν. . . ἐκ δύο φύσεων [ἐν δύο φύσεσιν],[31] then clearly here we are dealing with more than just a paradox. "Two natures" has the structure, but not the logic of paradox. And this is important for assessing any "apophatic" intentions of the text. There are varieties of paradox, but let's take three: Jesus's statement that to lose one's life is to gain it (Mark 9.33–35); Paul's statement divine folly is wiser than human wisdom, and divine weakness stronger than human strength (I Cor.20–1, 25); and Pseudo-Dionysius's darkness beyond light that became the English poet's, Henry Vaughan's, "dazzling darkness." The first two statements have not only a structural play of contradictions, but also a logic that reveals that play; a logic that avoids contradiction. In the first, self-denial and a total trusting in God leads to true life, a life of grace. In the second, there is an articulation that God's thoughts are higher than our human thoughts and so what seems wise or strong to us, can be folly and weakness in God's eyes. The third phrase is an oxymoron, a configuration of two antithetical images that invokes an *excessus mentis* in which there is a suspension of self-consciousness. The paradoxical structure does not have a logic—that would associate it too closely with rational consciousness—but rather it is itself indexical. It becomes a deictic that points away from itself to intimations of what is hidden in God (μιστηριον). The alpha privative was often employed in Greek with respect to the Godhead as an index of transcendence. The *symbolum* does employ alpha privatives, as we will see, but not directly about the Godhead.

---

to the Pauline *en Christō* in which Christ is recognized as a domain in which all things subsist. It is significant that Schwartz has demonstrated that out of the vast majority of Greek codices, only two have *ek,* and as he concludes that "*in* two natures" is standard and original. This also concurs with the Latin translation: *in duabus naturis*. For debates over the first draft of the "Definition" concerning *ek* as it stands in the minutes of the V Session, see Richard Price, "Truth, Omission and Fiction in the Acts," in *Chalcedon in Context: Church Councils 400–700*, eds. Richard Price and Mary Whitby (Liverpool: Liverpool University Press, 2009), 97.

31. In the English translation provided above, the second "in" two natures is preferred; "from" two natures opens an ambivalence—the difference in wording has been put down to an earlier draft of the *symbolum*, but there is textual evidence of both phrases in the dissemination of the *symbolum*.

With "two natures" any paradoxical logic is made more difficult to discover given the semantic ambivalences surrounding "nature," and the phrase is a technical formulation, not a kataphatic index of apophatic hiddenness (though, it does, suggest that divine nature and human nature are not of the same order because of a fundamental distinction between divinity and humanity). I want to call this phrase "scandalous," rather than paradoxical—σκανδαλον being a "stumbling-block."

Four uses of "nature" begin to emerge as we have seen with Cyril. While the properties of these "natures" remained obscure and undefined, particularly the divine and incarnate natures, the difference, and their union in Jesus Christ, was insisted upon and the cause of continuing fracas between the Alexandrine insistence on Christ's 'one nature' and the Antiochene view of the concurrence and lack of confusion between two; although the Latin employed for "nature" in Cyril is *substantia* that, in Greek, is *hupostasis* rather than *phusis*, as I have said. It is possibly not insignificant that, as a property of Christ's person χωρὶς ἁμαρτίας or "without sin," does not use any alpha privative. That is, using a positive term and then negating it: "sin" is itself a negative term and, as a property of humankind it is negated to constitute a positive property in Christ.

Whatever the ambivalence of "nature" this is not a condition that can be understood in the way we have come to understand the word in post Enlightenment and post the scientific enquiries into the orders and operations if the natural world. The Classical and New Testament scholar, Dale Martin, observes: "Almost without exception the Greek term *phusis* (nature) refers to 'all that is.'"[32] Human nature, under Martin's prescription, would therefore be "all that is determinative of being human" and Divine nature, would be "all that is determinative of being God." This is certainly more general and abstract than Aristotle, who defines πυσις as things having in themselves "a source of change and staying unchanged [αρχην κινησεως στασηως]"[33]—that is, self-subsistence, movement and rest. What contemporary biologists call "autopoesis"—one of the key conditions for determining whether something has "life." The divine even as the "unmoved mover" for Aristotle, could not have a "nature" for he relates "nature" to processes.[34] The way *phusis* is used in Greek prior to Aristotle suggests it is related to birth, generation, growth, outward appearance, constitution, temperament, and even instinct. It is the way things are, the way they are observed to

---

32. Dale Martin, *Inventing Superstition* (Cambridge, MA: Harvard University, Press, 2004), 14

33. *Phys.* II, 1,192b,13, trans. William Charlton (Oxford: Oxford University Press, 1992), 23.

34. *Phys.* II.1.193b.12

behave in their environments. It is that which is subject to change and mutability (things grown and die), subject to confusion (of the rational soul and the physiology of flesh), subject to separation (a plant is not an animal), and constituted of different, divided, elements (bi- or tripartite in the case of human beings depending on whether spirit or breath is distinct from soul). In other words, nature is constrained by the contingencies of materiality and causality.

The use of *phusis*, then, with respect to God and 'incarnate nature' in the Chalcedon *symbolum* is problematic when understood in terms of a human nature that is itself ambivalent because there is human nature in its perfection and human nature under the condition of sin. At this point I only want to emphasize is how plastic the use of "nature" was. Of course from Hippocrates to Celsus and on to Galen orders of nature were being defined; hierarchies in which men came above women, for example. Physiological systems and operations were being investigated and theories (of sexual generation, for example) proposed. But there was no nature as distinct from the supernatural. There is no *huperphusis* in Greek; the physical and the metaphysical interrelated hierarchically. Similarly, there was no human embodiment distinct from a soul.

The point here is twofold: first, "two natures" is a decidedly odd phrase because how can there be two forms of "all there is" when we do not know how "nature" might be applied to God or the human being under the condition of sin? Secondly, "nature" with respect to the human condition in Christ, in itself and under sin is far more fluid, porous, and unbounded than anything we later determine to be the nature of being human. Later, that is, when it is shorn of the complexities of the impact of both divine operations and innate spiritual interactions with human physiology. Any understanding of "nature" implodes in and through the juxtaposition.

Nevertheless, Jesus Christ is one person [*prosopon*] and one subsistence [*hupostasis*] in which the natures are united. As I said, although distinctions are made in the Chalcedon *symbolum* as if they were technical terms, the distinctions are not given any content. Although, a writer like Theophrastus can create different characters or personality types, there was nothing at the time sufficiently developed psychologically that approximated to our understanding of "person." And, besides, to appreciate that Jesus Christ was socially outward-going or an introvert, energetic, imaginative, or warm-hearted, was not to the point; could he heal, reconcile, redeem, forgive—save us—that was the point. What kind of God-Man was necessary in order that this salvation was possible? *Prosopon* indicated Jesus Christ was a distinct, historical figure. Nothing more. Mary, his mother, Mary the wife of Cleophas and Mary Magdalene were all *prosopa* on this score. It was much later that the theology of Persons with respect to Trinitarian relations began to emerge. Each of these gospel characters were *hypostases* as well, since this only indicated they had an actual existence; nature with qualities (as Aristotle understood it). In terms of human nature *hypostasis* meant we are psycho-physical entities—though the word was beginning to take on the ontological weight of "essence" (even though Aristotle distinguished between essence and *hypostasis*). This would indicate that Jesus Christ was a distinctive subsistent being because he was both God and human; though, again, the Chalcedon *symbolum* did not go into details.

In fact, exactly the opposite: for the properties "related to" this hypostatic union are presented in a series of four adverbs: *inconfusedly, unchangeably, indivisibly, inseparably* [ἀσυγχύτως, ἀτρέπτως, ἀδιαιρέτως, ἀχωρίστως]. It is important they are adverbs. They are not adjectives outlining the properties of a proper noun, the hypostatic union. Hence only tangentially, if at all, do they describe the nature of any person.[35] As I said above, the contingencies of nature (in which human nature participates) means that "all that is" (*phusis*) is subject to mixture, change, division and separation. These adverbs very much in use with respect to the Christological struggles that had led to and followed from the Council of Nicaea, and in debates with Jews.[36] In particular, ἀσυγχύτως is leveled at an Alexandrian rhetoric that suggested "mixture" and ἀδιαιρέτως and ἀχωρίστως is leveled at Antiochene rhetoric suggestive of "division" and "separation."[37] The apophatic appeal to these four adverbs, or at least three of them, drew attention to the heretical misconceptions on both sides that could arise from the employment of these words minus the privative alpha. To this extent, and only to this extent, did the Chalcedon *symbolum* offer a warning of what lay outside the grammar of orthodox faith, a safeguard against error, and a theological rule binding upon theology as a "craft-bound" discourse. The four adverbs then disavow each of these 'natural' constraints and do so by giving the Greek for mixture, change, division and separation and

---

35. Though, by inference, the adverbs do attest to, or confess, certain apophatic properties of the Godhead: immortality, impassibility, and simplicity. These are negated human properties, emphasizing the difference between divine and human natures, and employed as descriptors of God in the Bible.

36. As Sellers notes, Antiochene theology was developed in a context in which "there were more Jews in and around Antioch than in any other city of the Dispersion" (*Council of Chalcedon*, 158) and the debt they owed to the Hebrew Bible.

37. The concern with "confusion" has a further aspect within the Antiochene tradition where, following their emphasis upon the unity of the Godhead, or *ousia*, the three *hypostases* of Father, Son, and Holy Spirit were also distinct and "without confusion." The nature of intra-Trinitarian relations governs the concern with the soteriological and economic relations between the uncreated Godhead and creation.

then negating each of them with an alpha suffix. This is where discussions about the apophatic begin for Coakley. The apophatic is not ignorance. It is not the denial or absence of knowledge. It is a recognition of knowing in unknowing; and a recognition of some relation, undefined, between the knowing and the unknowing. The kind of relation, implicit but not spelled out, in the association of λογικος and λόγος; that is to say, between creator and creation. There are hierarchies of *phusis* that are permeable to and permeated with divinity; and there are realms in which what is divine is ontologically distinct. The four negative adverbs mark this distinction. But as I said, they are not adjectives descriptive of any divine *phusis*, of Jesus Christ as "the one and the same"—though the four adverbs do, syntactically, echo the four titles of "the one and the same" (Christ, Lord, Son of God and Only-begotten). They are adverbs of an action which is ours, translated, "to be acknowledged" though in Greek the verbal is a passive participle—γνωριζόμενον—of γνωριζω (to know, perceive or declare). I suggest the better translation here, since the document is an ecclesial document that reflects upon the Nicene Creed, is "to be declared" as in a "confession of the faith" or a "proclamation of the gospel."[38] In this way the phrase reiterates the opening of the *symbolum* where the bishops, following the Holy Fathers, ὁμολογεῖν υἱὸν τὸν κύριον ἡμῶν Ἰησοῦν Χριστὸν—where ὁμολογεῖν is the Greek "to confess." The *symbolum* is one, complex sentence governed by a double main verb "ὁμολογεῖν. . . ἐκδιδάσκομεν" that closely associates

---

38. The first draft of the Chalcedon *symbolum* opens with "We confess [ὁμολογοῦμεν]," this was changed in the second draft. The difficulty in translating this verb is evident in the use of the phrase "ἐν δύο φύσεσι γνωριζόμενος" in a comment of Basil of Seleucia on Cyril's Letters. The phrase may indeed lie behind the redrafting of the Chalcedon *symbolum*. It is translated, our one Lord Jesus Christ "made known to us in two natures." But translated in this way Basil would have been a fully paid-up member of the so-named Nestorians. We have no direct knowledge of Christ *as* two natures. As Cyril points out (in *Apol. adv. Theod.*, ed. Philip Edward Pusey, Cyrilli Archiepiscopi Alexandrini, 10 vols. [Oxford: James Parker & Co, 1875],VI, 418) we can only speak of "two" in contemplation [θεωρια]. We have knowledge only of one *hupostasis*, the union in one nature following the incarnation to which Scripture testifies that this *prosopon* is both fully God and fully human. We "confess" that which the Scriptures attest; that is our faith, and the faith of Nicaea. Frequently in the West, when referring to the "recognition" [*agnosco*] of the two natures, reference to the Scriptures is made while also insisting that Christ did not act as God in one scene and as a human being in another, since that would be to "divide" Christ. If indeed Basil's phrase "ἐν δύο φύσεσι γνωριζόμενος" did have some impact on the Chalcedon *symbolum* (see Sellers, *Council of Chalcedon*, 122f and 215f), it is significant that the passive participle is qualified there by the four apophatic adverbs. It is also important that Basil's phrase does not refer to *our* subjective perception and recognition of the natures, but to the objective proclamation "made known" to us in the Scriptures attesting to Jesus Christ. Both the LXX and the New Testament (24 x) use γνωριζω to mean "reveal" or "make known."

teaching with confessing. The auxillary verb—to γνωρίζω—indicates a certain understanding is available in what the church "teaches to confess." Significantly, the not-knowing that the alpha privatives express is ours; a condition of our being creatures not creator. But there is a knowing in this not-knowing otherwise we couldn't "acknowledge" or have anything to "confess."

## SO WHAT IS NATURE IN NATURAL THEOLOGY?

What does all the preceding analysis of the Chalcedon *symbolum* signify for Christian debates concerning natural theology? First: that such debates require from systematic theology an understanding of the incarnation of God as Jesus Christ. This event, in turn, has to be viewed cosmologically in terms of the relationship between Creator and creation. We cannot divorce Christology from creation. Such debates require both critical reflection upon the Scriptures and what the tradition, particularly the Chalcedon *symbolum*, teaches—because what it is stake here is salvation. If you like: the condition for the possibility of salvation. This return to Chalcedon is not undertaken because Chalcedon concluded the Christological debate. As its legacy showed, it did not. In fact, it "opened a Pandora's box."[39] But, secondly, in returning to the tradition, in this instance to Chalcedon because it acts as a quilting point for discussion on the nature of the body of Christ, we discover complex, unresolved and undefined understandings of "nature." And nature cannot be sidestepped, or symbolized too quickly. What Christ's being 'fully human' means has to appreciate the indissoluble relationship between the soul and the body, as well as the ways in which both are contextualized socially, culturally and historically. There is no internal/external for the embodied soul, as contemporary biological and neuroscience has revealed there is no internal/external for the body or the brain. There are myriad interchanges taking place continually across fields in which our living is situated that makes the ensouled body plastic and porous. Mary Jane West-Eberhard concludes her biological analysis of sex, its development and evolution, with: "beyond selection for success in survival, there are reproductively essential social factors that can exaggerate and maintain extravagant traits like sex."[40] The more we understand then about physi-

---

39. Richard Price and Michael Gaddis, *Acts of the Council of Chalcedon* (Translated Texts for Historians), 3 vols. (Liverpool, UK: Liverpool University Press, 2007), I, 75. The debate still rages over whether Chalcedon capitulated to the Antiochene position.

40. Mary Jane West-Eberhard, *Developmental Plasticity and Evolution* (Oxford: Oxford University Press, 2003), 637.

ological differences of sexual dimorphism and even intersex (since 1 out of every 100 people are born whose "bodies differ from the standard male and female"), and their impact upon affect, cognition and action, then the more we are trying to grapple with those questions about the natural, or following Cyril, the "natural otherness" [*eterotēta phusikēn*] of being human in Christ.[41] We were created, and created in such a way that we might know and not-know God as our creator. We were created in a way that, to employ a Mediaeval term, is "convenient." We need to understand somatically and spiritually, affectively and psychologically, the nature of that "convenience." And this requires systematic theology to be engaged with the social and physical sciences. What we need is a Christologically informed theology of "nature" that is altogether different from the old models of natural theology McGrath rightly takes issue with.

## ADDED COMPLEXITY

All I have shown is that "nature" is not one, and that our grasp of the theological complexities involved in determining *phusis* or "all that is" is conditioned by three factors: a) God's self-revelation in Christ as attested by the Scriptures—those depictions that "make known," that we "contemplate," and by means of which we "recognize," "acknowledge" or "confess;" b) our finitude as creatures such that even though we were made that we might know, make known, recognize and confess our Creator we remain part of the orders we are trying to fathom and dependent upon the work of the Spirit, the operations of grace. We cannot separate what we understand about ourselves from what we understand about our world. We are continually constructing models of both. And c) our sin (systemic and individual) such that we are prone to fermenting distorted knowledges and the projections of what Melanchthon termed *affectus*—erroneous and misleading desires, beliefs and imaginings.

All three factors impact upon our grasp of what is "natural" and morph one into the other; the distinction between them made here is heuristic. These are the lived conditions under which we as Christian theologians, seeking to understand, exist. But with respect to our theme, God in God became fully human, God submitted Godself to the social and cultural conditions of a particular historical time, in a particular geographical space, under sets of overlapping political and economic pressures, and what is constructed and interpreted (by others) in and through a shape-shifting

---

41. *Adv. Nest.* ii, Pusey, VI, 94. In Leo the Great's influential *Tome*, we have a similar phrase in Latin, "singular nature" [*natura singularis*] (*Tome* 6)—*singularis* is both "single" as "one," but also "unique."

*habitus*. The theological here in Christ encounters the biological and the sociological, and both are involved in the economic operations of God with respect to our salvation and the redemption of creation. EVEN SO we have arrived here only through the *horus*, our orientation point delivered by the Chalcedon *symbolum*. In other words, the aporias and ambiguities of *phusis* have been made known to us in and through Christ. "All that is" does not take on such complexities outside of our creation by the triune God out of nothing. In brief: Christ reveals nature (as its Creator) to us—putting into question all we might mean by nature and the natural. Christ reveals and is the revelation of another kind of natural. We have to recognize a certain "ontology" that creation announces and draws our attention to in Christ.

## CONCLUSION

It might appear that theology, like other intellectual disciplines, investigates in order to find answers to questions. For example, we could transpose the Christological debates leading to and from Chalcedon into a series of questions about the nature of Christ. But we will never intellectually be able to understand the nature of Christ. Having come a long way, down to the genome project and genetic drift, we still don't fully understand the nature of being human, and we're still exploring what differences there are that uniquely distinguishes us from clever apes. There is important research ongoing at the moment, sponsored by the Templeton Foundation, examining alternative, nonhuman intelligences. Theology is not about finding answers. It is intrinsic to a pedagogy of discipleship concerned with responding to the presence of God that puts everything into question the way any major and genuine encounter with the other, the unfamiliar, the traumatic, calls into question much of what we had taken for granted as the ways things are. Faith seeking understanding is not a purely intellectual pursuit just as contemplation is not a purely intellectual pursuit. It is not anti-intellectual either. But our knowing, and our knowledge, is more akin to knowing another person rather than knowing the properties of an object. It is more an affective, libidinal and imaginative pursuit than a logical one, as McGrath points out. It seeks to know in this way, such that Pseudo-Dionysius can speak of "an unknowing inactivity of all knowledge, knowing beyond mind by knowing nothing."[42] While we can label such phrasing apophatic that doesn't get us anywhere or really inform us at all. Or rather it informs by providing us with concepts but not in a way that enables us to conceive

---

42. *Mystical Theology*, 1025B, in *Pseudo-Dionysius: The Complete Works*, trans. Colm Luibheid (New York: Paulist, 1987), 138.

the meaning of those concepts. It informs us about the double movement in theological knowing—active acquirement, inactive acquirement—such that there is a third movement (of ascent "beyond") that acquires "nothing;" itself a paradox if by "acquire" we assume an object grasped. At best, we are intellectually informed about a state of mind beyond mind—which is hardly helpful, intellectually.

Theology's pursuit may begin but it does not end in analysis from which conclusions can be drawn and questions posed answered. We are questioned or everything is put in question, by God, by paradoxical descriptions of faith seeking understanding and by the interruption of what is not us and external to us and cannot be accommodating within the logics we have learnt. Enigma remains enigmatic. The questions remain. For if the answer is "nothing," then the questions are not answered and not, ultimately, important. What is important is the movement, the shifts from mind to beyond mind, the process and the transformations wrought in us by that process (for they are not transformations wrought in God but out a perception of and response to God).

We have to recognize, then, that whether we are treating the work of Nestorius, Cyril of Alexandria or Leo the Great, over and above the local politics (and the political cannot consume these discourses, that would be absurdly reductive of the passions invoked), they seek to know Christ as they are known by Christ. In other words, they write in faith, through faith, towards the furtherance of faith. And what each theologian is encountering is that answers to the question of *how* Christ can be both God and human leads them into the profound ambivalences of what the Godhead, Christ, nature and being human actually are. (Though *they* assume and do not question that whatever God is He is male; and maleness defines being human). They are being brought up against the utterly human words and the utterly human imaginative capacity we employ for that which is beyond human intelligence to know. They are exploring in and through their language and pushing at the edge of the indefinable that they might understand better what fits and what doesn't fit.

This is not a task undertaken unaided. There is Scripture, though that has to be interpreted (and all of them employ it or interpretations of it), and there is the Spirit of Christ, and that has to be discerned. There is then "revelation" or what has disclosed of Godself in ways accommodated to our condition. But the *pursuit* of truth is paramount. The risks of misinterpretation, the risks of taking a rhetorical trope literally, and the risks that when this said in Greek and that is said in Latin then some nuance will be lost and some nuance gained in translation. But what they do know is that despite the ambiguities in trying to understand the Godhead, Christ, nature and being human all four elements do fit together somehow. There is a theo-logic.

For God the Father is the maker of heaven and earth through God the Son, so whatever "nature" is and whatever "being human" is and whatever God incarnate as a human being is, all proceeds and returns back to the Godhead. Nestorius, Cyril of Alexandria or Leo the Great each then is contributing to a collective, ecclesial act of faith seeking understanding. The politics lie in the anathemas, the depositions and the excommunications. The politics lie in sectarianism and the desire for homogeneity and hegemony.

It follows from this that there we should be concerned about all our attempts to find the "right" definition, for, as Denys Turner points out, "In a pious vocabulary of unshocking, 'appropriate' names, lies the danger of the theologian's being all the more tempted to supposed that our language about God has succeeded in capturing the divine reality in some ultimately adequate way."[43] And we won't. We can't. Though there may be some articulations that are more successful and some that are more misleading. I doubt there has ever been any theologian who has not, at times, fallen into the misleading even when attempting to be successful (and perhaps achieving it). Nestorius actually profoundly revised his position in his later work—and came more in line with Cyril. But that's okay—because what is primary is the movement, as I said; the movement of faith to faith through faith recognizing through we treat not only ambivalences and inadequacies, but also invisibilities.

In talking about "success" and "failure" we are judging adequacies of description. We cannot be prescriptive. That the divine and human remain entirely distinct in Jesus Christ is a failure to describe incarnation adequately. That the two 'natures' (neither of which we are certain about) are united as one is a more adequate description of incarnation IF incarnation is to do the divine work Jesus Christ purports to do: redeem the human condition. How adequate the second description is unknown; for we have no way of calibrating the accuracy of the description. The difference between the divine and the human, the uncreated and the created is infinite (this radical difference is what Nestorius was insisting upon). There can be no calibration of difference between that which is infinite and that which is finite, since there is no difference *as such*. To differ and to calibrate that difference requires a relation that can be measured, because a comparison is possible, according to similarity and dissimilarity. No such relation exists between the divine and the human, and when Jesus Christ establishes a relation then it is only He who can measure the measure in that relation. So, finally, there is no answer to my governing question: what is nature in natural theology? There are only nonreductive ways of keeping the question open.

43. Denys Turner, *The Darkness of God* (Cambridge: Cambridge University Press, 1995), 24.

## Chapter 10

# "Looking for Overland"
## Fact and Fiction in Children's Literature

BENEDICTA WARD

OXFORD, MATTHEW ARNOLD'S "HOME of lost causes, and forsaken beliefs, and unpopular names, and impossible loyalties,"[1] has for centuries been a center of scholarship based on factual exploration, with research in many fields, mathematics, theology, philosophy, and history, to name only a few. The truth found in facts is of major importance to both permanent and transient Oxfordians alike; in every sphere this stern exploration of facts by strict method is vital. Alongside this, there is always the work of teaching of the young which is also based on dialogue about the true basis of facts. Textual truth matters and the works of both C. S. Lewis and Alister McGrath were concerned, as were their tutorial teaching and lecturing, with "facts," although they are better known for their contributions to the world of fiction. Indeed other great names in fiction at Oxford were known for their "factual" works first. For example, Lewis Carroll as Charles Dodgson was known for his for mathematical works; Tolkien for his analysis of Norse and Anglo-Saxon vocabulary; Lewis for his allegory of love; and Alister McGrath for his scientific dialogue with Richard Dawkins.[2] The work of

---

1. Matthew Arnold, *Essays in Criticism*, First Series. (London: Bloomsbury, 1997), xix.

2. Alister McGrath, *The Dawkins Delusion* (London: SPCK, 2007).

those who have lived and worked here, refining and applying the skills of textual, factual, scientific, and mathematical analysis, has made great advances possible in many spheres, but their contribution to fiction has provided an approach to deeper truth in wider areas.

There is a difference between fact and fiction and it is vital to know which is which. Both can convey a truth. Fiction, produced by imagination, is embedded in its own time, historical or not, and it should not be held to be teaching the other factual kind of truth, that of scholars, historians, or scientists. In order to convey the truth of fiction, it is often thought necessary to make the original background comprehensible in today's world in image and in language, in words, pictures, and sounds accessible by the human senses, and therefore such work is transitory and needs to be examined with caution. Fiction can mislead, but the presentation of facts also can mislead, especially when linked with fiction. Films of the past, especially documentaries, are often said to be based on "facts," but the very presentation distorts them; a film will not tell you what the world of the Anglo-Saxons was actually like: the pictures, conversations, clothes, and behavior are all constructs presented to give a context that is comprehensible today by the use of modern plastic materials and electronic techniques. Care must be taken that inner truth is not changed by attempting to see the past as being made in our own image. Truth is not an object to be analysed, but a life to be known and lived, and here the use of the imagination can be of paramount value. Through true fiction, a deeper reality can be known:

> Not everything has a name. Some things lead us into a realm beyond words . . . By means of art we are sometimes sent—dimly, briefly, revelations unattainable by reason, or as Dostoyevsky put it, "Beauty will save the world."[3]

Among all the works produced about human life, the most influential today are the works of fiction; they affirm truth through products of the imagination, whether in literature, prose, poetry, music, or art. And they should not be condemned as being only for amusement. Jane Austen wrote indignantly in reply to such a critic of the novel:

> It is only a novel. . . ! Or, in short, only some work in which the greatest powers of the mind are displayed, in which the most thorough knowledge of human nature, the happiest delineation

---

3. Alexander Solzhenitsyn, "One Word of Truth..." (The Nobel Prize Speech on Literature, Bodley Head, London, 1970. Translation by members of the BBC Russian Service, 1972), 5.

of its varieties, the liveliest effusions of wit and humor, are conveyed to the world in the best-chosen language.⁴

Similarly, in defense of poetry, Keats wrote to a friend:

> I am certain of nothing but of the holiness of the heart's affections and the truth of the imagination. What the imagination seizes as beauty must be truth—whether it existed before or not.⁵

Certainly there is more writing and speaking about the past by analysis of facts here in Oxford than anywhere else. In a way, Oxford is both past, present, and future in its literature.

> Noon breaks on England, noon on Oxford town,
> Beauty she was statue cold
> There's blood upon her gown
> Proud and godly kings had built her long ago
> With her powers and tombs and statues all a row
> With her fair and floral air
> And the love that lingers there
> And the streets where the great men go.⁶

Oxford is a world of facts but it is also the cradle of fiction as can be seen in many novels and especially in the detective series of Michael Innes, Dorothy Sayers, Edmund Crispin, Colin Dexter, etc. Besides their serious published works, it seems clear that many academics here are also quietly writing some kind of fiction, which may be privately printed or just personally shared. Such stories, in prose or poetry, can make the past uniquely available and truly known. For instance, one of the most obscure of medieval theologians, Duns Scotus, is revealed not by acute analysis of his works, but through a poem by G. M. Hopkins:

> Towery city and branchy between towers; Cuckoo-echoing, bell-swarmèd, lark-charmèd, rook-racked, river-rounded; The dapple-eared lily below thee; that country and town did Once encounter in, here coped and poisèd powers;
>
> . . . . . . . . . . . .

---

4. Jane Austen, *Northanger Abbey* (New York: Barnes & Noble Classic Series, 2005), 25.

5. John Keats, "On the Imagination and a Life of Sensations rather than of Thoughts": Letter to Benjamin Bailey, 22 November 1817, in *Letters of John Keats*, ed. M. B. Forman (Oxford: Oxford University Press, 1935), 67.

6. J. E. Flecker, "The Dying Patriot," *Poems of Today* 37 (London, 1924) 40.

> Yet ah! this air I gather and I release He lived on; these weeds and waters, these walls are what He haunted who of all men most sways my spirits to peace;
>
> Of reality the rarest-veinèd unraveller; a not Unrivalled insight, be rival Italy or Greece; Who fired France for Mary without spot.[7]

These lines about Duns Scotus set him fairly in his thirteenth-century Oxford context as true fact, but the main point is the lasting and living influence of his philosophy on the poetry of Hopkins centuries later. Facts are to be explored and established and used by "great men" in the search for truth; and they can be given life by being combined with fiction and fantasy.

Fact and fiction are not confined to the streets "where the great men go." Oxford is also the home of children's stories which grow out of the same academic soil: Wilbert Awdry invented Thomas the Tank Engine at Wycliffe Hall; Lewis Carroll created *Alice at Christ Church*; *The Wind in the Willows* is set on the Thames; the *Lord of the Rings* was initially set in a Cotswold-style Hobbiton; Lewis's *Narnia* was shaped by and in Oxford, as was Philip Pullman's imaginary world.

Good writing for children can be a breath of fresh air, a light in dark places, provided it is not sentimental or soppy, full of both danger and threat but also of hope, laughter, and natural lovingkindness.

> We have hands that fashion and heads that know,
> But our hearts we lost—how long ago!
> In a place no chart nor ship can show
> Under the sky's dome.[8]

Stories can lead us into the truth of a world which shows what its Creator is really like, not by imagining clever tricks of magic but by wonder at true life:

> There's many a crafty alchemist in Mecca and Jerusalem;
> And Michael Scott and Merlin were reckoned very wise;
> But I know a wizardry can take a wisp of sun-fire
> And round it to a planet and roll it through the skies,
> With cities, and sea-ports, and little shining windows,
> And hedgerows and gardens, and loving human eyes.[9]

---

7. Gerard Manley Hopkins, "Duns Scotus' Oxford," in *Collected Poems*, ed. W. H. Gardner (Oxford: Oxford University Press, 1970), 79.

8. G. K. Chesterton, "The House of Christmas," *Collected Poems* (London: Methuen, 1933), 140.

9. Alfred Noyes, "Wizardry," *Collected Poems* (London: John Murray, 1950), 2:74.

This positive aspect of truth embedded in fiction is clearly set out in Lewis's Narnia novel *The Silver Chair*, when Puddleglum answers the White Witch's entirely factual and negative view of life, saying

> One word, Ma'am, one word. All you've been saying is quite right, I shouldn't wonder. I'm a chap who always liked to know the worst and then put the best face I can on it. So I won't deny any of what you said. But there's one thing more to be said, even so. Suppose we have only dreamed, or made up, all those things—trees and grass and sun and moon and stars and Aslan himself. Suppose we have. Then all I can say is that, in that case, the made-up things seem a good deal more important than the real ones. Suppose this black pit of a kingdom of yours is the only world. Well, it strikes me as a pretty poor one. And that's a funny thing, when you come to think of it. We're just babies making up a game, if you're right. But four babies playing a game can make a play world which licks your real world hollow. That's why I'm going to stand by the play-world. I'm on Aslan's side even if there isn't any Aslan to lead it. I'm going to live as like a Narnian as I can even if there isn't any Narnia. So, thanking you kindly for our supper, if these two gentlemen and the young lady are ready, we're leaving your court at once and setting out in the dark to spend our lives looking for Overland. Not that our lives will be very long, I should think; but that's small loss if the world's as dull a place as you say.[10]

The truth of life is thus illuminated through fiction as much as by facts; so it is also in death. The search for truth is carried on at several levels in fiction and in many stories and death is seen as opening for children as well as adults into beauty beyond thought. As Peter Pan said, "Death-that would be a very big adventure."[11]

The classic fictional accounts of death-into-life are of course in John Bunyan's *Pilgrim's Progress*. For instance, at the end of book 2, which describes the pilgrimage of Christiana and her children, there is the well-known account of death of Mr Faithful-for-the-Truth:

> Then said he, "I am going to my Father's; and though with great difficulty I have got hither, yet now I do not repent me of all the trouble I have been at to arrive where I am. My sword I give to him that shall succeed me in my pilgrimage, and my courage and skill to him that can get it. My marks and scars I carry

---

10. C. S. Lewis, *The Silver Chair* (London: Collins, 1953), 43.
11. J. M. Barrie, *Peter Pan* (London: Hodder & Stoughton, 1951), 106.

with me, to be a witness for me that I have fought His battles who will now be my rewarder." When the day that he must go hence was come, many accompanied him to the river-side, into which as he went, he said, "Death, where is thy sting?" And as he went down deeper, he said, "Grave, where is thy victory?" So he passed over, and all the trumpets sounded for him on the other side.[12]

Equally memorable is the account of the death of Mr. Standfast:

> Then there came forth a summons for Mr. Standfast. Now there was a great calm at that time in the river; wherefore Mr. Standfast, when about half way in, stood a while, and talked with his companions that had waited upon him thither. "I see myself now at the end of my journey; my toilsome days are ended. I am going to see that head which was crowned with thorns, and that face which was spit upon for me. I have formerly lived by hearsay and faith; but now I go where I shall live by sight, and shall be with him in whose company I delight myself. I have loved to hear my Lord spoken of; and wherever I have seen the print of his shoe in the earth, there I have coveted to set my foot too." Now, while he was thus in discourse, his countenance changed; his strong man bowed under him: and after he had said, "Take me, for I come unto Thee," he ceased to be seen of them. But glorious it was to see how the open region was filled with horses and chariots, with trumpeters and pipers, with singers and players upon stringed instruments, to welcome the pilgrims as they went up, and followed one another in at the beautiful gate of the city.[13]

These entirely imaginary passages have been used by many writers. They provided a theme in *Little Women* and in John Buchan's *Mr. Standfast*. The children's author Violet Needham quoted them at the end of her novel *The Stormy Petrel*, relating it to the tragic death of a child, Christopher; here his sorrowing friends are given a new perspective on the little boy's death by this from the child Judith, who sees a glorious sunset and exclaims, "It is for Christopher now: all the trumpets are sounding for him on the other side."[14] This theme is present also in *Narnia*: at the end of *The Voyage of the Dawn Treader*, the mouse Reepicheap goes happily alone through death by a great wave into a new and ultimate country:

12. John Bunyan, *Pilgrim's Progress* (London: Longman, 1890), 365–66.
13. Bunyan, *Pilgrim's Progress*, 367.
14. Violet Needham, *The Stormy Petrel* (London: Collins, 1942), 317.

'This, said Reepicheep, is where I go alone. . ..' Then he bade them goodbye, trying to be sad for their sakes but he was quivering with happiness.'[15]

and in *The Last Battle* all the children are vividly alive as well as already dead:

'There was a real accident . . . your father and mother and all of you are . . .already dead.'[16]

This kind of "truth" is also conveyed in the nineteenth century in stories for children, a happy spin off from the austere theology of Oxford Movement. Beginning in Oxford 1833, a group of friends in Oxford determined to revitalize the Church of England. They were all were ordained clergymen, well trained in theology. Their leader at first was John Henry Newman (1801-90), a major theologian, subsequently a convert to Roman Catholicism and a cardinal; among them was Richard Hurrell Froude (1803-36), a fine scholar; John Keble (1792-1866), both a scholar and a poet; and Edward Pusey (1800-82), a most influential and austere professor. Their next generation companion was John Mason Neale, an Anglican priest, scholar and hymnodist (1818-1866). He was a Cambridge rather than an Oxford man but was nevertheless an heir and disciple of the earlier leaders. Like them he was a most careful classical scholar and like them some of his of actions were viewed with suspicion and hostility, not only his encouragement of the restoration of religious life in the Church of England but his translation of Latin and Greek hymns into English. John explained why he was doing it:

Among the greatest inconveniences that followed from the adoption of national languages in the prayer books of the Reformation, must be counted the abrupt end to using all the hymns of the Western church. That treasury, into which the saints of every age and country had poured their contributions . . . became as a sealed book and as a dead letter.[17]

To remedy the problem, he turned ancient Latin hymns into English such as the immensely popular "All glory, laud and honor" and "O Come, O Come, Emmanuel." He wrote and translated many more hymns which are still in use. The Tractarians were so called for publishing their scholarly insights in ninety tracts for the times. They did so without the help of J. P.

---

15. C. S. Lewis, *The Voyage of the Dawn Treader* (London: Collins, 1952), 219.

16. C. S. Lewis. *The Last Battle* (London: Collins 1956), 183.

17. John Mason Neale. *A Commentary on the Psalms from primitive and medieval writers from the various office-books and hymns of the Roman, Mazarabic, Ambrosian, Gallic, Greek, Coptic, Armenian and Syriac rites.* 4 vols (London: Joseph Masters, 1879-1887).

Migne's compilation of patristic texts, *Patralogia Latina et Graeci et Orientalis,* that invaluable tools for modern patristic scholars. Their excellent research issued in serious publications as well as being used in debates and preaching, but they were also accompanied by fiction for children, especially in many beautifully told stories John Mason Neale, the major scholar of the next generation. He was educated at Selwyn College, then lived in Cambridge, until ill health cause him to live in Sussex. His commentary on the psalms in four volumes is an amazing work, in which Neale incorporated comments on the psalms translated from eastern and well as western Fathers. But Neale and his colleagues also aimed to teach Christian life by fictional tales, in for instance *Deeds of Faith, The Quai of the Discori,* and *The Triumph of the Cross.*[18] They contain accounts of lives and deaths of and for children from the early church through the Middle Ages to modern times. They are meant as reminders that death is not an end into nothing but a gateway into the real world of God's love. Some of Neale's stories were dedicated to a child, "my dear little Emma," all were meant for children. Sometimes the ideals of Tractarianism may seem to have misdirected the moral of the stories but more often these stories about people in the past of the church reveal them more deeply than do accounts of their writings. The obscure doctrinal controversy between Arius and Athanasius, for instance, is presented here in story form, in which the truths discussed by the great heretic and his opponent are rendered available for all. They encouraged the use of the imagination in life, in prayer and in worship, a daring approach where one strand of the faith had insisted that the imagination should be disciplined and indeed shunned in the life of prayer. Here again, the Tractarians followed the pattern proposed by Anselm in the eleventh century in his prayers:

> Would that I with happy Joseph
> might have taken down my Lord from the cross...
> Would that with the blessed band of women
> I might have trembled at the vision of angels
> and have heard the news of the Lord's resurrection,
> news of my consolation.[19]

This positive use of personal imagination in meditation has had a long history, reaching without question, for instance, from Anselm's eleventh century prayers into the modern spiritual, "Were you there when they crucified my Lord?" This is not a scientific exploration of the truth of the New

---

18. John Mason Neale, *The Triumph of the Cross* (London: SPCK, 1849).

19. Anselm, *Prayers and Meditations of Saint Anselm with the Proslogion,* trans. Benedicta Ward (London: Penguin Classics, 1973), 96.

Testament but a way of being present within those texts by imaginative participation. This was not entirely new in the eleventh century but it received a major impetus from Anselm, a major theologian and philosopher, making imagination a firm part of the use of fiction as an aid to prayer without pretending that fact is the same as fiction. Anselm used picture language as an aid to prayer and also to depict heaven in his major philosophical work, the *Proslogion*; at the culmination of reasoning, heaven is to be explored not only be the mind but by all the senses and the creative imagination:

> God of truth, I ask that my joy may be full. . .
> let my mind meditate on it
> let my tongue speak of it
> let my heart love it,
> let my mouth preach it,
> let my soul hunger for it,
> my flesh thirst for it,
> and my whole being desire it
> until I enter into the joy of my Lord,
> who is God one and triune blessed forever.[20]

It is participation in the integrity of the inner world that matters. It is noteworthy that in the ultimate book for Christians all four Gospels show that what Jesus used most to convey his teaching was the story, the imaginary account, the parable. Noteworthy perhaps for illustrating the double kind of truth found in fact and fiction is the tale of 'Good King Wenceslas'[21] (21). Written in story form by John Mason Neale, as well as this prose version he wrote with it the carol which is now among the most popular of such songs. Neale makes it clear that this is not historical fact but true fiction. In fact, Wenceslas of Bohemia was venerated as a martyr since he was murdered by his brother at the age of thirty-three but as Neale says the idea of following the footsteps of a saint in caring for the poor may not have been fact in this case but the story presents an eternal dimension and indeed could have happened many times and in many places. Putting a moral into a story-form is not an affirmation of historical truth but an appealing presentation of ultimate truth through fiction made available for all.

The same is true of the story of St. Frideswide of Oxford, a particularly appropriate figure to examine. For the historian it is clear that the "facts" about her story were invented in the eleventh century when the details of the cult therefore were invented. This is not to say such things could not have happened anywhere, only that there is no firm factual knowledge of how she

20. Anselm, *Prayers and Meditations*, 267
21. Neale, *Deeds of Faith* (London, SPCK, 1902), 74–79.

lived, when, and where and her legend should not be used as historical fact. But in plays, poetry, paintings, illuminated glass, Frideswide's legend has a lasting place in the modern imagination which still draws people to the holy well at Binsey and her supposed tomb at Christ Church. For the serious historian the "facts" about her legend may well be shaky, but the basis of fiction still presents healing and salutary truth.

While the analysis of facts is basic to knowledge, it is often through fiction that true life can be seen. There life is not examined as series of molecules for our analysis and use, but as a personal pilgrimage from exile towards home, with others or alone, a journey short or long, sad or merry, known by speaking which is personal and immediate, or by writing which reaches more people and lasts longer. Seeing what has happened or what was thought to have happened, requires careful thought but shining through all attempts to understand both facts and fictions, is the golden light of ultimate truth. It is not surprising therefore that Alister McGrath should be praised most of all for his serious attention to his fellow Oxfordian's novels for children:

> "Not everything has a name. . . beauty will save the world."

## Chapter 11

# Models and Cultures in Science and Theology[1]

Bethany Sollereder

ALISTER MCGRATH HAS OFTEN used the central concept of "models" to help readers and students understand the complex relationships between science and theology.[2] The use of models and model-based reasoning are common in pedagogy, used to understand complex realities, and have even been instrumental in the process of scientific discovery.[3] Models help us categorize and observe interactions. A model train set helps us think about how tracks and trains and points work. That is a simple model: visual and kinaesthetic. Nonvisual models are more complex, such as Iain Barbour's famous four models of interaction between science and religion. They have illuminated historical narratives and theological options.[4] Very simple models are often

---

1. I am grateful to Amy H. Lee for her very helpful comments on a draft of this paper.

2. I will use "science and theology" rather than "science and religion" throughout this essay because "theology" describes more accurately what I am interested in: the academic discipline of Christian beliefs. "Religion" as a title offers too expansive a landscape, including practices and other religions.

3. Marta Spranzi, "Galileo and the Mountains of the Moon: Analogical Reasoning, Models and Metaphors in Scientific Discovery," *Journal of Cognition and Culture* 4 (2004) 451–83.

4. Alister E. McGrath, *Science & Religion: A New Introduction*, 2nd ed. (Chichester, UK: Wiley & Sons, 2010), 45–50.

scaled down versions of reality that help us understand the more complex reality. Bohr's model of the atom, for example, gives a visual and imaginative grasp on something that is too small to be seen and demonstrates certain realities about the behaviour of electrons. The theological model of God as a good shepherd highlights aspects of God's character and care in easily graspable and concrete ways. This paper will explore how my thinking on models began and expand on an underexplored model: science and theology as two cultures.

I've written elsewhere of my favourite way to conceive of the relationship between science and theology—that they are like maps.[5] Discussed by Mary Midgley and Christopher Southgate, the metaphor of maps is easily understood: a map *has* to be a simplified—and to some extent, incorrect—version of the reality. A map that was the same size as the territory portrayed would be useless. A good model draws attention to the most important information for its intended use, even if by doing so it portrays intentional inaccuracies.

One of the best examples of this is Harry Beck's justly famous map of the London Underground system. In 1931, Beck broke with the convention of a geographical map of the tube, imposed over a roadmap, with a topological map that only depicts the relationship of tube stations in relation to one another. The map is not to scale and does not even bear true for the direction of travel at all points. The tube map takes a tangled reality and depicts it as clear, straight lines with evenly-spaced stops. It does so by intentionally distorting reality. The result is a clear, easy-to-read, intuitive map that you can find your place on and find your destination at a glance. The few geographical maps left in the stations that depict the complex reality are almost impossible to read by comparison.

The advantages of the tube map are clear. The map is a highly effective way to communicate how to navigate the London underground. But there is also a significant downside. It leaves one without any idea how to navigate the city on foot or by car. You can use the tube for years, and yet have no idea how the stations are situated geographically. When lines or stations are closed for repairs, the passenger is left with no resources for navigating the city by other means. When I used to travel frequently in London, I remember the occasional vague sense of helplessness I felt when I was forced off the train one stop early and had absolutely no sense of which direction I should be walking in, nor how long it might take to get there. I was lost, and the

5. Bethany Sollereder, "Lost in a World of Maps," *Faith and Science Seeking Understanding* (blog), *Biologos*, 7 October 2015, https://biologos.org/blogs/jim-stump-faith-and-science-seeking-understanding/lost-in-a-world-of-maps-relations-between-science-and-theology.

simplified tube map—in itself so efficient—gave me no aid when I needed information it was not designed to provide.

The same is true of all models, whether scientific or theological. They convey certain types of information, but they do not provide comprehensive data of the reality they point to. If they did, they would cease to be useful.

There are important differences in comparing theological to scientific models. Both use imagination and analogy, but they regularly work in opposite directions. The Christian Scriptures do not offer clear, systematic theory of God. Theological theory like the doctrine of atonement is built on the back of revealed models like Christ as Lamb or ransom. But the Scriptures offer only models and stories: God is like a king, like a shepherd, like a lover. Theological models of God act like doors, opening up the poetic imagination to new possibilities. They point to mystery. Like the stable to Narnia in C. S. Lewis's *The Last Battle,* theological models are doorways to wider worlds, bringing color and light to dark and colorless concepts of God.

Models in science tend to move in the other direction. They reduce possibility, and act to save the phenomena. Someone thinking about the movement of gas in a container as billiard balls moving around and knocking into each other will generally have to move away from the model in order to make a new discovery. This is not always the case, as sometimes models themselves are generative. But generally speaking, the theory exists and the models are used to explain the theory, to help make the theory graspable. Scientific models tend to move from an abstract, complex reality (often described in mathematical terms) to a simplified and often visual model that helps understanding, whereas in theological circles we usually start from the revealed models and analogies and head into the mystery of complexities that cannot be fully grasped.

Models of interaction between science and theology have tended to center on epistemology and domains of knowledge: What content does each one cover? What sort of truth claims does each one make? Which one has epistemic priority in any given situation? But these models tend to lack practical advice for how one might go about actually engaging with the other domain of knowledge. I want to suggest that using intercultural models can provide a practical, rather than epistemic, approach to bridging the two different understandings of reality provided by science and theology.

## INTERCULTURAL MODELS OF SCIENCE AND THEOLOGY

In 1959, C. P. Snow delivered the annual Rede lecture in Cambridge. Snow defined two cultures at play in the university: the "literary intellectuals" of the humanities and the empirical culture of physical scientists.[6] Snow represented these two cultures as having a deep gulf of understanding between them, aliens to the discussion of the other.

Science and theology are also depicted as cultures—often cultures at war or deeply divided.[7] However, although the idea of science and theology as two cultures is around, I have not found anyone that has used the resources of intercultural studies to address how these two cultures can reasonably be crossed. What follows in the rest of this essay is a "beginner's guide to crossing-cultures" applied to science and theology. I use resources from anthropology and particularly from cross-cultural missions literature and apply it to crossing the cultures of science and theology.

What is culture? Although there is no agreed upon definition, Ron Scollon et. al. suggest that culture can be thought of as a *heuristic;* a tool for thinking.[8] Cultures guide how we shape meaning, how we decide what it means to behave appropriately towards others, and how we interpret what goes on around us. If theology and science are indeed to be thought of as two cultures, then they are not simply sets of knowledge or methodologies of practice, but provide frames of understanding the world in far more complex and foundational ways than we might initially assume. We can think of the entire process of finding one's career or identity as a "scientist" or "theologian" as a process of enculturation. Becoming a scientist or theologian takes years of higher education, and education is one long process of enculturation. It shapes thought patterns, trains questions, encourages certain lines of enquiry, and devalues others. A scientist emerging from a PhD will have dramatically different questions and interests from a theologian at

---

6. Charles P. Snow, *The Two Cultures and the Scientific Revolution* (Cambridge: Cambridge University Press, 1959), 4.

7. See, for example, the excellent SCIO program called "Bridging Two Cultures" in Oxford, and the way their promotional material uses the model of culture: "Science and religion are often presupposed to be antagonists, and debates in the field are often bad-tempered and reliant on caricature. Part of the problem stems from the cultural differences that exist between the humanities and the sciences, differences which make cross-disciplinary discourse and collaboration in science and religion problematic," para. 2, http://www.scio-uk.org/wp-content/uploads/2017/03/Bridging-two-cultures-II-double-sided-US-ltr.pdf.

8. Ron Scollon, et al., *Intercultural Communication*, 3rd ed. (Malden, MA: Wiley-Blackwell, 2012), 3.

the same point, even if they are working on related questions. So, how can these two talk to each other?

The first step in cross-cultural training is to learn to recognise cultural values and the ways they are endorsed by practice. Everyone undergoes a process of enculturation from birth that shapes the basic contours of life. But many of the assumptions and values that underlie cultural training are not universal or obvious—in fact, they tend to be highly contingent. What is the best utensil for eating? A fork, chopsticks, or one's hand? The answer will be shaped (in this case almost entirely) by cultural training.

The person crossing cultures has to learn to see both their native values as the contextually-specific values they are: not assume that their own perspective is the obvious or right way to go about thinking of the world. In Edward Hall's anthropological analysis, *The Silent Language*, he identifies ten patterns of cultural messaging that communicate a multitude of values. These include language, interaction (responses to irritable stimuli), association (group behaviour), subsistence (diet and economy), bisexuality (differentiation along sexual roles), territoriality, temporality, (patterns for) learning, play, defense, and exploitation (use of material goods and what is now called "niche construction").[9] Hall writes: "it is important to remember that culture is not one thing but a complex series of activities interrelated in many ways."[10] These activities organise values in the culture, teaching patterns of behaviour and prioritizing actions based on perceived needs. Anthropologists stress that these values are culture-specific, not human universals. One set of values does not have ontological or moral priority over another.

Take the temporality aspect of messaging as an example. This deals with how a culture perceives and values time. If a person is event-oriented rather than time-oriented, it will not matter to that person or others in the community if someone shows up late to a meeting. The meeting only begins when the person arrives. Nor would the meeting have a specific time for conclusion: the meeting is finished when the business at hand has come to a natural conclusion. For the time-oriented person, being late is an insult to the other party, a demonstrated contempt for the wasted productivity of the time they spent waiting. "Time is money," they say. Western, European cultures tend to be time-oriented cultures. Latin American or Polynesian cultures, by contrast tend to be event-oriented cultures. For the Canadian, respect is shown by being punctual to meetings. An allowable "lateness" is arriving within five minutes of the appointed time. Anything after that, an

9. Edward Hall, *The Silent Language* (New York: Doubleday, 1959), 62–81.
10. Hall, *Silent Language*, 80.

apology is expected. After fifteen minutes, not only is an apology expected but also an explanation for why one was late. Half an hour late provokes open hostility. In the Polynesian island of Yap, time is treated differently: the culture is event-oriented rather than time oriented. Arriving anytime within two hours of an appointed meeting time is treated with the same lax attitude as someone being five minutes late in Canada.[11] Three hours late might require an apology, but it is not until one is four hours late that any offense is generated. For the Yapese, time is not a measure of possible productivity, and so waiting is not a "waste of time." The Canadian worry about "lost time" indicates a particularly high value for productivity, and a high value of productivity indicates particular biases about exploitation, or use of material culture. One perspective on time is not ontologically superior to another; rather each one is a solution to other cultural pressures. In North American culture where achievement and productivity take precedence over most other considerations, wasting another's time and therefore taking from them their most important currency in achieving success, is a grave sin. In Yapese culture, where avoiding shaming another is far more important than productivity, having a flexible concept of punctuality avoids many potential conflicts—conflicts that would not have the same anxious weight for North Americans. Who thinks twice before apologizing for being late? But in a culture where vulnerability is perceived differently, admitting one has made an error can be a major crisis.

Cultural webs are intricately interwoven, and it is rare for one value to stand as an independent variable within the whole composition. What does this look like applied to the cultures of science and theology? Science and theology hold different sorts of values, desire different ends, and use different means to get there. A full exploration of either the culture of science or theology is well beyond the scope of this paper, but we can explore a few case studies.

In scientific culture, time is in short supply and value is placed almost exclusively on the most current thought. I've heard scientists say many times that reading any scientific literature more than ten years old is a waste of time. Paper publishing happens on a scale of weeks, rather than months. Because of this rapid pace, books are considered nearly irrelevant for research, since by the time the information in a book has been through all the hoops of publication, the information in it is likely to be out dated. By contrast, books are still the major source of research in theology. They take years to research and write, and stay relevant for many years after they are published.

---

11. Sherwood G. Lingenfelter and Marvin K. Mayers, *Ministering Cross-Culturally: An Incarnational Model for Personal Relationships* (Grand Rapids: Baker, 1986), 39.

Theologians regularly find new inspiration by reexamining ancient texts, and whole theological movements (like Radical Orthodoxy) are founded upon recovering rather than discovery. Establishing conclusions may take centuries, and refining an argument may take centuries more. Theology is not generally in a hurry.

Methodology is another area where science and theology show cultural differences. When I talk to scientists, one of the most common questions I face is: "What is it that you actually *do*?" They cannot comprehend doing research without a lab, without new empirical evidence guiding new theory. When I try to explain that I think of myself as joining a conversation, they look puzzled. That doesn't count as research for natural scientists. Simply defining how two interlocutors interact on a certain subject is considered a valuable contribution in theology, but is seen as odd in the sciences. However, perhaps the biggest methodological difference is usually the size of the question asked. Scientists ask specific, measurable questions that contract variables and that can be answered within the few pages of a journal article. Theologians tend to ask huge, complex, and even unsolvable questions that multiple monographs cannot comprehensively cover.

Importantly, in intercultural work, these differences of values cannot be thought of in hierarchical terms. One set of values is not inherently better than others. Rather, each set of values leads to strengths in one area and drawbacks in another. Scientific knowledge leads to technological advances, for example. Theology does not do that: the understanding of the world it provides does not control physical processes. But theology, for its part, can investigate complexities that science itself cannot comment on: the nature of the human condition, for example, or how to use wisely the technology that scientific knowledge develops.

## EXPECT CULTURE SHOCK

The concept of dialogue between science and religion gained considerable traction through Ian Barbour's typologies. But the practical outworking of dialogue could benefit from models of cross-cultural experience. When we attempt cross-cultural dialogue, what can we expect?

One of the first experiences most people have when they cross cultures is culture stress or culture shock. The familiar touchstones of culture are removed, replaced by unfamiliar values and behaviours. People's reactions are no longer predictable, and patterns of conversation are no longer natural. When I first moved to England from Canada seven years ago, I followed North American patterns of introduction. I would walk up to a stranger at a party and begin with "Hi! I'm Bethany!" extending my hand with a smile, expecting them to smile back, shake my hand and say "My name is . . ." and we would proceed from there. In England, this strategy did not work at all. Reponses varied, but there was usually a startled look, often a few mumbled words, or even just a stunned silence. What I meant as a friendly breaking of the ice was too abrupt. I slowly learned that the proper way to begin talking to a stranger in England was to complain about the weather. Then one might talk about the venue, or the event we were attending. Then it was appropriate to talk about work, country of origin, and all the rest. Introducing names comes last, almost as an afterthought. (One advantage of this is that when the name comes last, I usually remember it.) Yet, until I learned these different patterns of conversation, meeting new people without painful amounts of embarrassment felt impossible!

In the same way, someone moving from science to theology or vice versa can expect different interests, different beliefs and academic instincts, and different standards of success. Conflict arises over whether a person has reasonably defended a point, what counts for evidence, or what solutions are deemed satisfactory. None of these are standards set in stone: they are cultural guidelines that have been instilled in the practitioners over years of training.

## A CASE STUDY IN THEODICY

Different instincts about what is interesting, convincing, and rigorous can lead to polarisation between the different approaches to common questions. Take, for example, two different cultural approaches to the theodicy of natural disasters represented by David Bentley Hart's *The Doors of the Sea: Where Was God in the Tsunami?* and Robert White's *Who is to Blame? Disasters, Nature and Acts of God*.[12] Hart is a philosopher and theologian in the Orthodox tradition while White is a geophysicist who specialises in volcanoes. I have chosen these two because they represent the ends of a spectrum: Hart's approach is thoroughly theological, while White's approach is largely a scientific appraisal of a theological problem. There are other books that stand in the middle ground, drawing from both theological and scientific traditions more evenly, but these two help us see the cultures clearly.[13]

---

12. David Bentley Hart, *The Doors of the Sea: Where Was God in the Tsunami?* (Grand Rapids: Eerdmans, 2005); Robert S. White, *Who is to Blame? Disasters, Nature and Acts of God* (Oxford: Monarch, 2014).

13. An example of a more evenly sourced book is Christopher Southgate's *The Groaning of Creation* (Louisville: Westminster John Knox, 2008).

Hart begins by rejecting theodical approaches that attempt to justify a universal harmony that makes (or will make) every piece of suffering fit an overall plan. Rather, "the New Testament teaches us that, in another and ultimate sense, suffering and death—considered in themselves—have no true meaning or purpose at all."[14] He moves on to explore the tradition of *privatio boni*—that evil is not a reality in itself, but only a deprivation of reality—and of divine *apatheia*. Hart wanders around the narrative of a fallen world, but never clearly expresses how fallenness manifests itself. He argues for the centrality of the Cross, the hope of redemption, and trust in the providence of God in bringing about the eternal kingdom. Hart does not argue that every event is determined by God, or that every event had to happen for the greater glory of God's plan. Yet, it would be hard for a scientist to affirm that God created the present world without ever intending any death, or the planetary system without ever intending an earthquake. Hart shows at a few places that he knows about the scientific narrative of the world: "All life feeds on life, each creature must yield its place in time to another, and at the heart of nature is a perpetual struggle to survive and increase at the expense of other beings." But nowhere does Hart seem to recognize precisely what "life feeds on life" necessitates: instead, he claims that "the entire history of sin and death is in an ultimate sense a pure contingency, one that is not as such desired by God."[15] A biologist would likely object to this, insisting that you cannot have it both ways. You cannot have God willing a physical world with developmental properties and reproductive capacities and not have death. Without death there could be no new life. Without death there would be no evolution, no complex life, no humans to have such discussions. If God did not intend any death at all, then the whole history of the world is so entirely corrupted that there is no sign of God's grace left. Nor can an earthquake be easily attributable to evil, or to the working of a "rebellious rational free will,"[16] instead of to the inevitable result of large bodies of rock in contact with each other.

Hart ends by acknowledging that he "clearly ventured far from any direct discussion of the sufferings of those who fell victim" to the Indian Ocean tsunami.[17] This, perhaps, is the greatest shortfall of typical theological and philosophical theodicy: it gets so caught up in the minutia of abstract concepts of God that it forgets those who first prompted it, and what might be done to help them—a complaint levelled by many anti-theodicists.[18]

14. Hart, *Doors of the Sea*, 35.
15. Hart, *Doors of the Sea*, 83.
16. Hart, *Doors of the Sea*, 97.
17. Hart, *Doors of the Sea*, 92.
18. John Swinton, *Raging with Compassion: Pastoral Responses to the Problem of Evil*

White's approach is startlingly different. White confidently embraces the human ability to control aspects of nature, and roots the theological blame for suffering in natural disasters squarely on human failure. The world is unambiguously God's good creation, and White explains that: "natural processes make this a fertile, fruitful world in which to live. Indeed, without them the earth would be a barren, infertile place without the possibility of human life."[19] The entire first half of the book emphasises that God made a perfectly good world and it is only human agency that turns natural processes into "natural disasters." White contends that natural disasters "are not natural at all—in fact, we might even go so far as to call them 'unnatural disasters,' because human agency has turned an otherwise good feature of the natural world into a disaster."[20] How is this so? White's approach is entirely scientific. Scientific reasons populate the necessity of natural disasters. The earth relies on plate tectonic movement and volcanoes to maintain a liveable surface, and so on. Scientific learning in technology is then used to argue that it is human agency which makes natural processes into disasters: "So although we can neither prevent earthquakes happening, nor predict exactly when or where they will next occur, we can take steps to mitigate their effects in areas known to be hazardous. The shaking caused by earthquakes is generally well understood, and buildings can be constructed to withstand it without catastrophic failure."[21] It is our failure to use this knowledge that turns a shaking ground into catastrophic, death-dealing tragedies.

White's argument for the cause of suffering in natural disasters comes down largely to the line he attributes to Nicholas Ambraseys: "Earthquakes don't kill people; buildings do."[22] A theologian would likely feel tempted to object at this point. Yes, modern building codes could largely reduce the number of deaths in major earthquakes, and developed countries have mitigated earthquake deaths, as seen in Japan's major earthquake in 2011.[23] But what about all the centuries and millennia of countless deaths when building codes did not exist? We can rejoice that science is able to prevent needless death, but that hardly gets God off the hook for creating a world that relies on such massive and destructive events to keep a liveable earth

---

(Grand Rapids: 2007); Kenneth Surin, *Theology and the Problem of Evil* (Eugene, OR: Wipf & Stock 2004).

19. White, *Who is to Blame?*, 11.
20. White, *Who is to Blame?*, 11.
21. White, *Who is to Blame?*, 47.
22. White, *Who is to Blame?*, 47.
23. Nearly 16,000 people died in Japan from the tsunami caused by the 2011 earthquake, despite all the tsunami barrier technology in play. Nature is always, and will likely continue to prove herself to be, ultimately uncontrollable.

surface in the first place. Nor does it justify the countless lives that have been lost prior to the development of modern technology. To argue that we have the power now to reduce deaths (not eliminate them) makes little impact in a discipline shaped by Dostoyevsky's objection in *The Brothers Karamazov* through Ivan. Even one child, tortured needlessly, was enough to motivate Ivan to hand back his ticket to the glories of divine harmony in creation. But many more than one child died even in the "best case" scenario of the Japanese earthquake, let alone the Indonesian or Haitian earthquakes that have claimed hundreds of thousands of lives. White is not acculturated into the wider theological discussion, and Ivan Karamazov makes no appearance in his book. From a theologians' perspective it is not enough to either simply reduce the number of dead (though this undoubtedly is good to do) nor to "spend a few moments considering what the new creation will be like"[24] since the future harmony should be rejected if the price is too high. And one child suffering a miserable death is too high a price.

In light of the theological objections I raise above as problematic, White offers a few theological responses. These are also instructive, as they are similar to how some theologians might respond, but have important differences. White points to the sinfulness of Adam and Eve in the Garden of Eden as the source of human misery in the world: "Humans lost their immediate access to God, and the rightness and orderliness of life in the Garden of Eden."[25] While White does not say it plainly, his argument is that prior to the entrance of sin, God would have warned people of impending earthquakes or tsunamis, giving them the knowledge and wisdom to flee in advance, or perhaps to build shake-proof and water-proof houses. Perhaps this would have happened through direct words of knowledge from God, or perhaps humans would have had some now lost super-intelligence. The "lost super human" argument is not alien to the Christian tradition and some of the earliest people we might call "scientists" in the modern sense (like Francis Bacon) drew on the narrative of lost super knowledge as motivation for scientific inquiry.[26] But it is not a line taken by theologians or Biblical scholars who tend not to read the early chapters of the Bible as historically accurate or Adam and Eve as literal people.[27]

---

24. White, *Who is to Blame?*, 180.

25. White, *Who is to Blame?*, 134.

26. Peter Harrison, *The Fall of Man and the Foundations of Science* (Cambridge: Cambridge University Press, 2007), 4.

27. White does not require others to accept the historicity of Adam and Eve, but he does, although he does not think they were the direct genetic progenitors of all other humans (*Who is to Blame?*, 123).

White ends his argument through a number of biblically-inspired approaches. He speaks of Joseph's famine, Job's whirlwind, and the Tower of Siloam. He emphasises the importance of human action and responsibility. He also, after all his scientific explanations for why God uses violent natural processes, advances a very strong argument for the inscrutability of God's sovereignty in nature. God's thoughts are not our thoughts and Scripture, he says, "makes it clear that humans, being created beings, cannot second-guess the motives of their creator."[28] Hart, by contrast, does not say that we cannot second-guess God, but rather that silence is often the best course. "There are moments, simply said, when we probably ought not to speak. But, of course, we must speak."[29]

These two different approaches to the same questions about natural disasters have perhaps revealed something about my own biases, and perhaps the reader too has found themselves nodding along to one line of argument and gritting teeth in frustration at the other. The sense of rightness or wrongness in either case may be considered a type of academic, interdisciplinary culture shock.

Anthropologist Kalvero Oberg has described culture shock as a hostile and aggressive attitude towards a host culture, which grows "out of the genuine difficulty which the visitor experiences in the process of adjustment."[30] When you enter a new culture, you become like a little child again. From the fluency of your own culture, you are immersed in an unfamiliar language, unfamiliar social norms, and you may even become illiterate. The same is true of interdisciplinary conversation. The theologian is lost by the formulas and graphs in scientific work, whilst the scientist cannot understand the fuss over how a missing article in the first line of Genesis ends up seriously challenging the doctrine of *creatio ex nihilo*. Slowly, time spent in the other culture builds proficiency and comfort until it becomes natural and the discomfort passes.

Oberg notes four stages of cultural transition.[31] The first is a honeymoon stage in which all is exotic and fascinating. In the second stage, culture shock, the person begins to critique the host culture and glorify one's own native culture in all respects. After culture shock, there is a third stage of acculturation, where although there is still frustration and strain, the person accepts the new environment and its strange ways, accepting rather

---

28. White, *Who is to Blame?*, 155.
29. Hart, *Doors of the Sea*, 7.
30. Kalvero Oberg, "Cultural Shock: Adjustment to New Cultural Environments," *Curare* 29 (2006) 142–46, 143.
31. Oberg, "Cultural Shock," 143.

than fighting the differences. Humour becomes an ally in adjusting. Finally, there is the fourth stage of new cultural fluency—what I will explore further down as becoming a 150 percent person.

By far the most difficult time is the second stage. There is a tendency at the second stage to band together with other expats and create a sub-culture within the host culture. In full-fledged culture shock, these groups do little more than to critique the wider culture and try to (unsuccessfully) recreate the home environment in order to restore the lost sense of belonging. They become echo chambers that isolate themselves, and their disdain can be noticed and can earn disdain in return. Oberg writes: "If you are frustrated and have an aggressive attitude to the people of the host country, they will sense this hostility and in many cases respond in either a hostile manner or try to avoid you."[32]

Crossing cultures is always full of frustration, not just for the person who has crossed cultures, but for the receiving culture as well. The earliest societies in science and religion, the American Scientific Association (est. 1941) and Christians in Science UK (est. in the 1940's as the Research Scientists' Christian Fellowship), both began as groups of Christian scientists who wanted to discuss theology. They were crossing from their own disciplinary cultures into a foreign land. Yet there was not close integration with theologians—these were groups for scientists, rather than interdisciplinary groups. Indeed, for the ASA, full membership was only open to those who had at least one degree in the sciences. Although this requirement has now changed to include theologians and philosophers interested in science, it meant that for many years the members of those organisations created an enclave of people with a predominantly scientific culture within a wider theological culture: they have been an expat community within the wider theological community.

Equally, theologians in universities face a similar sense of culture shock. Universities pour resources into scientific equipment, promote scientific discoveries, and prioritise scientific research. Theology departments are often forced to fight for their very existence, justifying their existence in terms and by standards that are utterly foreign—defined by scientific measures. So they band together, perhaps with colleagues from the humanities, to form a cultural enclave.

Once that expat community is formed, it has the potential for deleterious consequences.[33] The ex-pat community might avoid meaningful

---

32. Oberg, "Cultural Shock," 144.

33. Craig Storti, *The Art of Crossing Cultures*, 2nd ed. (Yarmouth, ME: Intercultural, 2001), 53–59.

interaction with the host community, do their own activities (imported with all the cultural assumptions they find comfortable) and in return earn the disdain of the local community. Whether and to what extent this has happened between scientist-led groups and the wider theological community, and vice versa for theologians in universities, I leave the reader to decide. What the intercultural literature warns is that it is possible and even likely. How does one avoid the destructive effects of closed-in communities and move into the last two stages? First, by challenging one's own ethnocentric (or, perhaps, discipline-centric) impulses.

## CHALLENGING THE ETHNOCENTRIC IMPULSE

Ethnocentrism is the belief that our own cultural beliefs are the *human* norm, rather than a local expression of cultural values. Because of our cultural training, it seems natural to trust a P-value, or to argue over the slight nuance of Aquinas's use of *concupiscience*. But encountering those who really are different is startling and off-putting. What do you do with the person who does not care what the value of P is at all? Or someone who insists that the reliability of the Bible can be increased by scientific experiments? These encounters leave us reeling: we thought that deep down, the other side would be like us. As Craig Storti writes, "In fact, we *do* know better than to expect foreigners to behave like us. But that knowledge doesn't make any difference... It's entirely possible—indeed, it's inevitable—that we can cheerfully subscribe to the view that foreigners are different and still be stunned the first time we see a Hindu drink cow urine."[34]

It is precisely the moment when we are stunned and even offended that we begin to have the opportunity for proper intercultural work. Frustration shows that a cultural expectation is being contravened, and this gives us the conscious awareness to choose a path other than reacting in anger and avoidance. "Awareness, then, brings us to the brink of solving the problem of cultural incidents."[35]

Once aware of the problem, we can begin real dialogue about what is at stake in our different cultural systems, and learning can begin. When the moment of frustration hits, instead of reacting with anger, taking the opportunity to ask questions and dig deeper opens a new way forward. "What can you do to get over culture shock as quickly as possible? The answer is get to know the people of the host country."[36] It is also important in learning

34. Storti, *Art of Crossing Cultures*, 69.
35. Storti, *Art of Crossing Cultures*, 78.
36. Oberg, "Cultural Shock," 145.

to avoid characterizing individual particularities as the character of all the wider culture. If I am loud or rude, it does not mean that all Canadians are loud and rude. Similarly, if one scientist has odd views of theology, it does not follow that all share those same peculiarities. If a particular frustrating view is expressed commonly, then we can begin to think of it as representative of the host culture. As we understand representative behaviour we also begin to expect it, that is, we expect members of another culture to behave like themselves. Our expectations reduce our frustrations, and cause fewer moments of intense frustration.[37]

As fluency in the new culture increases, what is the final goal? Is it simply to move into two different, independently held patterns of behaviour? No.

## BECOMING A 150 PERCENT PERSON

In Sherwood Lingenfelter and Marvin Mayers's valuable little book on cross-cultural ministry, they speak of crossing-cultures as opening up the possibility of becoming a "150 percent person."[38] Cultures exist because they help us live together in society by rewarding or coercing certain types of behaviour from people regardless of whether the behaviour is natural to the individual or not. As we are trained in cultural values and perceptions from a young age, these become our natural ways of seeing the world, of finding identity and belonging. Those who work cross-culturally have a unique challenge and a unique opportunity. The challenge is that they begin 100 percent one culture or another. One hundred percent Canadian, in my case, is then exposed to 100 percent of another culture. Everything feels wrong. Ways of thinking make little sense. Values are incomprehensible and the ways of determining the right action are opaque. In order to learn from the new culture, and not simply conflict with it, one has to examine, and make room for the new culture by becoming less than 100 percent of one's own culture. When I came to England, I had to give up some of my engrained cultural perceptions. I had to stop introducing myself to strangers right away and learn to wait until I had grumbled about the weather and shared some life stories before broaching the intimate subject of what my name is. I was exposed to the elaborate liturgy of Anglo-Catholic worship, far from the charismatic evangelical tradition I was used to. I had to give up ways that I understood the world works, and learn new patterns of friendship and conversation. I had to become less than 100 percent Canadian.

37. Storti, *Art of Crossing Cultures*, 85.
38. Lingenfelter and Mayers, *Ministering Cross-Culturally*, 117–24.

But this also gave me a wonderful opportunity to learn new values and new ways of seeing the world. I learned that J-walking is not a violation of the natural law of the universe, and that round-abouts (or traffic circles, as we call them in Canada) are far more efficient than the Canadian propensity for 4-way stop signs at every intersection. I've learned of the settled identity attached to place, borne of tracing family back for hundreds of years in the same location: an impossible dream for most Canadians descended from recent immigrants. Different cultural expectations (like tiny attached houses) can lead to surprising outcomes (a sense of neighbourliness). I learned, bit by bit, to become part British. By adapting myself to a different culture, I lost part of the identity and values I once held, but gained new pieces of belonging and new perceptions of the world. And these can lead to being more than a 100 percent person. We will never be 100 percent of the new culture, so being a 200 percent person is impossible. But we can aim for being a 150 percent person: some bits of Canadian culture lost, and many pieces of British culture gained. A multiplicity of perspectives is gained, which brings with it a richer outlook on the world, and a deeper understanding of human nature.

The notion of 150 percent people can perhaps offer a goal for science and theology dialogue. Scientific training prioritises certain types of analysis: mathematical, inductive, empirical. It finds some kinds of question interesting and others uninteresting. It solves questions in carefully methodical ways. Certain types of answers are satisfying to a scientifically-trained mind, while others are not. Scientific training creates a scientific culture. The same is true of theological training. While there are rigorously methodological disciplines, such as textual criticism, many theological disciplines emphasise the place of critical judgment, creative metaphor, and imaginative engagement with mysteries beyond our mastery. Theology is an expansive discipline, where breaking new territory leaves one less rather than more certain about the nature of the world. To become a 150 percent person is to develop a third culture in oneself: one that is neither wholly the first nor the second.[39] To do so requires the humility to take on an identity that is neither this nor that: to let go of mastery and embrace the uncertainty of the in between.

---

39. The concept of "third-culture kids" is a common one: where children are raised in a culture different from that of their parents.' But my use of the term "third culture" should also be distinguished from John Brockman's use of the term in *The Third Culture: Beyond the Scientific Revolution* (New York: Simon & Schuster, 1995), where he uses it to refer to scientists who write for popular audiences directly rather than through the intermediary of journalists or literature specialists.

The 150 percent person gives up the highest mastery: no one can keep up with all the possible reading in two related sub-fields, let alone two completely different disciplines. Embracing the role of the 150 percent person is to give up being a master in either individual discipline. Yet, it may be the creative confluence of these identities that offers a breakthrough to the monocultural practitioners.

Finally, the 150 percent person, standing on the continental divide of disciplines may simply be content that their perspective allows them a glimpse of a wider view of human experience and knowledge than is generally perceived. It is in the widening of perspectives that wisdom is born, and pursuing science and theology may just offer one possibility amongst many paths for the recovery of wisdom in a world inundated by information.

## CONCLUSION

Models are key features of understanding complex realities. Science and theology are sometimes spoken of as two cultures, and this paper has taken that seriously as a model for understanding how practitioners can deal with the frustrations of engaging in interdisciplinary work. Avoiding isolation in ex-pat communities, challenging the discipline-centric impulse, and working towards becoming a 150 percent person are ways to begin to build bridges across the oft-divided cultures of science and theology.

Alister McGrath stands prominently amongst those who have modelled successfully what it looks like to live as a 150 percent person in science and theology, embracing the two different cultures with fluency and skill. It is a joy to have the chance to celebrate his work and impact in this *Festschrift* volume. He is a lucid writer, a lauded teacher, and a most valued colleague.

Chapter 12

# Alister McGrath's Theodicy

Michael Lloyd

This chapter will explore Alister McGrath's theodicy, and, in so doing, might be likened to a tree surgeon attempting to extract a friend's tooth with a chain saw, not because a chain saw is particularly suited to the task, nor even because the friend had anything other than the mildest tooth ache—but simply because it was the only tool that the tree surgeon possessed. Alister is not particularly known for his theodicy. It is not where his most important contributions—and they are myriad—have been made. Furthermore, the only book he has written on it was at a popular level—and that was twenty-six years ago![1] For all I know, he may have changed his mind significantly since then (but I couldn't ask him, or it would have given away the secret of this *Festschrift*).

However, theodicy is the only tool in my tool box, so I shall set to work on Alister's theodical tooth, accordingly. I have two defences for this potentially unfair and, indeed, probably painful operation. The first is the fertility of Alister's mind. To whatever subject he turns, he brings the incisiveness, clarity and creativity of an exceptional thinker. Even in an area that is not central to the main preoccupations of his intellectual journey and has only been addressed at popular level, I hope to show that his writing will repay careful academic attention.

1. McGrath, *Suffering* (London: Hodder and Stoughton, 1992).

My second justification for wielding my chain saw in this worryingly dental pursuit is the importance of the subject. Alister's book on *Suffering* was prompted by a conversation he had, while a tutor at Wycliffe Hall, with a student whose father had died:

> He was devastated. He talked about how much he loved his father, and the deep sense of loss that his death evoked. He told me about his sense of sadness in knowing that his father would never know of his future life and career. He wondered what God might be saying to him through all this. Rather than discussing his essay, he was thinking out loud about the place of suffering in his own life, and meditating on what he could learn through it.[2]

Alister accepted that "Theology may not be able to abolish suffering," but insisted that "it can allow that suffering to be seen in a new light."[3] Theology is nothing if it is not pastoral—knowing the essentially pastoral nature of theology is one of the strengths of all Alister's writing—and nowhere is that truer than when attempting theodicy. That does not mean that theodicy should be deprived of the rigour, and exempted from the mutual critique, of academic thinking. As I have written elsewhere, "I don't believe that one pays respect to suffering by denying it the homage of the most careful thought, by cutting it off from the resources of academic discipline and theological tradition, by isolating it from other areas of life and other dimensions of what it is to be human."[4] It *is* to say that "When the intellectual and pastoral dimensions of the problem of evil are addressed in isolation from one another, it is to the impoverishment of both. If we are not to cut off the sufferer from the resources of rigorous thought, no less should we deprive academic deliberation of the critique and the constraint of being confronted by the reality of personal suffering."[5] That is similar, I think, to what Alister means when he draws on John Mackay's image of the Balcony and the Road:

> By the Balcony . . . I mean that little platform in wood or stone that protrudes from the upper window of a Spanish home. There the family may gather of an evening to gaze spectator-wise upon the street beneath, or at the sunset or the stars beyond . . .
> By the Road, I mean the place where life is tensely lived, where thought has its birth in conflict and concern, where choices are

---

2. McGrath, *Suffering*, 1.
3. McGrath, *Suffering*, 7.
4. From my forthcoming book on the problem of evil, under the working title, *The Evil of Suffering and the Goodness of God* (henceforth *Evil of Suffering*).
5. Lloyd, *Evil of Suffering*.

made and decisions are carried out. It is the place of action, of pilgrimage, of crusade, where concern is never absent from a wayfarer's heart. On the Road a goal is sought, dangers are faced, life is poured out.[6]

Mackay seems to prioritise the Road—"Truth is found upon the Road."[7] Alister, by contrast, insists that "Those high above the Road on the Balcony could be of help to those on the Road—above all, if they were fellow travellers, engaged on the same journey":

> For at its best, the Balcony perspective can be profoundly helpful. Those on the Balcony can see further, on account of their elevated position. They can see the full glory of a sunset or a starlit sky and not just the potholes and the puddles; where those on the Road see only to the next bend, those on the Balcony can see where the Road is going, and what it avoids. The Balcony provides a perspective to make sense of the Road.[8]

Of course, it works the other way round, too. Those on the Balcony can see problems ahead that those on the Road cannot see, and those on the Road can encounter ground-level glories beyond the vision of those on the Balcony—which is why the two need each other.

Alister wrote his book in the hope that its balconian perspective might help make sense of the Road. This chapter is also written in the hope that it might indirectly help those for whom the problem of suffering is personal and acute. I do not entertain the fond illusion that it would be *directly* helpful to someone who was going through the crucible of suffering: my hope is that it may challenge views of God that make the sufferer's path a harder one than it need be, and that it may thereby equip the academy and the church to articulate, to worship, and to serve a God who is the Helper, the Sustainer, and the Fellow-Sufferer of those in pain—and not the Inflictor of that pain.

This chapter will first draw a map of the problem of evil. It will then locate Alister's theodical views on that map, attempt to subject them to that critique which can be the anvil and furnace of more burnished truth,

---

6. James Mackay, *Preface to Christian Theology* (London: Nisbet, 1942), 29–30, cited in McGrath, *Suffering*, 3–4. I believe that Mackay overdraws the distinction between the Balcony and the Road, thus perpetuating the myth of the academic ivory tower. Having been a college chaplain in two different universities, I do not believe that there is any such thing as an ivory tower. Academics are just as prone to the vicissitudes and pains of life as everyone else. And those "on the Road" think about the implications of human suffering. Balcony and Road are simply different modes of every human life.

7. Mackay, *Preface to Christian Theology*, 39. Mackay is here drawing on a comment by Unamuno.

8. McGrath, *Suffering*, 5.

exploring their strengths, weaknesses, and a putative inconsistency. Finally, it will expound Alister's belief in the passibility of God. This is not a rare belief today, but Alister helpfully unpacks *why* he considers it to help with the problem of evil. Thus we conclude with what in my view is Alister's most creative contribution to theodical thought.

## A MAP OF EVIL[9]

J. L. Mackie, in his famous essay, "Evil and Omnipotence," articulates where the problem of evil lies:

> In its simplest form the problem is this: God is omnipotent, God is wholly good; yet evil exists. There seems to be some contradiction between these three propositions, so that if any two of them were true the third would be false. But at the same time all three are essential parts of most theological propositions; the theologian, it seems, at one *must* adhere and *cannot consistently* adhere to all three.[10]

The basic claim here is that the following set of beliefs is inconsistent:

1. "God is omnipotent"
2. "God is wholly good"
3. "Evil exists"

Mackie does accept, however, that "the contradiction does not arise immediately," and that, in order to demonstrate that a contradiction does arise from holding all three, 'we need some additional premises, or perhaps some quasi-logical rules connecting the terms "good" and "evil" and "omnipotent."' He suggests adding . . .

4. "There are no limits to what an omnipotent thing can do"[11] (as an unpacking of 'omnipotent')

and

---

9. This section draws heavily on the first chapter of my doctoral thesis, *The Cosmic Fall and the Free Will Defence* (DPhil., Oxford: Bodleian Library, Oxford University, 1997).

10. J. L. Mackie, "Evil and Omnipotence," from *Mind*, Vol. LXIV, No. 254, 1955, reprinted in *God and Evil*, ed. N. Pike (Englewood Cliffs, New Jersey: Prentice-Hall, 1964), 47.

11. I have reversed the order of these additional premises for my own evil (actually, structural) purposes—the change of order makes no difference to Mackie's argument.

5. "A good thing always eliminates evil as far as it can" (as an unpacking of 'wholly good')

Most Christian philosophers have complained that "There are no limits to what an omnipotent thing can do" is an overstatement of the concept of omnipotence. There are *logical* limits to what an omnipotent thing can do. For example, an omnipotent being could not make a round square—not because that being is not omnipotent, but because the concept is logically incoherent. Mackie accepts this, so he suggests rewording (5) as:

5. "There are no *nonlogical* limits to what an omnipotent thing can do"

This would give us the set of beliefs:

1. "God is omnipotent"
2. "God is wholly good"
3. "Evil exists"
4. "There are no nonlogical limits to what an omnipotent thing can do"
5. "A good thing always eliminates evil as far as it can"

The question is, is this an inconsistent set of beliefs? No, because evil might be a logical necessity. As Nelson Pike put it, "An omniscient and omnipotent being *could* prevent evil in the world only if it be admitted that evil is not a logical necessity, i.e. only if the statement "all worlds contain evil" is not a tautology."[12] If evil is a logical necessity, then the existence of evil falls within the area of *logical* limitations and is therefore no contradiction of the omnipotence of God. So let's take account of that by reformulating our set of propositions accordingly . . .

1. "God is omnipotent"
2. "God is wholly good"
3. "Evil exists"
4a. "There are no nonlogical limits to what an omnipotent thing can do"
4b. "Evil in the world is not logically necessary"
5. "A good thing always eliminates evil as far as it can"

We have now arrived at a set of propositions that is generally regarded as being logically contradictory. If we believe all of them, we are guilty of logical error. Mackie believed that theists are committed to all of them, but

---

12. Nathan Pike, "God and Evil: A Reconsideration," *Ethics* 68.2 (1958) 119.

is that the case? All a theist need do is to reject any one of them, and there is no logical error. We may therefore use this set of propositions as a grid on which to map responses to the problem of evil within Christian theology. Different families of theodicy reject different propositions. We shall look briefly at each of them.

## 1. "God is Omnipotent"

Very few Christian theologians have rejected this proposition. The Process theologian, Charles Hartshorne, did write a book with the provocative title, *Omnipotence and Other Theological Mistakes*,[13] but more careful expositions of a Process theodicy have tended to redefine omnipotence rather than reject it, and are therefore better seen as rejecting Proposition 4a than Proposition 1.

## 2. "God is Wholly Good"

Even fewer Christian theologians reject Proposition 2. This is hardly surprising, given the fact that the goodness of God is part of the Christian gospel: "This is the message we have heard from him and declare to you: God is light, in him there is no darkness at all" (1 John 1:5). It is even less surprising that there are virtually no Christian theologians who reject Proposition 2 in the modern era,[14] given that it has become a widely accepted view that, as Bishop John Davies writes, "At the heart of all things, the motive of power is subservient to the motive of love."[15] Throughout Christian history, however, the goodness of God has generally been seen as so central to the Christian faith as to exclude Christian theologians from denying it *by definition*.

---

13. Hartshorne, *Omnipotence and Other Theological Mistakes* (State University of New York Press, Albany, 1984).

14. Two exceptions would be John K. Roth, "A Theodicy of Protest," in *Encountering Evil: Live Options in Theodicy*, ed. S. T. Davis (Atlanta: John Knox, 1981), 7–37, and Martin Israel, *Angels—Messengers of Grace* (London: SPCK, 1995). Roth's "A Theodicy of Protest" is more protest than theodicy, given that he declines to defend the goodness of God. And it is not clear how far Israel's view in *Angels* is characteristic of the corpus of his thought.

15. Davies, *A Song for Every Morning: Dedication and Defiance with St Patrick's Breastplate* (London: Canterbury, 2008), 10.

## 3. "Evil Exists"

This is really the realm of the Christian Science tradition, which tends to see suffering as appearance and not reality. It is of course possible to consider Augustine here, as one who definitely—and helpfully—insisted that to talk of evil "existing" is a category mistake. He did, however, allow that evil *events* occur; thus, the problem of evil persists—it is just to be located in the realm of history, not ontology. His *privatio boni* position is hugely important, but I argue elsewhere[16] that it does not solve the problem of evil, and that Augustine did not think that it did. What it does do is to help us to conceive of that problem—and of creation, and of ourselves—more accurately.

## 4a. "There are no Nonlogical Limits to What an Omnipotent Thing can Do"

As suggested above, Process Theology is the position that is best known for rejecting this proposition. Process Theology, building on the philosophical foundations of Alfred North Whitehead and Charles Hartshorne, offers a framework of thought in which freedom is essential—but that freedom (which is characteristic, not just of human beings, but of all existent realities, for to exist is to have power) is not given to creation by God, but is a surdic fact in an eternally existing and not divinely derived metaphysical operating system. This cuts the Gordian knot of theodicy, because it means that God is not the source of all reality, is not the owner of all power, and is therefore not able to control what "choices" are made by the "actual occasions"[17] of which reality is made up. His only power is the power of persuasion, not of compulsion. He is therefore not culpable for the choices made by actual occasions against the flow of His attempted persuasion, and in defiance of His divine advice. It absolves God of responsibility for evil and suffering in the world, however, at the cost of confident eschatological hope. For if God is not the source of all reality and the owner of all power, if God can only persuade and not compel, then He does not have the power to ensure that justice is finally done, that the old order of suffering, sorrow and death passes away, and that all things are made new. For that, He is dependent

---

16. Lloyd, *Evil of Suffering*.

17. "Actual occasions" is the term Whitehead uses for the slices of space-time which are the building blocks of all beings and events. See his *Process and Reality*, Corrected Edition, ed. David Ray Griffin and Donald W. Sherburne (New York: Free Press, 1978), 18f.

upon the co-operation of every other being and every other event. And their track record is not encouraging.

## 4b. "Evil in the World is not Logically Necessary"

Mackie sees that belief in the logical necessity of evil would constitute a way out, for the theist, from the horns of his logical trilemma, and he argues compellingly against it. I know of no Christian theologian who rejects this proposition, for the obvious reason that, if evil is logically necessary, if it is true that good cannot exist without evil, then it would seem to follow either that there is evil within God Himself, or that the world has always existed. If there is evil within God, then we have denied the message of the gospel, which is that God is light and in Him there is no darkness at all (1 John 1:5). And we have successfully attacked Proposition 4b at the cost of forfeiting Proposition 2. If the world has always existed, that may be perfectly possible to state in a theologically acceptable form. But to suggest further that the world, with its evil and suffering, exists as the pillar upon which the goodness of God is founded would seem to render the goodness of God an incoherent concept. Furthermore, if evil is necessary for the existence of good, then the eschatological hope for the removal of evil would seem to be undermined.

Here is probably the place, however, to locate Karl Barth's view of evil as Nothingness. Barth held, not that evil is a logically necessary concomitant to *good*, but that evil is a logically necessary concomitant to *creation*. "In willing and affirming a good creation God has unwilled, or willed against, a contrary possibility, and has thereby given that which was rejected and excluded a negative but nevertheless virulent power over against the real creaturely world" is John Hick's summary of Barth's position.[18] If evil is a logically necessary concomitant to creation, then God cannot be held to account for all that happens in His world—only for the overall decision to create at all, given the inevitable consequences. Barth offers no reason to believe that God's creation of the world does inevitably entail the unwilling into being of a negative and de-creative power. Indeed, the idea would appear to be logically flawed. Not willing, not affirming, not electing, saying No, do not confer anything on anything: they are themselves precisely a *privation* of conferring, and thus it is not possible to attribute anything to them. It is therefore not surprising that Barth has not had many theodical followers.[19]

18. John Hicks, *Evil and the God of Love* (Basingstoke, UK: Macmillan, 1988), 135.
19. See, however, Neil Messer's "Natural Evil after Darwin," in *Theology After*

Which leaves us with . . .

## 5. "A Good Thing Always Eliminates Evil as Far as it Can"

Nelson Pike insists that the rejection of this proposition is a live and logically acceptable option for the theist: ." . . . a perfectly good person could allow evil, or for that matter be himself an evildoer—though it were avoidable—providing only that there be some other 'good reason' for His tolerance of evil or His evil. . . . If the proposition, 'there is a good reason for evil in the theistic universe . . . *could* be true, then the logic of the phrase 'perfectly good person' allows that the propositions, 'God is a perfectly good person' and 'God allows evil in the world even though He could prevent it' *could* be true together."[20]

Proposition 5 is therefore the proposition that has been rejected by many—indeed, most—Christian theologians. They have given different answers as to what that 'good reason' might be. The *Free Will Defence* favours the good of "freedom": unless human beings are free to choose good, their good choices and actions are meaningless, but, if they are free to choose, then they may choose to do evil rather than good. The *Non-Identity Theodicy*[21] favours the good of particular women and men like you and me existing, dependent as we are on the whole nexus of events (morally good and morally bad, pleasurable and painful, vital and lethal) in our event horizon, which has made us the particular people that we are, and which is believed to be justified by the good of our existence. The *Skeptical Theism* theodicy does not claim to know what God's reason is for permitting evil, but believes that there is one, and that "it is only *hubris* which would tempt us to think that we could so much as grasp God's plans here, even if He proposed to divulge them to us."[22]

On the co-ordinates of this admittedly sketchy map, let us attempt to locate the theodicy of Alister McGrath.

---

*Darwin*, ed. Michael S. Northcott & R. J. Berry (Milton Keynes, UK: Paternoster, 2009), 139–54.

20. Pike, "God and Evil," 119.

21. The Non-Identity Theodicy was developed by Vince Vitale, based on ideas of Robert Adams. See his "Non-Identity Theodicy," in *Finding Ourselves after Darwin: Conversations on the Image of God, Original Sin, and the Problem of Evil,* eds. Stanley P. Rosenberg et al., 306–25. Grand Rapids: Baker Academic, 2018.

22. Alvin Plantinga, from the unpublished handout accompanying his 1998 Wilde lectures in Oxford.

## THE LOCATION OF ALISTER MCGRATH'S THEODICY

At first sight, Alister might be thought of as rejecting Proposition 1. The third chapter of his book is entitled "God Almighty?"—and the clue is in the title: he wants to qualify what is meant by "omnipotent." In particular, he wants to challenge the understanding of omnipotence as meaning that "God can do anything he chooses to." He does so first by pointing out that there are logical limits to what God can do—as we noted above and as Mackie allowed. He goes on to argue that there are also *moral* constraints on what God can do. He is constrained by His character (such that He could not "command someone to hate him, for example"[23]), by His promises (such that He could not "prevent every human being that has ever turned to him in faith from being saved"), and by His choices (such that, having decided to create the universe, which He did not need to do, He cannot now will that it cease to exist, because "Once God acts, he is bound by his actions"[24]). Alister expresses these qualifications strongly: "God is faithful and reliable. And for that very reason, he cannot be omnipotent."[25]

He supports this view by appeal to William of Ockham's distinction between the absolute power of God and the ordained power of God. The former refers to God's potentiality "before he had committed himself to any course of action or world ordering."[26] The latter refers to His circumscribed potentiality subsequent to decisions, creation, covenant and promises:

> For Ockham, God cannot now do everything. He has deliberately limited his possibilities. In his omnipotence, God chose to limit his own options. Is that a contradiction? No. If God is really capable of doing anything, he must be able to commit himself to a course of action—and stay committed to it. Otherwise, there is something which God cannot do, thus calling into question his omnipotence.[27]

That passage shows that Alister is not actually denying God's omnipotence. He is merely, and in a perfectly orthodox fashion, qualifying what it can mean in the context of the biblical understanding of God. He clearly prefers the more biblical term "almighty" to the more philosophical (and fraught) term "omnipotent":

---

23. McGrath, *Suffering*, 6.
24. McGrath, *Suffering*, 17–18.
25. McGrath, *Suffering*, 19.
26. McGrath, *Suffering*, 20.
27. McGrath, *Suffering*, 20.

So where does this leave all the abstract talk about God being omnipotent? In something of a state of ruin, is the short answer. The neat simplifications of the philosophers are left in tatters. God is indeed almighty. But that does not mean that he can do anything and everything. His choices are limited. This limitation does not arise from any weakness or failure upon the part of God, but from a decision to deliberately restrict his own options. It is a self-imposed limitation, not something that is imposed upon God. Only God had the right and the ability to limit his own course of action.[28]

The fact that Alister is allowing only *self*-limitations to the potentiality of God, the fact that he is uncomfortable with any other suggestion that "there is something that God cannot do," and the fact that he never uses this qualification of the potentiality of God to suggest that God *could not* remove the suffering of the world[29]—these facts together demonstrate that Alister's theodicy is not to be located in the rejection of Proposition 1, nor in the rejection of Proposition 4a.

His appeal to the faithfulness and reliability of God shows that he is not rejecting Proposition 2. The pastoral focus on the grief of his student in the book's Introduction, and the exultant recapitulation of "The Hope of Glory" in the final chapter—"Just as the suffering is real, so are the promises of God and the hope of eternal life"[30]—demonstrate that he is not rejecting Proposition 3. The promise that "God will wipe away every tear from their eyes" and that "There will be no more death or mourning or crying or pain" (Revelation 21:4) that he holds out to the reader at the end of the book is simply incompatible with the rejection of Proposition 4b.

Committed as he is to logical coherence, Alister has to deny one of the propositions, and it is Proposition 5 that he clearly rejects. Further, it is the Free Will argument that he seems to favour. In his chapter on "Blaming God," he writes of blaming God for all the ills of the world as "the easy way out," insisting that . . .

> . . . it wasn't God who engineered the holocaust. It was human beings. It wasn't God who developed the atom bomb, nor he who dropped it on Hiroshima. It wasn't God who directed the

---

28. McGrath, *Suffering*, 21.

29. He only uses it to suggest that God *can* choose to be passible. We shall consider Alister's account of the passibility of God later.

30. McGrath, *Suffering*, 104.

liquidation squads during Stalin's purges. It was sinful and fallen human beings.[31]

Why does God allow us to do such things to one another? What is the good for which God is warranted in allowing such suffering? It is human freedom:

> Freedom implies that we are free to make mistakes; to do things that hurt others; to cause evil. . . . So we have freedom—a freedom to do evil, a freedom to avoid and disobey God. God leaves us room to be human. He makes space for us to make mistakes. God pulls himself back from his creation, in order to allow it to exercise the freedom which he chose to allow it. It is pointless to speak of God endowing his creatures with freedom, only to refuse to allow them to exercise that freedom. And in the exercise of that freedom, we may see the origins of much of the tragic suffering of the world.[32]

Into this reasonably classic statement of the Free Will argument, Alister has inserted a combination of Moltmann's concept of God's withdrawing into Himself in order to make space for us to be free, and Hick's notion of God creating us at epistemic distance from Himself, again for the sake of our freedom. It is only if God "pulls Himself back from His creation" that it can be free. As I have written elsewhere:

> What these two concepts have in common is the assumption that the overt presence of God would render creaturely freedom impossible, and that, therefore, the creation of a free, self-creating universe requires that God, in some sense and to some extent, absents himself from his handiwork. . . . But this raises the questions: Is the power and majesty of God overwhelming? Is the absence of God more creative, fertile and liberating than his presence? Is it not a pagan (mis)conception of God to see his presence as a threat to creaturely freedom? Where can creatures be more fully themselves and more free than in the direct presence of God? When Moltmann writes of God's withdrawal into himself as 'a movement which allows creation the space for its own being,'[33] do we not have to ask whether space can ever rightly be conceived as a zero-sum game between God and creation? Would that not make God himself a spatial being? A

---

31. McGrath, *Suffering*, 12.
32. McGrath, *Suffering*, 57–58.
33. Jürgen Moltmann, *God in Creation: A New Theology of Creation and the Spirit of God* (Minneapolis: Fortress, 1993), 87.

part of his own creation? As Rowan Williams likes to say, 'God does not compete with us for space.' God's presence does not cramp, warp or misshape—it is his presence, surely, rather than his withdrawal, that lets be.[34]

However, the concept of freedom, which does involve the self-*limitation* of God, does not require His self-*withdrawal*, and nothing in Alister's theodicy depends on this supporting framework. (The language of "self-withdrawal" is probably best seen, in Alister's use of it, as a metaphor or picture of "self-limitation." Nothing is lost, I suggest, and much is exorcised, if that metaphor is dropped.)

So Alister rejects the Proposition that "A good thing always eliminates evil as far as it can." He believes that there is a good reason why God does not eliminate evil or suffering. He believes that that good reason is the freedom that alone can make moral good and love meaningful, because it makes human beings genuine agents whose actions are genuinely their own, and whose characters are (to a significant extent) self-made.

The Free Will argument, however, has one obvious gaping hole in it, which is that it seems to account well for *moral* evil (the wrong, hurtful and harmful acts of human beings), but it does not seem to account at all for *natural* or *physical* evil (that suffering that is not caused by human agency). The Free Will argument can account for murder and war and violence and spite, but it does not seem to be able to bear the weight of accounting for drought, disease, predation and pre-human animal suffering. This lacuna in the explanatory power of the Free Will argument is accepted by nearly all theistic thinkers.[35] They therefore accept the need to supplement or to extend the Free Will argument in order to equip it to cover natural evil as well as moral evil. So, at this point, we need another map.

---

34. From "The Fallenness of Nature: Three Non-Human Suspects," in *Finding Ourselves after Darwin: Conversations on the Image of God, Original Sin, and the Problem of Evil*, eds. Stanley P. Rosenberg et al. (Grand Rapids: Baker Academic, 2018), 268–69.

35. One writer who attempts to explain all suffering by reference to human agency, despite what we know from Darwinist biology and genetics about prehuman natural evil, is William Dembski, *The End of Christianity: Finding a Good God in an Evil World* (Nashville: B&H Academic, 2009). For a critique of his position, see my "Theodicy, Fall and Adam," in *Finding Ourselves after Darwin: Conversations on the Image of God, Original Sin, and the Problem of Evil*, eds. Stanley P. Rosenberg et al. (Grand Rapids: Baker Academic, 2018), 258–61.

## A MAP OF NATURAL EVIL

I have argued elsewhere[36] that the arguments put forward by Christian theodicists to account for natural evil can be revealingly analysed under three headings: 1) Natural Evil as Instrumental to the Purposes of God, 2) Natural Evil as Inevitable within the purposes of God, and 3) Natural Evil as Inimical to the purposes of God. A brief explanation of these three categories is necessary here.

### 1. Natural Evil as Instrumental to the Purposes of God

Instrumental accounts of natural evil believe that God allows events of natural evil to happen because He is able to use them to further His purposes for His creatures. They become "instruments" in His hands. They may be unpleasant, injurious or destructive, but they are not wholly negative because of the good which God may bring from them. Different theologians have focused on different "goods" which they see as dependent upon the "evils" of humanly-unintended suffering. The goods may be . . .

#### a. Educational

God uses suffering to educate us. It is His "megaphone to rouse a deaf world."[37] It teaches us hard but important lessons, which we would otherwise eschew. A key proponent of this position is Eleanor Stump:

> Natural evil—the pain of disease, the intermittent and unpredictable destruction of natural disasters, the decay of old age, the imminence of death—takes away a person's satisfaction with himself. It tends to humble him, show him his frailty, make him reflect on the transience of temporal goods, and turn his affections towards other-worldly things, away from the things of this world. No amount of moral or natural evil, of course, can guarantee that a man will seek God's help. If it could, the willing it produced would not be free. But evil of this sort is the best hope, I think, and maybe the only effective means, for bringing men to such a state.[38]

---

36. See "Theodicy, Fall and Adam."
37. C. S. Lewis, *The Problem of Pain* (London: Collins Fontana, 1972), 81.
38. Eleanor Stump, "The Problem of Evil," *Faith and Philosophy* 2.4 (October 1985) 409.

Michael Lloyd—*Alister McGrath's Theodicy*   215

The penultimate sentence of that quotation shows that Stump accepts the Free Will argument, and is using this educational argument to supplement the Free Will argument, so as to cover the phenomenon of natural evil as well as moral evil.

### b. Aesthetic[39]

This takes two forms. First, there is the aesthetic argument of Augustine that, just as a good painting requires dark colors as well as light, for the painting to have contrast and interest, so evil—both moral and natural—contributes to the overall beauty of creation:

> A picture may be beautiful when it has touches of black in appropriate places; in the same way the whole universe is beautiful, if one could see it as a whole, even with its sinners, though their ugliness is disgusting when they are viewed in themselves.[40]

The idea, however, that God takes any sort of aesthetic pleasure in either the sin or the suffering of His creatures seems abhorrent.

Secondly, there is the argument that it is suffering that prompts great art: "In a world devoid both of dangers to be avoided and rewards to be won we may assume that there would have been virtually no development of the human intellect and imagination, and hence of either the sciences or culture."[41] However, "Human beings seem to be innately curious and creative: they do not need to be pushed into science or art by hunger or want."[42] To see evil and suffering as generative of knowledge and creativity, is, I suggest, to pay them too much respect, and to overlook their intrinsically destructive teleology.

## 2. Natural Evil as Inevitable within the Purposes of God

"Inevitable" accounts of natural evil believe that it was not possible for God to create a physical world that was free of the violent clash of systems and

---

39. There is also an instrumental account of natural evil that sees it as necessary to provide knowledge of how to commit morally wrong acts, and therefore a requisite to moral freedom. See my *Cosmic Fall and the Free Will Defence*, 70–75.

40. *City of God*, Book XI, chapter 23, trans. Henry Bettenson (Harmondsworth, UK: Penguin, 1986), 455–56.

41. John Hick, "An Irenaean Theodicy," in *Encountering Evil*, ed. Stephen T. Davis (Edinburgh: T. & T. Clark, 1981), 47.

42. Lloyd, *Cosmic Fall*, 68.

species. Christopher Southgate has helped establish the term "Only Way" arguments, arguing that a competitive, conflictual set of processes necessarily involving parasitism, predation, pain and waste "was the only way in which God could have given rise to a biosphere containing all this value and beauty, including the eventual evolution of a species capable of bearing the image and likeness of God."[43]

Such a view has to face (at least) two sharp question. First, does it pay too much respect to violence, seeing it as creative of value? "Surely a religion built on the cross of Christ would shrink from allowing violence so fertile a role in the creation of values? Does not the cross of Christ suggest that, contrary to all perception to the contrary, it is the *refusal* of violence that is the most creative of value?"[44] And secondly, inevitable approaches have their eschatological work cut out, for, if the only way in which God can create a physical world is by allowing it to create its values through violent clash and destructive conflict, then how will it be possible to remake the world in such a way as to enable the wolf to lie down with the lamb? Southgate believes that the world will be remade in that way, and insists that "it must have been impossible for God simply to create directly the eschatological state that Christians believe will follow from the ultimate redemption of the cosmos."[45] But how does the Atonement change the potentialities of the physical constitution of the cosmos? Some account needs to be given of how what is physically impossible at creation becomes physically possible at recreation. And, ideally, an approach needs to be found that does not set up such a tension between the two.

## 3. Natural Evil as Inimical to the Purposes of God

Inimical accounts of natural evil look to the healing and nature miracles of Jesus, and see within them the divine attitude to natural evil—and they find it to be hostile. They see the cleansings of lepers and the stillings of storms and the raisings to life as the divine assault upon disease and death. They therefore find a contradiction in those theodicies that seek to *justify* disease and death. They find the movement of the Cross (dying for others) to be in the opposite direction from the movement of a predatory system (killing others), and therefore resist any suggestion that the latter is intended by the

---

43. Christopher Southgate, "'Free-Process' and 'Only Way' Arguments," in *Finding Ourselves after Darwin: Conversations on the Image of God, Original Sin, and the Problem of Evil*, eds. Stanley P. Rosenberg et al. (Grand Rapids: Baker Academic, 2018), 294.

44. Lloyd, "Theodicy, Fall and Adam," 254.

45. Southgate, "'Free-Process' and 'Only Way,'" 302.

God we meet in the former. They look at the doctrine of the Trinity and they find there the otherwise unknowable truth of what John Milbank calls "the ontological priority of peace"[46] and they therefore forbear to make the Trinitarian God of peace the deliberate author of an essentially violent creation. They define theodicy as the justification of *God*, not of suffering. And they therefore seek to find a creaturely cause for the hiatus they discern between the way the world is and the way it was intended to be (and will one day be) within the purposes of its loving Maker. Three possible creaturely causes in particular have been put forward:[47]

### a. The Fall of the World Soul

N.P. Williams posited the existence of a corporate creaturely being, encompassing within a unity all the elements of the created world—a being with consciousness, other than God, and free. He posited the pre-cosmic rebellion of such a World Soul and the consequent vitiation of the creative process, marring God's harmonious purposes for creation with such defiance of His purposes as the venom and destructiveness of "the cobra, the tarantula and the bacillus of diphtheria."[48]

### b. The Fall of a Free Process

John Polkinghorne[49] suggests that, not only are human beings free, but the whole creaturely process is free—free from divine determination, and free to a significant extent to create and shape itself. If, therefore, creation develops in such a way as to produce the destructiveness of cancer, then we are in no way to mistake that as remotely the will or purpose, let alone the action, of God.

---

46. John Milbank, *Theology and Social Theory: Beyond Secular Reason* (Oxford: Blackwell, 2003), 432.

47. For a critique of a) and b), see my "Fallenness of Nature," 263–70. For a critique of c), see Christopher Southgate's *The Groaning of Creation: God, Evolution and the Problem of Evil* (London: Westminster John Knox, 2008), 28–35.

48. N. P. Williams, *The Ideas of the Fall and of Original Sin* (London: Longmans, Green, 1927), 522.

49. See, for example, his *Science and Providence: God's Interaction with the World* (Philadelphia: Templeton Foundation, 2005), 69–79.

### c. The Fall of the Angels

Eric Mascall,[50] C. S. Lewis,[51] Stephen Davis,[52] Gregory Boyd[53] and others suggest that there is some reality to the language of the angelic and the demonic, and some referent to the tradition of the Fall of the Angels. They further suggest that, so interconnected are the different dimensions of creation, a declension away from the will of the Creator in one sphere may have destructive implications within another, luring the material world away from its Creator's harmonious purposes for it.

Having drawn our Marauder's Map, we now need to find Alister on it.

## THE LOCATION OF ALISTER MCGRATH'S NATURAL EVIL THEODICY

And, confusingly, we see him at two different places at the same time—without a Time Turner! On the one hand, he seems to plum squarely for an Instrumental account of natural evil—and the Educational version, in particular. His assertion that . . .

> Suffering and the death of those we know and love break down the pretence of human permanence. . . . Suffering . . . batters down the gates of the citadel of illusions. It confronts us with the harsh facts of life. And it makes us ask those hard questions which have the power to erode falsehood and propel us away from the false security and transient rewards of the world towards our loving God.[54]

. . . sounds very like the quotation of Eleanore Stump above. And when he goes on to write that "We learn through suffering. There is much truth in the old Greek saying, "pathemata mathemata—suffering is education,"[55] it seems clear where on the map he is to be found.

---

50. Eric Mascall, *Christian Theology and Natural Science* (New York: Ronald, 1956), 32–36, 299–304.

51. Lewis, *Problem of Pain*, 121–24.

52. Stephen Davis, "Free Will and Evil," in *Encountering Evil: Live Options in Theodicy*, 69–99.

53. Gregory Boyd, *God at War: The Bible and Spiritual Conflict* (Downers Grove, IL: IVP Academic, 1997), and *Satan and the Problem of Evil: Constructing a Trinitarian Warfare Theodicy* (Downers Grove, IL: IVP Academic, 2001).

54. McGrath, *Suffering*, 30.

55. McGrath, *Suffering*, 56.

But then he also appears in the Inevitable region of the map. Talking about the 'armchair critics of God,' he writes that *"they* could have created a universe devoid of any suffering and pain. But could they really?"[56]—a question he later answers in the negative: "Suffering is part of life—not an add-on feature we can dispense with, but a vital aspect of our existence as humans. To eliminate suffering is to eliminate life itself."[57] Southgate could not have put it more clearly himself.

So, is this bilocation contradictory? Is this the "inconsistency" which I mentioned at the start of this chapter? No, they are quite reconcilable. It may be that there is no physical world that could be created that is free of suffering, but that God is justified for going ahead and creating it, because of the good He can bring out of it. It may be that suffering is inevitable, but that God can make it His instrument. There is no contradiction here, but that does not mean that there is nothing to critique.

## A CRITIQUE OF ALISTER MCGRATH'S THEODICY

Alister's Inevitable arguments are subject to the same criticisms we made of Inevitable arguments generically, above. So let us focus on his Educational approach. First, if the purpose of suffering is to "propel us away from the false security and transient rewards of the world towards our loving God," then what is its justification for those who have already turned towards Him? Alister gives some idea of how he would answer that question. Suffering can not only turn us into Christians: it can deepen us as human beings: "Suffering makes us more sensitive and compassionate people."[58]

So the second question that needs to be asked of the Educational view, is, granted that it can make us more sensitive and compassionate, can it not equally make us deflated, defeated, depressed, exhausted, cynical and bitter? It can deepen us, but can it not equally destroy us? And is it necessarily satisfactory to blame the individual themselves alone if it does the latter? If it is an instrument, is it not a rather faulty one?

Thirdly, when suffering has a good effect and deepens us, I suggest that it is God we have to thank—not the suffering. "Our experience of suffering can, by the grace of God, be converted into something positive,"[59] writes Alister. Indeed, but it is *by the grace of God*, not by the inherent grace of the suffering. Suffering can be *converted* into something positive—it is

56. McGrath, *Suffering*, 35.
57. McGrath, *Suffering*, 55–56.
58. McGrath, *Suffering*, 56.
59. McGrath, *Suffering*, 9.

not something positive in itself. It has to be turned 180 degrees to become something positive. Its natural teleology is not deepening, but destroying. That is why God assaults it in the person of His Son. Alister puts forward the idea that "At least some of the theological fuss about suffering" is because it is a "painful reminder of the limitations of human nature and human culture."[60] But who was more outraged at human suffering than Jesus? At the graveside of Lazarus, he broke down in anger and grief. He did not reassure Mary and Martha that their suffering could make them more sensitive and compassionate people. He did not encourage them to learn all they could from the experience. He told them that, if they believed, they would see the glory of God[61]—and that glory took the form, not of education but of revivification. "Suffering was once seen as our enemy, something which separated us from God. It can now be seen as something which can bring us closer to God."[62] St Paul, by contrast, describes death as *still* being an enemy now.[63] That is how Jesus treats it, and it is how we experience it. Gloriously, it is now a *defeated* enemy, but an enemy it remains, severing relationships, depriving children of parents and parents of their children, guillotining creativity, dissipating meaning, haemorrhaging hope. Similarly, suffering remains that which (the ministry of Jesus demonstrates) is properly assaulted and assuaged. If we do meet God more closely within it, then that is testimony to the radically miraculous work of the Spirit, rather than to any positive place for suffering within the purposes of God.

Fourthly, it seems to me that the instrumental accounts of natural evil fail to do justice to the example of Jesus. Alister asks, "could we really believe in a god who just pampers individuals, making them 'happy'?"[64] But Jesus did attack pain and suffering wherever He came upon them. A good, loving human parent would not pamper their children. They would make them do things they didn't want to, like homework and household chores. But they wouldn't let them get cancer if they could possibly avoid it. Nor does Jesus, and therefore, given the fact that Jesus is our window onto the nature of the Father, nor does God—which drives us, I suggest, to one of the Inimical understandings of natural evil.

And lastly, the putative inconsistency. There seems to be a tension in Alister's thinking between moral evil and natural evil, which relates not just to their causation but to their effects. Moral evil, he seems to see as

60. McGrath, *Suffering*, 61, 60.
61. John 11:40.
62. McGrath, *Suffering*, 77.
63. 1 Cor 15:26.
64. McGrath, *Suffering*, 26.

abhorrent and something the world would be better off without. Natural evil, he seems to see as something that has a "purpose and place . . . in the Christian life."[65] It is not clear to me that there is such a difference in human experience. If someone suffers concussion and experiences incessant headaches as a consequence, that could result from the blow of a mugger or from a climbing accident. The physical pain, at any rate, will be the same—as will be many of the other potential consequences. The tension seems rather to stem from a proper desire not to justify sin. To describe humanly intended suffering as having a "purpose and place . . . in the Christian life" would seem to embed sin in the purposes of God. But if sin is held up as abhorrent (partly at least) through its horrible effects in the lives of human beings, and if the effects of natural evil are no different from the effects of moral evil, do we not have to take as negative a view of the one as we do of the other? Do we not need to see them both as inimical to the purposes of God?

This is what I meant at the beginning of this chapter by attempting to articulate a view of God "who is the Helper, the Sustainer, and the Fellow-Sufferer of those in pain—and not the Inflictor of that pain." Instrumental views make God more directly responsible for suffering, more "behind" the suffering—albeit for good and loving purposes. Pastorally, this is in danger of making God the enemy—the One who took away my father, wife or child. Inimical views mean that God is *not* "behind" the suffering, *not* the Inflictor of the pain or the loss. Inimical views make God—like Jesus at the tomb of Lazarus—the One who weeps with us, and who is angry at the distortion of His good creation that causes His creatures to suffer.

## ALISTER MCGRATH'S UNDERSTANDING OF THE PASSIBILITY OF GOD

Despite the fact that almost all the fathers and the reformers were passionate defenders of the Impassibility of God, Alister expresses the opposite view confidently: "just as we are moved by the sufferings of those whom we love, so God is moved by the pain and sorrow of those whom he loves."[66] He is careful to stress that this is a self-chosen vulnerability on God's part, and not an enforced passivity or impotence: "God *decided* to be hurt by our pain. God *allowed* himself to suffer as we suffer . . ."[67] Nor is it just in the person of Jesus that pain is taken into the Godhead: no, "the entire Godhead—Father, Son and Spirit—are brought together in the pain of the

---

65. McGrath, *Suffering*, 6.
66. McGrath, *Suffering*, 14.
67. McGrath, *Suffering*, 21, my emphasis.

loving redemption of sinful humanity."[68] This is a common—probably the majority—view amongst academic theologians today. As Bonhoeffer said, "Only the suffering God can help."[69]

But *how* does the suffering God help? Many simply assert as obvious that "to our wounds only God's wounds can speak":[70] few unpack wherein lies the help. Alister does—almost in passing, but quite extensively. He highlights five aspects. First, "we are able to relate better to someone who has shared our problem."[71] When I was suffering from depression and doubt, the year before my ordination, a wise friend pointed me towards the first chapter of C. S. Lewis' *Voyage to Venus*. The way in which Lewis describes the "barrage" which obstructed the narrator's walk to Ransom's cottage and made everything in him want to turn back—that was a huge relief to me, as it made me feel that someone understood. It made me feel less alone.

Secondly, Alister goes on to suggest that "we are able to relate better to someone who has . . . been through already what we are going through now—and has triumphed over it." Part of what comforted me about Lewis' apparent understanding of my pain was that he had come out of whatever equivalent experience with his faith intact. Only the suffering God can help, but a God who only suffered could not. The Cross and Resurrection need to be held together.

Thirdly, the suffering of God helps because it is a sign of His love. It is a sign of His love because it was voluntary: "Our place is on that Road; he chose to join us. He didn't have to; he wanted to."[72] Here we see the importance—the pastoral importance—of Alister's insistence that the passibility of God is a self-chosen vulnerability.

Fourthly, shared suffering creates a shared bond: "he has shared it, and thus created a powerful bond of sympathy between himself and ourselves."[73] Just as soldiers who have been through conflict together experience a shared understanding and a bond between them, so the omni-passibility of God (implied in the parable of the sheep and the goats in Matthew 25), forges a bond between Him and us.

Fifthly, the first four points play a particular role in building a relational rapport, intimacy and confidence in prayer: "We can pray to him with

---

68. McGrath, *Suffering*, 66.

69. Dietrich Bonhoeffer, *Letters and Papers from Prison* (London: SCM, 1967), 361.

70. Edward Shillito, "Jesus of the Scars," in *Jesus of the Scars and Other Poems* (London: Hodder and Stoughton, 1919), 11.

71. McGrath, *Suffering*, 45.

72. McGrath, *Suffering*, 46.

73. McGrath, *Suffering*, 69.

confidence, knowing that he already knows our needs, and has experienced them before us."[74]

However, as will have become all too apparent, we have now trespassed even beyond the (somewhat limited) competence of the chain saw, so it is time to stop. Besides, it is appropriate to end here, as it reminds us of the essentially pastoral nature of Alister's work—both his academic work, and his personal engagement. This essay comes as my tribute to his extraordinary contribution to academic and popular-level theology, but also to his kindness and support to me personally as I stepped into a role he himself filled with such distinction. Wycliffe and I are enormously grateful.

---

74. McGrath, *Suffering*, 73.

## Chapter 13

# Alister McGrath's Exemplary Theology

Jeffrey P. Greenman

This volume honors the remarkably prolific and valuable theological contribution made by Alister McGrath. Any *Festschrift* is a celebratory occasion, a "festive" or "party" writing, yet these authors sense that the best way to pay grateful tribute to Alister's rare achievement is to engage him—to take his arguments and agendas seriously, to probe and extend his key ideas, and to move ahead with the varied conversations that he has prompted. Together we celebrate him with gratitude yet also with critical appreciation rather than uncritical flattery.

Stepping back from the particularities of McGrath's arguments on specific topics, my purpose is to suggest that the overall shape of his theologizing has been exemplary. This does not mean that his every position or interpretation is faultless or the final word on the topic. Theologizing is the faithful church's continual task in every age. One does not expect to arrive at perfection or finality. Theology is a frail and finite undertaking. One hopes to say something intelligent and worthwhile in pursuit of God's truth. Saying that McGrath's theologizing is exemplary instead means that the quality of his vision, purpose, and achievement have an attractive and compelling excellence that should inspire others to follow in his path. McGrath's comment about one of his mentors, J. I. Packer, therefore seems quite apt as a description of McGrath himself: "His rare combination of theological competence, spiritual wisdom and a clear and accessible style of writing places him alongside the great spiritual writers of the evangelical tradition, such as John Owen, Richard Baxter, Jonathan Edwards and J. C. Ryle."[1] This is elite company. Yet in a century or two it would be no surprise to find gospel-loving Christians still reading Packer and McGrath alongside those other luminaries. Insight, wisdom, clarity, and accessibility are rarely found together in one author as richly as they are found in Alister McGrath's wide-reaching corpus.

McGrath's career has provided an admirable model well worthy of being imitated as an evangelical theologian, as an Anglican theologian, and as an ecclesial theologian. With McGrath, "a threefold cord is not quickly broken" (Eccl 4:12, a favorite verse in Anglican circles). He has been, and continues to be, all of these in one person, inseparably and creatively holding together an evangelical, Anglican, and ecclesial identity as a church-man-scholar-teacher. My point is that if you would understand McGrath's achievement, you need tri-focal vision to see all three interrelated facets of his life and work which are so thoroughly woven together.

McGrath is perhaps best known as an evangelical theologian. Many North American readers from across the denominational spectrum would point to McGrath as one of the clearest contemporary expositors of the "classic" evangelical Christian theological viewpoint. For them, his Anglican identity is almost incidental and often not even mentioned. This is because he has never shied away from embracing a clearly evangelical identity, and serving the evangelical wing of Christendom, even when that loyalty sometimes represents an embattled minority position within academic theology. He has explored quite candidly the strengths and weaknesses of evangelicalism as a movement, seeking to deepen its theological and spiritual roots.

In doing so, McGrath has had a strategic agenda. Evangelicalism needs to unapologetically embrace its intellectual vocation, renouncing any lingering vestiges of anti-intellectualism. Spiritual vitality cannot be disconnected from renewed minds apprehending and living the message of Scripture. He has written that "the essential precondition for a renewed evangelical engagement with intellectual life is confidence in its own coherence and credibility."[2] This quotation suggests one of the secrets of McGrath's influence as an evangelical theologian: he is able to give reasons for a "proper confidence" in the gospel. McGrath tells us that his work "as a

---

1. Alister McGrath, *J.I. Packer: A Biography* (Grand Rapids: Baker, 1997), xii.

2. Alister McGrath, *A Passion for Truth: The Intellectual Coherence of Evangelicalism* (Downers Grove, IL: IVP, 1996), 23.

scholar, speaker and writer has centered on the defense of the intellectual foundations of the gospel."[3]

What do evangelicals need most? Confidence in the gospel. Where will that confidence be found? In understanding the "coherence and credibility" of the evangelical account of the gospel. What kind of evangelical account is McGrath giving? Most basically, a centrist, mainstream, "classic" evangelicalism, in whose service he is a theological spokesman, evangelist, and apologist. His kind of evangelicalism is never ornery and it never devolves into fundamentalism. What are the major tenets of this expression of Christian faith? McGrath has articulated six "controlling convictions" (going slightly beyond David Bebbington's well-known quadrilateral): the supreme authority of Scripture; the majesty of Jesus Christ; the lordship of the Holy Spirit; the need for personal conversion; the priority of evangelism; and the importance of Christian community.[4] His version of evangelical is particularly "classic" in its cross-centeredness. McGrath has written, "I regard the cross as the foundation and criterion of true Christian thinking and living."[5] Perhaps here McGrath reveals the influence upon his thought of the early writings by Martin Luther, who said: "The cross alone is our theology."[6] Confidence in the gospel can only mean confidence in the divine foolishness of the cross as the supreme revelation of God's wisdom.

Methodologically, McGrath has exemplified the posture of "classic" evangelicalism in his affirmation of the centrality of Scripture for theologizing. The place of the Bible in theologizing goes beyond encyclopedically compiling proof-texts. He holds that

> theology is fundamentally an attentiveness to Scripture and encompasses a desire to express and communicate what is found there to the church and to the world. Christian theology is under an obligation to pay respectful and obedient attention to the biblical testimony and to allow itself to be shaped and *re*shaped by what it finds there. Theology therefore has both catechetical

---

3. Alister McGrath, *Evangelicals and the Future of Christianity* (London: Hodder & Stoughton, 1994), 100.

4. See Larry S. McDonald, *The Merging of Theology and Spirituality: An Examination of the Life and Work of Alister E. McGrath* (Lanham, MD: University Press of America, 2006), 13–14.

5. Alister E. McGrath, "Contributors: An Appreciation and Response," in *Alister E. McGrath and Evangelical Theology: A Dynamic Engagement*, ed. Sung Wook Chung (Grand Rapids: Baker Academic, 2003), 338.

6. WA 5.176.32–33.

and apologetic facets, just as it has immense relevance to spirituality and ethics.[7]

This statement reflects most of the core ingredients in his theological vision. His variety of evangelicalism is rooted in Scripture, fueled by a commitment to shape the life of the church (which is called to particular way of living, in spirituality and ethics) while sharing its message with the world. McGrath repeatedly writes about keeping together the connections between gospel-Scripture-church-world. The Scriptures form the church for the sake of the world. At bottom, his theology is missional—that is, oriented toward advancing the church's mission to the world as witnesses to Christ.

This missional focus is evidence of McGrath's embodiment of a main thread in "classic" evangelicalism. His concern for sound doctrine conveying the teachings of Scripture is valued for its extension into the church's catechetical and apologetic tasks. Catechesis is in the process of being discovered by evangelicals, not least by Anglican evangelicals. Apologetics has historically been a strong concern for evangelicals. Evangelical theology is therefore not intended for the academy alone but also for the church's ministry and witness. We see the tri-focal vision of McGrath coming together.

What is less typical of evangelicalism but arguably just as much an element of "classic" evangelicalism is McGrath's affirmation of the value of "listening respectfully to the view of our forbearers." McGrath's variety of evangelical theology is what we could call "Great Tradition Evangelicalism." McGrath gives credit to J.I. Packer for this emphasis in his own approach. He writes, "I am indebted to J.I. Packer for many aspects of my thought, not least his emphasis on evangelical theologizing within the 'great tradition.'"[8] He explains: "As an evangelical, I was also concerned with the question of how evangelicalism could be intellectually enriched without losing its distinct identity and values...My own view, which I shared with the noted evangelical writer J.I. Packer, was that evangelicalism was at its best when it saw itself as standing within the 'Great Tradition' of reflection on the Bible, drawing from its strengths of past engagement, while able to discard its weaknesses."[9] This is the posture of critical yet appreciative engagement with the church's tradition. McGrath "encourages evangelicals to value history and engage with the 'great tradition' in its totality. [This

---

7. Alister E. McGrath, "Engaging the Great Tradition: Evangelical Theology and the Role of Tradition," in *Evangelical Futures: A Conversation on Theological Method*, ed. John G. Stackhouse, Jr., (Grand Rapids: Baker, 2000), 140; italics his.

8. McGrath, "Contributors," 333n2.

9. Alister McGrath, "Reading Reality," in *Theologians in Their Own Words*, eds. Derek R. Nelson et al. (Minneapolis: Fortress, 2013), 130.

approach] invites evangelicals to enter into dialogue with the past—with Athanasius, Augustine, Anselm, Aquinas, Luther, Calvin, and Edwards, to mention but a few. To do so is to learn from the past without in any way being bound by that past. It is to be nourished, encouraged, challenged, and excited by the witness of those who have wrestled with Scripture before us, without allowing these servants of the gospel to become our masters."[10] This kind of "Great Tradition Evangelicalism" is fully congruent with McGrath's statement that he is "a firm supporter of what C. S. Lewis termed 'Mere Christianity' and have little personal interest in the boundary disputes that so frequently break out between different types of Christians."[11] McGrath's instinct has been that what evangelical theology urgently needed was probing the core of the historic, creedal faith, about which the church has always agreed, rather than focusing on "boundary disputes" that so easily capture the evangelical imagination. In my view, this is a way of wisdom worthy of emulation.

Beyond McGrath's evangelical identity, he is clearly and unapologetically an Anglican theologian. Throughout his writings he discusses a wide variety of Anglican thinkers from the advent of the English Reformation to the present day; he has sought to make Anglican theological resources better known and more widely more available.[12] It should be no surprise that three renowned Anglican authors, C. S. Lewis, John R.W. Stott and J.I. Packer are high among his list of favorite Christian thinkers. Yet McGrath is no smug or narrow Anglican triumphalist, either. In a variety of writings he seeks to demonstrate that there no inherent contradiction between his evangelical identity and his Anglicanism. After all, he is ordained as a priest in the Church of England, served in parish ministry, and gave leadership for an extended period as principal of a major institution of Anglican theological training at Wycliffe Hall in Oxford. He has contributed to denominational forums and has published extensively on questions of the Anglican identity and its future, without being unduly consumed by the deeply contested disputed about sexual ethics that have characterized Anglicanism in the past decade or so.

Again, McGrath has had a strategic agenda, this time for Anglicanism's self-understanding—namely, "to insist that evangelicalism is, historically and theologically, a legitimate and respectable option within Anglicanism. At no point is evangelicalism inconsistent with any of the Thirty-Nine

---

10. McGrath, "Engaging the Great Tradition," 158.

11. McGrath, "Engaging the Great Tradition," 140.

12. For example, Alister E. McGrath, ed., *The SPCK Handbook of Anglican Theologians* (London: SPCK, 1998).

Articles, the only document, apart from Scripture, the creeds and the Prayer Book, regarded as authoritative for Anglicans."[13] Characteristically, McGrath avoids a fundamentally defensive posture in advancing this viewpoint. He puts the case positively and assuredly, on the basis of a typically Anglican appeal to Scripture, reason, and tradition, another "threefold cord not quickly broken."

Like other leading Anglican theologians over the centuries, his temperament has been formed to be insistent upon the church's historic, orthodox confession of faith yet unperturbed by diverse expressions of churchmanship and by diverse theological visions of "secondary" matters of faith. This instinct is one of the reasons why evangelical Anglicans such as Stott, Packer and McGrath have had an extensive influence on contemporary evangelicalism worldwide. Since both Anglicanism and global evangelicalism are (in a political sense) broad-based coalitions featuring diverse communities composed of people who share common commitments yet have their own distinct emphases and concerns, my suggestion is that Anglicans often are particularly well-suited to be evangelical leaders, calling people to a shared core commitment to Christ and his service without being insistent that every theological detail of every sub-group be uniformly expressed.

At the heart of McGrath's Anglicanism is his underlying and foundational "Great Tradition" allegiance. Anglicanism is, for him, a particularly edifying way to be a creedal, orthodox, believing Christian, but not the only way. It is impossible to understand his affirmation of Anglicanism apart from his "Great Tradition Evangelicalism" and vice versa. I would argue that he values the Anglican tradition chiefly insofar as it enables its adherents to find their spiritual roots in the church's mainstream, historic great tradition, to which the Scriptures bear witness.[14] Again, he appears to be following in the path of Packer, about whom he wrote: "Packer has come to see himself as representing Anglicanism as an example of 'great-tradition Christianity' stemming from the mainstream Reformation."[15] What we might call the Packer-McGrath synthesis runs like this: The church's historic, orthodox confession of faith (its vibrant and enduring "mere Christianity"), articulated by thinkers across the ages in the theological Great Tradition, is given robust and wise theological and pastoral expression substantially

---

13. Alister McGrath, "Evangelical Anglicanism: A Contradiction in Terms?" in *Evangelical Anglicans: Their Role and Influence in the Church Today*, eds. R. T. France and A. E. McGrath (London: SPCK, 1993), 13.

14. See Alister E. McGrath, "Anglicanism and Pan-Evangelicalism," in *Oxford Handbook of Anglican Studies*, eds. Mark D. Chapman et al. (Oxford: Oxford University Press, 2016), 314–25.

15. McGrath, *J.I. Packer*, 283.

in the Reformation heritage (especially in the magisterial Reformers and the subsequent Puritan tradition), in its Anglican expression (especially in Thomas Cranmer's gospel logic in the Book of Common Prayer), and in "classic" evangelicalism (especially in its embrace of biblical fidelity and cross-centered preaching and piety).

McGrath's way of being an Anglican theologian has rather strong affinities with evangelicalism's favorite nonevangelical, C. S. Lewis. As Graham Tomlin astutely remarks in his preface to this volume, "Reading Alister's biography of Lewis can't help make you think of the parallels between them — an Irish background, the setting in Oxford, the journey to Christianity, engaging at both popular and academic levels with sceptics and the robust defence and imaginative presentation of the riches of a classic, orthodox Christian faith."[16] It strikes me that there is another instructive parallel between McGrath and Lewis that arises in McGrath's exploration of the "intellectual world" of Lewis. As McGrath sets out to discover Lewis's Anglican identity, he comments that "many younger Anglicans, anxious to affirm both theological orthodoxy and their denominational commitment, are coming to regard Lewis as a benchmark for Anglican identity. For them, Lewis embodies — and, for some, even defines — what Anglicanism ought to be: a theologically orthodox, culturally literate, imaginatively engaged, and historically rooted vision of the Christian faith."[17] The parallel is that at least part of the explanation for why McGrath is so widely read and respected, both inside and outside Anglican circles, is that he also so thoroughly embodies that desirable constellation of attributes he ascribes to Lewis. In fact, he even goes beyond Lewis's achievement in some respects. He is theologically orthodox in a more robust and doctrinally sharpened way; culturally literate and skilled at contesting a very broad range of contemporary issues, pushing far deeper into the relation between faith and science; offering professional theological depth of exposition in championing a well-resourced, historically rooted vision of the Christian faith. In all these ways, he reflects an appealing Lewis-like Anglicanism that is likely to stand the test of time.

Finally, McGrath is an exemplary ecclesial theologian. His commitment to the centrality and vitality of the Christian community of the church is basic, not peripheral, to his overall evangelical-Anglican vision. He sees himself as an evangelist and apologist, primarily to intellectuals but also in the broader culture. His embrace of an ecclesial identity has meant for him that theology belongs properly to the realm of the church, since it arises

---

16. See p. xviii. See also Alister McGrath, *C. S. Lewis — A Life: Eccentric Genius, Reluctant Prophet* (Carol Stream, IL: Tyndale, 2013), 18.

17. Alister E. McGrath, *The Intellectual World of C. S. Lewis* (Oxford: Wiley-Blackwell, 2014), 158.

from revealed Scriptures and from the church's confessions, and therefore at its best should be intended to serve the church's witness and equip the saints for eager service of the triune God. Along the way, in light of this commitment, he is not shy about attacking the excesses and deviations of academic theology when it retreats to the ivory tower and becomes removed from real life questions and from Christian formation. The theologian's proper and necessary task includes supporting the faithful in developing what he has called "the passionate intellect" which embraces "the discipleship of the mind."[18] Alongside his steady output of academic monographs and specialized studies, he has been unashamed to write for the "ordinary" readers in our churches, offering balanced, insightful, and accessible treatments of everyday Christian concerns such as facing suffering or doubt. One of his recent more popular books is entitled *Mere Discipleship*—clearly a nod in the direction of C. S. Lewis, but seeking to articulate how Lewis-styled historic orthodox is relevantly lived out by God's people in the contemporary world. These efforts are McGrath's expression of his pastoral calling: he has taken to heart Jesus' instruction to feed his sheep (John 21:17). Addressing this lay audience so well is entirely commendable, if difficult to emulate. Very few scholars have anything near his ability to write effectively for the proverbial "ordinary person in the pew." We need more of them.

Moreover, as an ecclesial theologian, he has breathed new life into the practice of Christian apologetics. While rejecting a narrow rationalistic defense of the faith, he has championed the attractive reasonableness of Christian faith in a series of books and by speaking often in the context of congregational gatherings or conferences hosted by evangelical organizations. He appears to have a minor franchise on *Mere* titles, as perhaps the best example of his apologetic agenda is *Mere Apologetics: How to Help Seekers and Skeptics Find Faith*.[19] His overall posture in commending the gospel is well worth emulating: "Apologetics is to be seen not as a defensive and hostile reaction against the world, but as a welcome opportunity to exhibit, celebrate, and display the treasure chest of the Christian faith."[20] He invites Christians into a more confident yet always humble sharing of their vision of God and life with nonbelievers. McGrath's readers, regardless of their faith or lack of faith, are asked to discover how Christianity addresses life's perennial questions, captures our imaginations, and answers humanity's deepest longings. In a more assertive mode, McGrath has confronted

---

18. See Alister E. McGrath, *The Passionate Intellect: Christian Faith and the Discipleship of the Mind* (Downers Grove, IL: IVP, 2010).

19. Alister E. McGrath, *Mere Apologetics: How to Help Seekers and Skeptics Find Faith* (Grand Rapids: Baker, 2012).

20. McGrath, *Mere Apologetics*, 11.

the naturalism and reductionism so commonly (but wrongly) assumed to accompany an affirmation of the importance of modern science. The most prominent example of this is his book, *The Dawkins Delusion? Atheist Fundamentalism and the Denial of the Divine*, which offers a forceful refutation of British biologist Richard Dawkins' best-seller, *The God Delusion*.[21]

His vision for theologizing to offer joyful service of the community of faith finds constant expression as a university teacher, conference speaker, and unparalleled author of textbooks. In fact, his teaching has been extended to the far reaches of the globe thanks to his textbooks. He explains the link: "My Oxford lectures on Christian doctrine set out to reclaim the Christian theological tradition, seeing this as a repository of wisdom and experience, nourished by and saturated in biblical themes, which could be reappropriated and applied in the life of the church."[22] Here we see how he considers his service to the academy and to the church as a seamless whole. Far more than any other recent first-class theologian, McGrath has become known for his best-selling and student-friendly texts, chiefly *Christian Theology: An Introduction* (at the time of this writing in its sixth edition) and its accompanying *Christian Theology Reader*. With his gift for classification and exceptional skill for producing clear, simple, and readable prose, he has sought to introduce, explain, and contextualize—as he says at the outset of one of his other textbooks.[23]

As I have reread a good deal of McGrath's writings in preparation for this essay, I have been struck by his repeated references to the importance of the idea of the "organic intellectual" championed by Italian Marxist Antonio Gramsci (1891–1937). At first glance, McGrath and Gramsci seem to make a rather strange pair. Perhaps surprisingly, McGrath turns to Gramsci for help in expounding the positive role for a theologian in service of a community. McGrath believes that evangelicalism, given its embrace of populism, has found it difficult to establish a valued place for the theologian with its ranks. The key distinction is between two types of intellectuals. What Gramsci calls "traditional intellectuals" are "those who are imposed upon a community by an external authority" as contrasted with "organic intellectuals" who "operate and are respected within a community, and who gain authority on account of their being seen to represent the outlook of that community. Their authority is thus not imposed, but emerges naturally, reflecting the

---

21. Alister McGrath, *The Dawkins Delusion? Atheist Fundamentalism and the Denial of the Divine* (Downers Grove, IL: InterVarsity, 2010).

22. McGrath, "Reading Reality," 129–30.

23. Alister E. McGrath, *Reformation Thought: An Introduction* (Oxford: Basil Blackwell, 1988), xi.

esteem in which the community holds them and its willingness to regard them as its representatives and thinkers."[24]

McGrath's favorite example is the noted evangelical Anglican leader John R.W. Stott (1921–2011), who was long-time rector of All Soul's, Langham Place in London.[25] One of the most prominent evangelicals of the twentieth-century, Stott was a renowned preacher and conference speaker, best-selling author, and perhaps the most influential networker and strategist of the worldwide evangelical movement. He never held an academic position, and never became a bishop. Some evangelicals during his lifetime likened Stott to an "evangelical Pope" on account of his magisterial, unifying voice speaking worldwide. McGrath comments that Stott possessed "no overwhelming academic or institutional authority but rightly [enjoyed] enjoys enormous status within the evangelical community (and beyond) on account of having earned that respect. There is an organic and natural relationship between Stott and the community for whom he has spoken and to whom he so clearly has held himself responsible."[26]

McGrath's insight is helpful not only because it casts a vision for a positive place for theology and theologians in the service of the church, but also because it reflects so accurately the internal dynamics of evangelicalism as a coalition movement. From its earliest days, evangelicalism's leaders have not been imposed but recognized. They have emerged from within diverse contexts and ministries on account of having contributed something that is broadly deemed to be highly valuable.

Again I want to propose that we find a clear case of déjà vu: what McGrath has ascribed to Stott can also be ascribed quite appropriately to McGrath himself. Unlike Stott, McGrath has held prestigious academic posts throughout his career. But notice that he has used that platform so energetically and effectively in service of the church's ministry and witness, while not neglecting specialized scholarship. McGrath has been highly esteemed by transdenominational, global evangelicalism for the past four decades. Again and again, especially across English-speaking contexts, a broad range of evangelical congregations, liberal arts colleges and seminaries, publishers, and conferences, often repeatedly, have turned to McGrath for insight across a wide array of themes and topics. They have sought him

---

24. McGrath, *Passion for Truth*, 19.

25. For more on Stott, see Jeffrey P. Greenman, "Stott, John R.W.," in *Biographical Dictionary of Evangelicals*, ed. Timothy Larsen (Leicester, UK: InterVarsity, 2003), 638–41.

26. McGrath, "Engaging the Great Tradition: Evangelical Theology and the Role of Tradition," in *Evangelical Futures: A Conversation on Theological Method*, ed. John G. Stackhouse, Jr., (Grand Rapids: Baker, 2000), 156.

out on account of his reliable excellence as a clear, consistent and passionate spokesman for a biblically faithful, intellectually grounded, evangelistically attuned, and culturally engaged evangelicalism.

As we conclude this volume, we as authors of the *Festschrift* together offer a celebratory and appreciative tribute to Alister McGrath's remarkable achievement as an exemplary and inseparably evangelical, Anglican, and ecclesial theologian. *Soli Deo gloria*.

www.ingramcontent.com/pod-product-compliance
Lightning Source LLC
Chambersburg PA
CBHW051053230426
43667CB00013B/2281